A Gospel of Doubt

The Legacy
of John MacArthur's
The Gospel According to Jesus

A Gospel of Doubt

The Legacy
of John MacArthur's
The Gospel According to Jesus

Robert N. Wilkin

Grace Evangelical Society
Corinth, TX 76210

A Gospel of Doubt: The Legacy of John MacArthur's The Gospel
According to Jesus
Copyright © 2015 by Grace Evangelical Society

Mailing Address:
P.O. Box 1308
Denton, TX 76202
www.faithalone.org
ges@faithalone.org

Wilkin, Robert N. (1952–).

ISBN: 978-1-943399-00-0

Unless otherwise indicated, Scripture quotations
are from *The New King James Version*, Copyright
© 1979, 1980, 1982, by Thomas Nelson, Inc.

Book and Cover Design: Shawn C. Lazar

Layout: Bethany Taylor and Shawn C. Lazar

Printed in the United States of America

For the doubters,
that you may find assurance in Christ,
not in your works.

Contents

Dedication

This book is dedicated to the partners of Grace Evangelical Society. Like Gideon's small band, we are not a large group. However, we are united in our commitment to the real gospel according to Jesus.

Special thanks to Brad Doskocil who spent untold hours editing and proofing the manuscript. Though he is a CPA, he is also a gifted theologian and editor. He helped improve the tone, style, and readability of the book.

Shawn Lazar made terrific suggestions and was excellent in the editing and proofing phases.

Kyle Kaumeyer too caught lots of errors and improved the style of the book significantly.

Pastors Paul Carpenter and Joe Lombardi also both carefully reviewed the entire manuscript and made many helpful suggestions.

I also dedicate this book to John MacArthur and his many ministries, Grace Community Church, Grace to You, The Master's College, and The Master's Seminary. While I disagree with you strongly on the gospel the Lord Jesus preached, I very much approve of the conservative stands you take on inerrancy, the role of women, verse-by-verse exposition, creation and the young earth, the Lordship of Christ, and much more. My hope is that you will return to the faith you had before you studied the Puritans in 1980. I also hope that those in your church and schools will come back to the actual gospel according to Jesus, regeneration by faith alone in Christ alone apart from works before or after the new birth.

Introduction

David vs Goliath? Auburn vs Alabama? Ali vs Foreman? Coyote vs Roadrunner? If you're expecting this book to be an all-out, take-no-prisoners competition with MacArthur, then think again. It's first and foremost a search for truth.

This book isn't written to smear John MacArthur. He holds Biblical positions on many important issues, such as on inerrancy (i.e., the view that the Bible has no errors of any kind in it), traditional marriage, verse by verse expository preaching, cessationism (i.e., the view that the signs gifts are not operating today), young earth creation (i.e., the view that the earth and man were created around 4200 BC), the universal Noahic flood (i.e., not a regional flood only), male leadership in the home and local church, elder rule, etc.

MacArthur's graduate school, *The Master's Seminary*, is a fine school. It takes conservative stands on all of the issues just mentioned. Faculty like Robert Thomas (retired), David Farnell, and Dick Mayhew are well known for their defense of the Scriptures.

In many important ways, John MacArthur is a champion for Biblical truth.

However, in *The Gospel According to Jesus (TGAJ)* MacArthur champions a view called Lordship Salvation. It is the view that in order to have everlasting life one must turn from his sins, submit to Christ's Lordship, obey Him, and persevere in faith and good works until death.

Lordship Salvation is not a minor issue. It is a major issue. The question of what one must do to have everlasting life is more important than any other (Gal 1:6-9). Proclaiming the right message is a matter of life and death.

So while this book isn't a competition, we should be like the Bereans who search the Scriptures to evaluate what is true (Acts 17:11). If we are, we will be able to discern what is true and what is false in what we read and hear. That is especially important when it comes to the message of everlasting life.

MacArthur has not always held to Lordship Salvation. The reason that the first edition of *The Gospel According to Jesus (TGAJ)* was not published before 1988 is because he did not embrace this view until 1980. At that time MacArthur went on a sabbatical and studied the Puritans, the English branch of Calvinism.

The reason why the title for this response to *TGAJ* is called *A Gospel of Doubt* is because MacArthur's Lordship Salvation produces doubt in those who accept its teachings. According to MacArthur's gospel one cannot be sure of where he will spend eternity until after he dies. It is true, however, that MacArthur, like the Puritan theology he follows, urges people *to search their works in hopes of finding reasons to believe they will end up in Jesus' kingdom.* But according to MacArthur that very search produces doubts that one is born again and secure because no one's works are perfect.

A Gospel of Doubt advocates the same basic view that MacArthur himself held before 1980. Before that time MacArthur said that certainty could be found simply in believing the promise of everlasting life, not in looking at one's works.

If you appreciate John MacArthur and his views, you should consider the Biblical evidence cited in *A Gospel of Doubt*. As he himself says, no man is a perfect expositor of God's Word. No man infallibly proclaims the Word of God. That includes MacArthur and me and every writer and preacher. Only Scripture is without error. I hope you will prayerfully read this book, asking God to show you if your understanding of God's Word and of the condition for receiving everlasting life are correct.

The first edition of *TGAJ* was published twenty-seven years ago. It was so popular that a second revised and expanded edition came out six years later in 1994. Its continued strong sales led to a remarkable twentieth year anniversary edition that was released in 2008 (with an additional chapter added).

Most books are lucky if they sell 5,000 copies and remain in print for six months. The importance of MacArthur's book on the gospel (i.e., the saving message, the message of everlasting life) is evident in that it has had massive sales and it is still in print twenty-seven years after its release.

After Zondervan first published *TGAJ*, they asked Zane Hodges to write a reply, one responding to MacArthur directly, chapter by chapter.

Hodges was not willing to write a direct response to *TGAJ* because he felt such a book would be limited in scope. Instead, he wanted to write a timeless response to Lordship Salvation. The book Hodges wrote was called *Absolutely Free! A Biblical Reply to Lordship Salvation* (Zondervan and Redención Viva, 1989; a second edition was released by Grace Evangelical Society in 2014). Not once did Hodges mention MacArthur in the main text. He only mentioned him in the endnotes. (MacArthur is mentioned occasionally in the text of the second edition since longer endnotes, many of which referred to MacArthur, have been moved to the text.)

A Gospel of Doubt fulfills the original assignment given to Hodges to write a response to MacArthur, section by section, chapter by chapter. This book is a labor of love. The evangelistic message is a matter of life and death. Hence clarifying the evangelistic message which our Lord proclaimed is of utmost importance.

It was difficult to keep this book approximately the same length as *TGAJ*, but we did. *A Gospel of Doubt* has to lay out MacArthur's arguments and then respond to them. Consequently, the summary of his arguments was brief in many places. Since readers of *A Gospel of Doubt* are expected to have *TGAJ*, there was no need for extensive quoting or restatement, except where it's especially important. The reader is able to verify the summaries of what MacArthur said, making sure they accurately represent him.

I hold no animosity toward MacArthur. I've met him on several occasions and I've found him to be a cordial person. He is obviously a gifted speaker and writer. My aim in writing is to clarify the message of everlasting life, not to win a debate.

I hope you find that *A Gospel of Doubt* causes you to think more deeply about Scripture. For as we meditate on God's Word, good things happen (Rom 12:2; 2 Cor 3:18).

Bob Wilkin
April 2015
Corinth, TX

CHAPTER 1

What Does Jesus Mean When He Says, "Follow Me"?

Introduction

Kunte Kinte was abducted from his village in Africa and sold into slavery in the United States. He was treated horribly by his master. After running away several times, his master disabled him. Alex Hailey's famed TV series *Roots* was a jarring introduction to the evils that often accompany slavery.

When you think of slavery, what comes to mind? Is it the millions of men, women, and children kidnapped by fellow Africans and sold to Europeans to work the colonies? Or maybe you think of the Hebrews escaping across the Red Sea from their Egyptian masters? Or Spartacus leading the revolt against Rome? Or modern-day Christian women being sold into slavery by the Islamic State in Syria and Iraq? Whatever image of slavery comes to mind, it is most likely a grim one. When we think of slavery, we think of the very worst kind of human existence possible. But when the Bible describes us as slaves to Jesus Christ, is that what we should think?

In the first chapter of *The Gospel[1] According to Jesus[2]* (hereafter *TGAJ*), John MacArthur argues that the Bible's description of Christians as slaves tells us something about the nature of saving faith. In sum, slaves were subservient to their masters, hence MacArthur believes that to be born again one must surrender to Christ as Lord. Is MacArthur right?

A Word about Words[3]

MacArthur begins by examining two words, *Lord* (*kurios*) and *slave* (*doulos*), and rightly sees the sovereignty of the Lord Jesus in the former term and our status in the latter term. He suggests that many New Testament translations have de-emphasized the word *doulos* by translating it as *servant*, rather than as *slave*, which he thinks minimizes its impact.

However, as is his practice throughout *TGAJ*, MacArthur makes pronouncements that are not backed by Scripture, such as this one:

> *Doulos* speaks of slavery, pure and simple. It is not at all a hazy or uncertain term. It describes someone *lacking personal freedom and personal rights* whose very existence is defined by his service to another. It is a sort of slavery in which "human autonomy is set aside and an alien will takes precedence of [sic] one's own." This is total, unqualified submission to the control and the direction of a higher authority—*slavery*, not merely service at one's own discretion (p. 28, emphasis added).

---

[1] MacArthur uses the term *gospel* to mean *the saving message*, the message of what one must believe, or in his case, *do*, in order to have everlasting life. I have chosen to use the term in the same way, even though technically it is rarely if ever used that way in the New Testament. It actually refers to the good news that the second member of the Trinity, Jesus Christ, became a man, lived a sinless life, died on the cross for the sins of the world, rose bodily from the dead, ascended to heaven, and is coming back soon to establish His righteous kingdom. The good news is the proof that Jesus' promise of everlasting life to all who simply believe in Him is true. See my book *The Ten Most Misunderstood Words in the Bible*, chapter 9, "Gospel."

[2] John MacArthur, *The Gospel According to Jesus*, Revised and Expanded Anniversary edition (Grand Rapids, MI: Zondervan, 2008).

[3] *A Gospel of Doubt* follows MacArthur's arguments chapter by chapter and section by section. All chapter titles in this book are taken from *TGAJ*. Nearly all section titles from *TGAJ* are the titles of the sections in *A Gospel of Doubt*.

On the one hand, MacArthur is right that *doulos* sometimes refers to a common slave. On the other hand, he fails to mention that it often refers to a king's official or to people who are officials for God Himself.

The leading dictionary of New Testament Greek lists two main senses of *doulos*: "1. male slave as an entity in a socioeconomic context, *slave*" and "2. One who is solely committed to another, *slave, subject*" (BDAG, p. 260AB, emphasis original). But under the second definition BDAG lists two types of uses: "a. in a pejorative sense," and "b. in a positive sense" (p. 260B). Under the positive use of *doulos* BDAG lists "α. in relation to a superior human being…of a king's officials" and "β. especially of the relationship of humans to God" (p. 260B).

When MacArthur talks about being a slave, his explanation does not appear to have any positive sense at all; yet BDAG lists slavery to God as a positive thing, just as being one of "a king's officials" is certainly a positive thing. Indeed BDAG lists being apostles and Christian prophets as positive examples of being a *doulos* (p. 260C).

MacArthur's interpretation of what it means to be a slave does not fit with many texts of Scripture. For example, MacArthur says that Christians *lack personal rights*. However, Paul asserts that he and Barnabas, both slaves of Christ (Acts 14:14; Rom 1:1; Gal 1:10; Phil 1:1; Titus 1:1), had rights:

> *Do we have no right* to eat and drink? *Do we have no right* to take along a believing wife, as do also the other apostles, the brothers of the Lord, and Cephas? Or *is it* only Barnabas and I *who have no right* to refrain from working? (1 Cor 9:4-6, emphasis added).

Also, MacArthur says that, since believers are slaves, they *lack personal freedom*. By contrast, Paul spoke of the freedom that believers in Christ have:

> If any of those who do not believe invites you to dinner, *and you desire to go*, eat whatever is set before you, asking no question for conscience's sake (1 Cor 10:27, emphasis added).

Accepting or declining an invitation certainly sounds a lot like freedom of choice for believers. And don't believers also have freedom in the matter of marriage? Aren't believers free to choose whom they wish to marry? Paul says they are:

> A wife is bound by law as long as her husband lives; but if her husband dies, *she is at liberty to be married to whom she wishes*, only in the Lord[4] (1 Cor 7:39, emphasis added).

When MacArthur says that Christians have no personal freedom or rights, he is misstating the meaning of *doulos* while ignoring contexts that do not support his explanation.

MacArthur goes on to mention five passages (Matt 6:24; Rom 14:7-9; 1 Cor 6:19-20; 2 Pet 2:1; Rev 5:9), evidently thinking that they prove that believers have no freedom and no rights. But none of the verses he cites supports what he is saying.

For example, MacArthur says, "We have a Master who bought us (2 Peter 2:1)" (p. 28). Of course, it is absolutely true that Jesus is our Master (*despotēs*). *Despotēs* is used four times in the New Testament of the Lord Jesus as our Master (2 Tim 2:21; 2 Pet 2:1; Jude 4; Rev 6:10). And it is certainly true that the Lord Jesus bought us (*agorazō*). The word *agorazō* is used four times in the New Testament in reference to redemption, whether for all mankind (Matt 13:46) or for believers (1 Cor 6:20; 7:23). But the verse MacArthur specifically cites is 2 Pet 2:1, which doesn't refer to the redemption of believers at all:

> But there were also false prophets among the people, even as there will be false teachers among you, who will secretly bring in destructive heresies, even denying the Lord who bought them, and bring on themselves swift destruction.

When MacArthur says, "We have a Master who bought us," he is referring to believers, not false teachers. Yet Peter is talking about false teachers.[5] MacArthur misses the distinction. The fact that the Lord bought false teachers does not in any way prove that believers have no freedoms or rights.

None of the other passages MacArthur cites indicate that believers lack freedoms or rights either (Matt 6:24; Rom 14:7-9; 1 Cor 6:19-20; Rev 5:9). He is simply citing verses that use the words

---

[4] The lone restriction is that Christians are only to marry fellow believers.

[5] Second Peter 2:1 is often cited as a leading verse proving unlimited atonement.

Master (*despotēs*) or *bought/redeemed* (*agorazō*) without examining whether they prove his point.

Why Such a Revolting Concept?

The title of this section shows that MacArthur thinks being a slave of Jesus Christ is "a revolting concept." It is true that being a slave (*doulos*) in the ancient world was a bad thing. No one would want to be in such a position, especially modern people who enjoy a wide range of personal freedoms. But MacArthur's arguments are misleading. While the New Testament does describe us as slaves, there isn't *an exact equivalence* between being the slave of a pagan and being Jesus' slave. It's a metaphor. And all metaphors have their proper limits.

The truth is, following Christ can involve hardships and sufferings. But to call it "revolting" may be good rhetoric, but poor exposition. On the contrary, being Jesus' slave is a good thing, not a bad thing. It's not revolting; it's an honor and a great responsibility. For the person who understands who Jesus is and what is to come, being His slave is a wonderful concept. Indeed, it's the very best thing you can be!

To say, "They understood far better than we do what a menial position He was calling them to" (p. 29) is another exaggeration of the slave metaphor. Yes, Christ's Apostles would experience debasement. But the kind of debasement they experienced was less like a Roman *doulos*, and much more like what Jesus Himself experienced. Remember that in His first coming, the Lord Jesus Himself came as a slave:

> "You know that the rulers of the Gentiles lord it over them, and those who are great exercise authority over them. Yet it shall not be so among you; but whoever desires to become great among you, let him be your servant. And whoever desires to be first among you, let him be your slave—*just as the Son of Man did not come to be served, but to serve,* and to give His life as a ransom for many" (Matt 20:25-28, emphasis added).

MacArthur fails to point out here that Jesus first came to serve (though he does later, on p. 34), which is an important omission.

In His First Coming, Jesus came to serve others, not to be served. In His Second Coming the Lord Jesus will come to be served. Will serving Him be revolting? Absolutely not! In fact, if we are faithful in our service for Him in this life, we will actually *reign* with Him in the life to come (2 Tim 2:12; Rev 2:26). Jody Dillow entitled his book on eternal rewards, *The Reign of the Servant Kings*. That captures the idea well.

Christians are slaves to Christ. But that kind of slavery is not a revolting concept!

The Problem with a Feel-Good Gospel[6]

MacArthur hopes his emphasis on slavery will help counteract what he perceives as a major problem today, namely, "a feel-good gospel" (p. 30). And what is that? He identifies it with what he calls "the no-lordship message" and "the no-lordship doctrine" (p. 30), the most disastrous form of the "feel-good gospel." He says that "the whole gist of the no-lordship message" is as follows:

> You can have Jesus as Savior and Friend here and now and decide later whether you really want to be submitted to His authority or not. It is hard to imagine a more disastrous twisting of what it means to be a Christian (p. 30).

It is unfortunate that MacArthur chose pejorative labels like "the no-lordship message" when the people he is criticizing call our view *Free Grace theology*. We believe in the Lordship of Jesus Christ and call for people to submit to Him and live for Him. The very name "no-lordship doctrine" is offensive to Free Grace proponents. And it is misleading.

Free Grace teachers say that only by following the Lord can anyone have meaning and significance in life. Believers who do not yield to Christ are miserable. Why would anyone want that?

But it is true that Free Grace proponents, unlike MacArthur, do not make submitting to Christ a condition of receiving everlasting life. Submission is a condition for discipleship and for the fullness of life which God wants us to have.

---

[6] This section title is taken from *TGAJ*. However, it incorporates the arguments MacArthur makes not only on pages 30-31 where this section is found, but also material found in the short section which follows, entitled "What Would Jesus Say?" (pp. 31-32).

Free Grace preachers call MacArthur's view what he calls it, *Lordship Salvation*. If we were to call his view the *no-grace doctrine, the no-grace message,* or *the feel-bad gospel*,[7] we would be using pejorative language that would offend people we hope to reach.

MacArthur does believe that the grace of God is essential for anyone to be born again. His church is called *Grace Community Church*. His radio ministry is called *Grace to You*. He speaks a lot about grace. He differs from Free Grace people in that in his view the grace of God motivates and enables "the elect" to repent, submit, commit, obey, and persevere so that they might gain kingdom entrance. In his view the grace of God must be wedded with our works in order for anyone to escape eternal condemnation.

Since the debate between Lordship Salvation and Free Grace Salvation will be discussed throughout this book, there is no need for a lengthy discussion of the differences here. Instead, a few observations about the basic differences follow.

First, the decision to submit to Christ, which MacArthur says one must make to be born again, is just that, a decision. But the new birth is not a decision. Decisionism is wrong in terms of the new birth, as MacArthur himself says elsewhere in *TGAJ* (pp. 37, 116). Of course, an unbeliever can and should decide to submit to Christ. But submitting to Christ won't save anyone.

Second, MacArthur points people inward for assurance. He wants people to look for "implicit obedience to His commandments," which MacArthur says is "the telltale mark of authentic saving faith" (p. 32). But the Lord Jesus pointed people away from themselves to Himself (John 3:16; 4:10-14; 5:24; 6:35; 11:25-26). Believing in Jesus' promise of everlasting life is the true basis of assurance.

Third, salvation, according to MacArthur, is hard work. It is work that does not end until death or the Rapture. But salvation, according to Jesus, is not hard work, it's a free gift received by faith alone, apart from any work (John 3:16; 4:10; 6:28-29).

---

[7] Initially I had the expression "the feel-good gospel" here. MacArthur obviously finds that expression abhorrent. So using it served to illustrate my point on pejorative language. However, a friend who reviewed chapter one, John Yantis, said I should change that to "the feel-bad gospel." He wrote, "the expression 'feel-bad gospel' pretty much describes what went through my mind when contemplating MacArthur's definition of 'slavery.' And I glory in calling Free Grace a 'feel-good doctrine,' because that's what assurance gives!"

Fourth, the message of justification by faith alone is not a "feel-good" message, contrary to MacArthur's claim. If it were, there wouldn't be 1.2 billion Catholics, 300 million Eastern Orthodox, and 25 million Mormons and Jehovah's Witnesses who reject the Free Grace message and instead believe in salvation by grace through faith plus works. And most of the 800 million Protestants hope to be saved by a mixture of faith and works. Clearly the message of Lordship Salvation is a much more popular message than the Free Grace message.[8]

Slavery and True Liberty[9]

MacArthur ends the chapter by saying that "the gospel is an invitation to slavery" (p. 34), and it's impossible not to see that he makes everlasting life depend upon a mixture of faith and works. How else can you understand the following?

> The gospel according to Jesus calls sinners to give up their independence, deny themselves, submit to an alien will, and abandon their rights in order to be owned and controlled by the Lord (p. 35).

Does the law require anything more or less than such complete submission? A bit later MacArthur adds:

> But remove that spirit of submission, and the most profound kind of "admiration" for Christ is not even true faith at all. Yielding completely to Christ's lordship is that vital an element of true saving faith, and therefore the proclamation of His lordship is an absolutely necessary component of the true gospel (p. 36).

Aside from the serious problems this raises for Paul's argument about justification and the law, a more fundamental question is, *what evidence is there that the call to follow Christ is the same as the call to be born again?* MacArthur offers no such evidence.

---

[8] Anyone who compares sales of MacArthur's books with those of Hodges or other Free Grace writers (certainly my own books included) knows this to be true. MacArthur is a giant in Evangelical publishing.

[9] This section title is taken directly from *TGAJ*. My discussion incorporates the arguments MacArthur makes both in this section (pp. 34-36) and in the related penultimate one entitled, "Not Mere Slaves, But Slaves Who Are Friends" (pp. 32-34).

Conclusion

No doubt the Bible teaches that believers are Jesus' slaves. And MacArthur is right to call attention to this neglected subject in preaching. But he also takes things too far. He exaggerates the analogy between grueling pagan slavery and slavery to Christ, and wrongly makes submission to Christ as one's Master a condition for receiving everlasting life without a shred of Biblical proof to support his claims.

CHAPTER 2

A Look at the Issues

After the first edition of *The Gospel According to Jesus* came out, I heard MacArthur give a message on the radio entitled, "Truth: The Boundary of Love and the Test of Loyalty (2 John 5-8)." In that message he said the following:

> I was sitting here in the church, I told you some years ago, with the leaders of the religion department of Brigham Young University, the Mormon leaders, the ones who are responsible for all the training of their students at BYU and are responsible for writing books on the Mormon theology. They said they wanted to meet with me for a day because they had so much in common with me. And so they came and I enjoyed their discussion very much and my heart went out to these two very fine men. And they said, "You know, we use your book, *The Gospel According to Jesus,* as a text book at BYU." And I was so stunned, I thought to myself, "What did I leave out? I've got to go back and edit that book." Are you kidding?
>
> Well they said, "We're very, very concerned because there isn't a love for Christ and there isn't a submission to His lordship among our students. And so we found that book helpful."
>
> And so that launched our discussion. And they said, "We just came down to talk to you and ask if you would come to

BYU and speak to our students and our faculty because we feel like, you know, we have so much in common."[1]

MacArthur assured these Mormon leaders that they had misunderstood what he was saying in the book.[2] But had they? Do Mormons believe in Lordship Salvation?

MacArthur does not think that Mormons are regenerate.[3] He rightly sees Mormonism as a cult that has a terribly distorted view of the deity of Christ, the Bible, special revelation, etc. But that does not mean that there are not some significant areas of agreement between MacArthur and Mormons on the question of what one must do to be born again.

Phil Johnson is MacArthur's right hand man and the editor of *The Gospel According to Jesus*. In a Sept 7, 2005 blog entitled "Peddling Mormonism as Mainstream Christianity," Johnson tries to rebut the efforts of Mormons, and particularly BYU Professor Robert Millet, to present their views as the same as MacArthur's.

In the blog Johnson writes,

> Tuesday I read an Internet forum where a Mormon missionary was attempting to convince some naive evangelical that MacArthur's "lordship doctrine" asserts the very same soteriology as Mormonism. The Mormon guy claimed the Bible is full of verses *that deny the principle of sola fide and make salvation a cooperative work between God and the sinner*, just the way the Mormon "gospel" teaches. That, he insisted, is also John MacArthur's view…
>
> Millet's book itself strives to leave that same impression. Although Millet hasn't really grasped the first principles of what MacArthur actually teaches, he quotes frequently but selectively from MacArthur, apparently *attempting to*

---

[1] http://www.gty.org/resources/print/sermons/63-3.

[2] He indicated three points of disagreement: the Trinity, the full deity of Christ, and salvation by grace alone. The Mormons went on to indicate that they do believe in salvation by grace.

[3] He *mentions* the deity of Christ on a dozen pages (pp. 44, 52, 75, 81, 82, 87, 120, 166, 168, 169, 227, 230). On another occasion he says, "A cultist who denies the deity of Christ could wholeheartedly affirm those four truths from 1 Corinthians 15:2-4, but that does not make him a true believer" (p. 81).

give the impression that MacArthur believes the sinner's own works are instrumental in justification (emphasis added).[4]

Does MacArthur teach that "salvation is a cooperative work between God and the sinner"? Does he teach that "the sinner's own works are instrumental in justification"? Johnson doesn't think so. But Millet is right. That is precisely what MacArthur believes and teaches in chapter 2 (and throughout *TGAJ*).

MacArthur begins chapter 2 by lamenting the fact that evangelistic presentations often call for people to "accept Jesus," "invite Him into your life," or "make a decision for Christ" (p. 37). He rightly says that those are misleading and unbiblical ways of evangelizing. Nowhere do we find such calls in Scripture.

Next MacArthur identifies what he considers to be the core truth that is missing in the "diluted gospel" of popular Evangelicalism, i.e., the truth that "The gospel Jesus proclaimed was a call to discipleship, a call to follow Him in submissive obedience, not just a plea to make a decision or pray a prayer" (p. 37).

Think about that statement. Phil Johnson adamantly denies that MacArthur believes that works are necessary for justification. And yet, here MacArthur is plainly saying that discipleship and submissive obedience are conditions of salvation. Don't submission and obedience require good works? If good works like "submissive obedience" are necessary for salvation, then, contrary to Phil Johnson, "the impression that MacArthur believes the sinner's own works are instrumental in justification" is absolutely spot-on.

The Lord Jesus did not say that submissive obedience is necessary to be eternally saved. He said that whoever simply believes in Him has everlasting life.

The Abandonment of Jesus' Gospel

MacArthur points out that some Evangelicals speak about a conversion to Christ that involves "no spiritual commitment whatsoever" (p. 38). He mischaracterizes this view as the promise that whoever "believes the facts about Christ" can claim eternal life.

---

[4] Phillip Johnson, "Peddling Mormonism as Mainstream Christianity." See http://phillipjohnson.blogspot.com/2005/09/peddling-mormonism-as-mainstream.html Accessed March 30, 2015.

MacArthur isn't entirely wrong on that point, but he's not quite right either.

The Pharisees of Jesus' day believed many facts about Jesus. So do Mormons, Catholics, and Muslims today. But they aren't saved. The facts about Jesus' life and identity are important, of course, but believing them won't save you. The reason is because one can believe a number of important truths about Jesus, and also believe in salvation by works. That isn't saving faith. What is?

A person is born again when he believes Jesus' promise to give everlasting life to the one who simply believes in Him. Just as Abraham believed in the coming Messiah for everlasting life and was justified (Gen 15:6; John 8:56; Rom 4:1-4), so too we believe in Jesus' promise of everlasting life to all who simply believe in Him (e.g., John 3:16; 5:24; 6:47). Knowing facts about Jesus (e.g., His sinless life, His death on the cross, and His bodily resurrection from the dead) gives us reasons to believe His promise, but many people believe the facts about Jesus' life, death, and resurrection and yet do not believe that by faith in Him they have everlasting life.

MacArthur says that some Evangelicals claim that one can have everlasting life without having to turn from sin or without experiencing a "resulting change in lifestyle" (p. 38).[5] He disagrees. In other words, he believes you need to turn from your sins and have a resulting change in lifestyle to be saved (i.e., you need to do good works).

How do we get eternal life—by faith in Jesus or by doing good works? Do we believe in justification by faith alone apart from works, or something else? That is the heart of the Lordship Salvation debate.

Faith in Christ, not commitment to work for Him, is the sole condition of justification (Rom 4:1-8; Gal 2:15-16; 3:6-14) and of everlasting life (John 3:16; 5:24; 6:35; 11:26; Eph 2:8-9). The words *commit* and *commitment* do not even appear in John's Gospel or Galatians in relation to men. Nor do they appear in Ephesians. There are two uses in John and one in Galatians, but these refer not to the commitment *of men*, but the commitment *of God* (John 5:22; 8:34; Gal 2:7). And while the words *commit* and *commitment*

---

[5] He says, "[They say] there need be no turning from sin, no resulting change in lifestyle, no commitment—not even a *willingness* to yield to Christ's lordship" (*TGAJ*, p. 38, emphasis his).

do occur in the Synoptic Gospels in relation to men, they are never used as conditions of everlasting life.

MacArthur thinks the reason why many church people are unregenerate is because they have not been sufficiently committed and obedient to God. However, the real reason why multitudes of people from within Christianity will end up in the lake of fire is because they never believed the simple promise of John 3:16.

The Problem of Assurance

MacArthur's emphasis on works inevitably leads to a view of assurance that is likewise entirely dependent on our works. As MacArthur writes: "Genuine assurance comes from seeing the Holy Spirit's transforming work in one's life..." (p. 39). So for MacArthur, if you want to be sure that you are saved, you need to look at your behavior.

There are two problems with that approach to assurance.

First, looking at one's works for assurance of salvation only feeds the delusion that salvation depends upon our works. It's entirely man-centered. Instead of looking to Jesus' work and promise, MacArthur wants us to see how we're living. The only way to have assurance, according to his view, is if you think that you're basically living a good life. That further deludes people into thinking they are good enough to be saved, when they are not (e.g., Isa 64:6; Rom 3:11).

Second, looking at one's works for assurance of salvation is absolutely demoralizing to anyone convinced that even their best works are like filthy rags before God (Isa 64:6).

Calvinist David J. Engelsma calls the Puritan view of assurance, which is MacArthur's view of assurance, "a gospel of doubt."[6] Engelsma shows that only the promise of life in Scripture to the believer, not an imperfect life (Rom 3:23), can provide assurance that we are born again.

Wrongly Dividing the Word

MacArthur accuses Free Grace Dispensationalists with wrongly dividing the Word, especially when we distinguish between Christ

---

[6] David J. Engelsma, *The Gift of Assurance* (South Holland, IL: The Evangelism Committee of the Protestant Reformed Church, 2009), p. 53.

as Lord and Christ as Savior. He criticizes Livingston Blauvelt for suggesting that one is born again by believing in Jesus as his Savior, not by committing himself to Him as Lord of his life (p. 43). MacArthur adds, "It is astonishing that anyone would characterize that truth as unbiblical or heretical, but a growing chorus of voices is echoing the charge" (p. 43).

Maybe it *is* astonishing—*to someone who believes in salvation by works.* The doctrine of *sola fide* would obviously be heretical to anyone who believes that one must work his way into the kingdom by repentance, submission, commitment, obedience, and persever- ance until death. The real tragedy is the growing chorus that labels as unbiblical and heretical the truth that justification is by faith alone apart from works.

There are two verses in particular that MacArthur argues teach the necessity of works for the new birth.

> The two clearest statements on the way of salvation in all of Scripture both emphasize Jesus' lordship: "Believe in the Lord Jesus, and you shall be saved" (Acts 16:31); and "If you confess with your mouth Jesus as Lord, and believe in your heart that God raised Him from the dead, you shall be saved" (Rom. 10:9) (p. 44).

Jesus is Lord. We can agree on that. But do these verses teach that eternal life depends upon our obedience? Let's take a closer look.

Acts 16:31. MacArthur cites part of Paul's famous answer to the Philippian jailer: "Believe on the Lord Jesus Christ, and you will be saved, you and your household." He suggests that the word *Lord* in Acts 16:31 proves one must yield to the Lord Jesus Christ to have everlasting life. But please read that verse carefully. What is the one condition that we must fulfill in order to be saved? The only condi- tion is *believing in* the Lord Jesus Christ. Where are the mentions of repentance, surrender, commitment, obedience, and perseverance? They aren't mentioned. The words *Lord Jesus Christ* are Paul's des- ignation of the Person who is the object of saving faith. He is the one we must believe in to be born again. Paul neither says nor implies anything about repentance, commitment, surrender, obedience, or perseverance. Acts 16:31 actually *refutes* Lordship Salvation.

Romans 10:9. MacArthur finds additional proof of his position in Rom 10:9, which reads, "...that if you confess with your mouth the

Lord Jesus and believe in your heart that God has raised Him from the dead, you will be saved."

He does not cite verse 10, which completes the thought of verse 9, "For with the heart one believes unto righteousness, and with the mouth confession is made unto salvation."

Romans 10:9-10 lists not one, but two conditions of being *saved*: confessing Jesus and believing in Him. Even if we granted MacArthur's view that believing in Jesus is insufficient for anyone to be born again, four of MacArthur's "five essential elements of genuine conversion" (p. 118) are missing. Paul does not mention humility, revelation,[7] repentance, or submission, which are all essential to the new birth according to MacArthur (pp. 118-23). Why this is not explained is puzzling.

Since elsewhere in Romans Paul taught justification *by faith alone*, not by faith plus confessing Christ (Rom 3:22-28; 4:1-6), MacArthur's use of Rom 10:9-10 does not make sense.

There are various explanations of Rom 10:9-10 which avoid the problem of suggesting that Paul contradicts himself within Romans.[8] Far and away the simplest solution is to recognize that salvation in Romans does not refer to salvation from eternal condemnation.[9] This is easily seen in Rom 10:13-14, which MacArthur does not discuss.

Romans 10:13 is a quote of Joel 2:32, which refers to salvation from *temporal difficulties* by believing Jews during the Tribulation. Romans 10:14a specifically says that the ones calling on the Lord

---

[7] Revelation (i.e., "the Word of God") is mentioned in Rom 10:14-16, but MacArthur does not mention those verses.

[8] See, for example, John Murray, *The Epistle to the Romans* (Grand Rapids, MI: Eerdmans, 1959, 1965), pp. 55-57 ("confession verifies and confirms the faith of the heart," p. 57); F. F. Bruce, *Romans*, Tyndale, Revised Edition (Grand Rapids, MI: Eerdmans, 1985), pp. 192-93 ("we should more probably think of the initial confession made in Christian baptism," p. 193); C. E. B. Cranfield, *Commentary on Romans*, ICC (Edinburgh: T & T Clark, 1979), pp. 526-31 ("Confession that Jesus is Lord meant the acknowledgement that Jesus shares the name and the nature, the holiness, the authority, power, majesty and eternity of the one and only true God," 529); Zane Hodges, *Romans: Deliverance from Wrath* (Corinth, TX: Grace Evangelical Society, 2013), pp. 299-309 ("To be justified by faith in the heart but to refuse to confess 'Lord Jesus!' with the mouth will leave the believer tragically still exposed to God's temporal anger," pp. 301).

[9] See Hodges, *Romans*, pp. 299-309.

are believers: "How shall they call on Him in whom they have not [already] believed."

In Romans, the Apostle Paul uses the noun, *salvation* (*sōtēria*), five times (Rom 1:16; 10:1, 10; 11:11 and 13:11), and the verb, *to save* (*sōzein*), eight times (Rom 5:9, 10; 8:24; 9:27; 10:9, 13; 11:14, 26), and in each case they refer to deliverance from God's temporal wrath.

Romans 10:10a refers to justification by faith alone: one is *declared righteous* (i.e., justified) by believing. And Rom 10:10b, following Joel 2, refers to the salvation *of the believer from God's temporal wrath* by confessing Christ.

Faith and True Discipleship

MacArthur says that "obedience and submission are [not] extraneous to saving faith" (p. 45).[10] In other words, MacArthur has arbitrarily redefined the meaning of faith or belief without any lexical or Biblical support. He simply announces that obedience and submission are a part of saving faith.

But if that were true, think of how that would radically change the meaning of several authentically evangelistic verses, such as John 3:16. It would have to be read as saying,

> "For God so loved the world that He gave His only begotten Son, that whoever *obeys and submits* to Him should not perish but have everlasting life."

Or think of Eph 2:8-9. It would actually mean,

> For by grace you have been saved *through obedience and submission*, and that not of yourselves; it is the gift of God, not of works, lest anyone should boast.

And Jas 2:19, though not evangelistic, would strangely mean,

> "You *obey and submit* to the one God. You do well. Even the demons *obey and submit*—and tremble!"

---

[10] We know that obedience and submission are extraneous to saving faith because Paul said, "a man is justified by faith apart from [*chōris*] works of the Law" (Rom 3:28b). BDAG says the meaning of *chōris* in Rom 3:28 is, "without relation to or connection with something, independently of something…without regard to the observance of the law Rom 3:28" (p. 1095D). Saving faith does not include works; it necessarily excludes them.

Whether or not you agree with MacArthur that obedience and submission are a part of faith, you have to admit that such a view results in a radically different understanding of justification by faith alone.

Two Different Objects of Hope

MacArthur's Lordship Salvation hinges our eternal destiny not on faith, but on works. If saving faith is simply believing that what the Lord promises the believer is true, then our eternal destiny relies solely on *Jesus being faithful* to His promise. But if saving faith involves obedience and submission to Christ until death, then the burden of our eternal destiny rests squarely on our own shoulders.

Can you see now why Mormons love MacArthur's book?

That MacArthur does not separate justification from sanctification, or the call to discipleship from the promise of life, is a fatal flaw in his thinking. The results are disastrous. It makes our salvation depend upon works. Obviously, following Jesus in discipleship involves more than just believing in Him apart from works. So once MacArthur equates discipleship and evangelism, belief cannot be the condition of everlasting life. While MacArthur decries what he calls "easy-believism" (p. 46), what he's actually rejecting is plain-old *believism*. Belief isn't enough for him. He thinks God requires a lifetime of good works for everlasting life. Belief must be joined with submission, commitment, obedience, and perseverance.

MacArthur thinks the people discussed in Matt 7:21-23 have the problem of relying on the wrong type of works. Might it not be that the people who will say at the Great White Throne Judgment, "Lord, Lord, have we not prophesied in Your name, cast out demons in Your name, and done many wonders in Your name?" (Matt 7:22) do so because they think their works will justify them? Could it be that these people, like MacArthur, hope that their works will be sufficient to get them into the kingdom?

But Jesus rejects them: "I never knew you." He does not reject their works. He doesn't say, "I never knew your works." Jesus' standards are higher than theirs. They think they did well, but Jesus will reject them for their lawlessness (Matt 7:23). He never knew them, because they never did the will of the Father, which is believing in Jesus for everlasting life (John 6:28-29, 40). Faith in Christ, apart from works (Rom 3:28; Eph 2:8-9), guarantees entrance into the kingdom.[11]

By Grace through Faith

Realizing that some will see in Eph 2:8-9 a salvation that is not of works, MacArthur does mention these verses, yet surprisingly without actually explaining them. We find no discussion of how Eph 2:8 harkens back to Eph 2:5 (showing that *saved* in Eph 2:8 clearly refers to everlasting life, or being made alive). We find no discussion of the perfect tense of the verb *sōzō* (signifying a past salvation which has an abiding result). Missing is the discussion of the neuter *that* which refers back to the *by grace through faith* salvation, not to *faith*, which is a feminine noun, not neuter (though see p. 188 where he has a brief, yet unconvincing, explanation). And what is it that Paul is saying is "the gift of God"? Is this expression used elsewhere in the New Testament (e.g., John 4:10) or in Paul (Rom 5:16; 6:23)? We aren't told by MacArthur.

Previously MacArthur had said that saving faith is surrender and obedience. Now he adds a third aspect of saving faith: repentance, which he defines as "a turning from self and sin to God" (p. 47).

So "by grace you have been saved through faith" really means, "by grace you have been saved through *turning from sins, surrender, and obedience*." Is it any wonder that people who hold to Lordship Salvation lack assurance of their eternal destiny? Sadly their motivation to obey God is a desire to gain entrance into the kingdom (Matt 7:22).

---

[11] Although I am convinced that MacArthur preaches a false gospel of salvation by works, I am not thereby suggesting that he is unregenerate. I've heard him say that prior to his study of the Puritans in 1980 he believed in justification by simple faith, apart from works. And I've met people who had been in his church for over twenty years who told me that only after he studied the Puritans in 1980 did his theology change. On that basis, I believe that MacArthur is regenerate and eternally secure. He, like all of us, will have to answer at the Judgment Seat of Christ for anything he has taught which is in error (Jas 3:1). Yet in the end, I expect to spend eternity with him as a brother in the Lord. MacArthur himself illustrates the beauty of once-saved, always-saved. Even if someone ceases to believe in justification by faith alone, apart from works, his later belief in works salvation cannot undo the new birth.

But people who have never believed in justification by faith alone, apart from works, remain unregenerate, no matter how committed and seemingly obedient they are, for they have failed to do the will of the Father concerning His Son.

Loosely commenting on the word *gift* in Eph 2:8-9, MacArthur writes, "Salvation *is* a gift, but it is appropriated through a faith that goes beyond mere understanding and assenting to the truth" (p. 47, italics his). Note the word *but*. It is a contrast word. He is saying one thing, only to take it right back again. MacArthur cannot simply say what Paul says, "Salvation is the gift of God." He needs to qualify that statement, and explain it, and hedge it in; otherwise the reader might think it really is a gift! MacArthur feels it vital that no one bases assurance on Jesus' promise; he is always trying to turn people's attention to their own works: "Genuine assurance comes from seeing the Holy Spirit's transforming work in one's life" (p. 39).

A Warning

The second chapter of *TGAJ* ends with a warning. "If we are truly born of God," MacArthur says, "we have a faith that cannot fail to overcome the world...the process of sanctification can never stall completely [in us]...God...will continue to perfect us until the day of Christ" (p. 48).

But who among us is certain that he will overcome the world? Who is sure that his sanctification will never stall completely? Who can be sure that God will continue to perfect him until Christ returns?

The answer is *no one*. Hence the second chapter of *TGAJ* ends with a warning that is in essence a call to doubt and despair since no one can be sure he will pass those tests.

CHAPTER 3

He Calls for a New Birth

Introduction

Doublethink," George Orwell once explained, "means the power of holding two contradictory beliefs in one's mind simultaneously, and accepting both of them." The third chapter of *The Gospel According to Jesus* reads like a case study in theological doublethink. MacArthur desperately wants to denounce legalism *and* to teach that everlasting life depends upon our obedience. If that seems contradictory to you, it is. And yet, that is how MacArthur interprets the famous dialogue between Jesus and Nicodemus about the new birth in John 3.

The New Birth

If you want to know what a person needs to do in order to be born again, then John 3 is one of the best passages to read. Obviously MacArthur agrees, or he wouldn't have one of his opening chapters on John 3.

The message is simple and easy enough for a child to understand. All we need to do is believe in Jesus for everlasting life and He gives it to us (i.e., we become born again). Rituals and law can't do it. Only faith in Jesus can.

But that way of understanding Jesus' talk with Nicodemus doesn't sit well with MacArthur. In *TGAJ* he calls that message *easy-believism* (pp. 20, 37, 52, 91, 187, 202, 205, 219, 270, 277, 279, 281), *the no-lordship doctrine/message/evangelism/gospel* (pp. 10, 13, 25, 30, 59), *cheap grace* (pp. 20, 51, 68, 205, 277), and *antinomian/ antinomianism* (pp. 46, 176, 197, 199, 200, 214, 266, 269, 277). He thinks that the faith-alone message leads to many fake Christians, people who believe in Jesus for their eternal destiny, but whose lifestyle does not reflect total submission to Him.[1]

MacArthur begins the chapter by repeating his concern about assurance, saying, "Not everyone who claims to be a Christian really is" (p. 51). As always, his concern is *cheap grace* and *easy faith*: "The softening of the New Testament message has brought with it a putrefying inclusivism that in effect sees almost any kind of positive response to Jesus as tantamount to saving faith" (p. 51).

What kinds of *positive responses to Jesus* does MacArthur have in mind? If he's saying that walking an aisle is not a saving response to Jesus, he is correct. Of course, that isn't a "positive response to Jesus." That is a positive response to a preacher and a man-made appeal. The only saving response is belief in Jesus' promise to give us everlasting life. But MacArthur does not believe that is what the Lord told Nicodemus. He wants to convince his readers that John 3 teaches that salvation is obtained by obedience.

Though the Lord does not mention repentance or obedience to Nicodemus, MacArthur says, "He was showing Nicodemus the necessity of repentance" (p. 59). "*Disobedience* is unbelief. Real faith *obeys*" (p. 60, emphasis added). "Real faith," he says, "has at

---

[1] In the Introduction of *TGAJ* MacArthur says, "The gospel in vogue today holds forth a false hope to sinners. It promises them that they can have eternal life yet continue to live in rebellion against God" (p. 19). Under the heading "Saying without Doing: The Sin of Empty Words," MacArthur writes in chapter 21, "Unlike preachers today who go to excessive lengths to avoid upsetting anyone's assurance, our Lord was determined to destroy the false hope of all who falsely thought they were redeemed" (p. 213). According to MacArthur the issue the Lord was addressing is not what one believes, but what one does or does not do. MacArthur speaks of *false professors*, whom he identifies as those who are not "loyal, abiding believers" (p. 188; see also p. 51); *false disciples*, whom he says "are friendly to Jesus…look and talk like disciples, but they are not committed to Him and are therefore capable of the worst kind of betrayal" (p. 115; see also p. 167); *professing Christians* "whose behavior is indistinguishable from the rebellion of the unregenerate" (p. 20); and *false believers*, whom he identifies as "shallow responders," as those who "respond positively," and "on the surface their faith looks encouraging…you might think these people stand taller and stronger than everyone else…[but they] are all smiles and cheers with no sense of repentance or humility" (p. 133).

its heart *a willingness to obey*" (p. 60, emphasis added). In the very last sentence of the chapter he says, "There is no promise of life... for those who will not identify with the sinful, dying Israelites *and turn from sin in obedient faith* to the One who was lifted up so that they would not have to perish" (p. 61, emphasis added).

Seven times in John 3:12-18 the Lord Jesus said that *the one who believes in Him* has everlasting life. Seven times in seven verses!

Not once does He say, "He who obeys Me has everlasting life."

Yet MacArthur wants his readers to think in terms of salvation *by works* by suggesting that in speaking with Nicodemus about how to be born again, "our Lord eschewed the quick, easy, or shallow response" (p. 51).

What the Lord demanded, MacArthur is saying, was a gradual (i.e., not quick), difficult (i.e, not easy), and deep (i.e., not shallow) response.

Does that sound like the message of John 3:16? Does that resemble the response of the woman at the well in John 4? Did she or Nicodemus gradually come to faith in Christ over the course of years? Was it difficult for them to come to faith? Was their response in some way *deep*?

No, no, no, no, and no.

The Futility of Religion

Of course, MacArthur knows that most Evangelicals look down upon salvation by works, at least in theory. So he needs to appear to be against it. MacArthur thinks that Jesus was rebuking Nicodemus for his legalism (or "hyperlegalism," p. 53). But just in case anyone starts to wonder what the difference between Lordship Salvation and legalism is, he distracts the reader with a generalization about the Pharisees and Nicodemus:

> The Pharisees were hyperlegalists who externalized religion. They were the very epitome of all who pursue a form of godliness with no reality (2 Tim. 3:5). Although they were fanatically religious, they were no nearer the kingdom of God than a prostitute. Their credo included fastidious adherence to more than six hundred laws, many of which were simply their own inventions (p. 53).

MacArthur implies that Nicodemus fit this mold:

> When Nicodemus heard Christ talking about a new birth, his mind must have been a bog. He had always believed that salvation was earned by good works. He probably even expected Christ to commend him for his strict legalism! (pp. 53-54).

Implying that Nicodemus was a hyperlegalist who externalized his religion and followed laws "many of which were simply [the Pharisees's] own inventions" allows MacArthur to denounce one form of legalism.

However, MacArthur wants the reader to know that the problem is not legalism but what he calls *hyperlegalism*. Too much attention to the commands and to works is a bad thing. But the right amount of attention to the commands and to our works is a life and death matter.

Jesus' solution, according to MacArthur, was to give Nicodemus an even more challenging demand: "Far from offering this man [Nicodemus] an easy conversion, Christ was challenging him with the most difficult demand He could make" (p. 54). MacArthur explains that sentence in the rest of the chapter.

The Unity of Revelation

After having said at the start of his chapter that being born again was not quick or easy, MacArthur now says, "People have always stumbled over the simplicity of salvation" (p. 56). So what is *the simple way of salvation*? We are not told here, other than "The message is simply that God saves repentant sinners who come to Him in faith" (p. 57). He continues, "There is no secret here, no mystery, no obscurity, and no complexity." According to MacArthur, to be born again one must repent ("repentant sinner") and "come to Him [Christ] in faith." But remember that MacArthur teaches that faith[2] is inseparable from submission, commitment, obedience, and perseverance.[3]

---

[2] MacArthur defines faith as persevering ("faith is neither transient nor impotent. It has an abiding quality that guarantees it will endure to the end," p. 189), as being "inseparable from obedience" (pp. 189, 190), and as "including surrender to Christ" (p. 189).

[3] MacArthur says that *commitment* is a condition of everlasting life on pp. 15, 19, 37, 38, 51, 62, 66, 70, 115, 144, 150, 172, 187, 225. He indicates that *obedience* is required for everlasting life on pages 10, 15, 19, 20, 29, 32, 37, 45, 58, 66, 80, 96,

MacArthur doesn't seem to realize how confusing these conditions are for his readers. How much obedience is enough for people who fall short of God's glory every day (Rom 3:23)? What if we find some measure of assurance in the fact that we appear to be more submitted, more committed, and more obedient than others (Luke 18:9-14)? What if we have assurance of being committed because we are blind to the extent of our own sinfulness? How can we be sure we will never fall away?[4]

The Reality of Redemption

MacArthur clearly rejects the view that *believing in Jesus* is *believing in Him*. I know that sounds odd. Let me restate that. MacArthur thinks that belief in the Bible is always being convinced or persuaded of the truth, *except in the case of saving faith*. To believe that Jesus is God is simply to be convinced He is God. To believe that the Bible is the Word of God is simply to be persuaded of that fact. But to believe in Jesus for everlasting life is not to be persuaded that He guarantees everlasting life to all who simply believe in Him. In this one case *to believe* means to submit to Him and to obey Him for the rest of one's life.

He champions the idea that believing in Jesus includes obeying His commands. MacArthur disapprovingly cites Zane Hodges who said, "there is no idea of committal of life…no possibility of surrender" (p. 59). Instead, MacArthur flatly says that "obedience to Christ [is] an element of saving faith" (p. 58).

MacArthur also says, "He [Jesus] was showing Nicodemus the necessity of repentance" (p. 59). However, repentance is not

---

149, 191, 211, 227, 230. *Submission* is repeatedly cited by MacArthur as required for spending eternity with the Lord (pp. 10, 11, 28, 34, 36, 44, 45, 47, 70, 80, 99, 116, 117, 122, 137, 158, 163, 187, 275). He also stresses the need *to persevere* in faith and good works in order to make it into Christ's kingdom (pp. 109, 187 n9, 217, 248-50, 262, 275). In many of the pages just cited he says that faith is inseparable from commitment, obedience, submission, and perseverance. He even coins the expression *obedient faith* (pp. 61, 113).

[4] MacArthur provides some answers to questions such as these in Appendix 3 in *TGAJ*, pp. 272-82. Twelve of the seventeen questions in that Appendix deal with assurance, showing that his book generates these types of questions. MacArthur thinks that "Periodic doubts about one's salvation are not necessarily wrong… Scripture encourages self-examination" (p. 213). He wants his readers to ask questions like this and he wants his readers to have periodic doubts about their salvation. He sees that as a healthy thing.

mentioned in John 3. In fact, it's not mentioned anywhere in John's Gospel. If that is a condition of everlasting life, why didn't Jesus mention repentance to Nicodemus? Why didn't John mention it?

MacArthur goes on to say that what is required to be born again is "obedient faith" (p. 61).[5] This is confusing. MacArthur just castigated Nicodemus and the Pharisees for overzealous obedience to God's law, arguing that hyperlegalism is wrong and that people must recognize that they are helpless sinners. Yet here he is arguing that they must also commit and surrender and obey in order to gain the new birth.

MacArthur's interpretation of this passage is at odds with the plain statements made by Jesus as recorded by the Apostle John in the Biblical text. Jesus didn't call Nicodemus to repentance, obedience, or commitment. He only asked him to believe in Him. That is all that is required to be born again.

By looking carefully at the conversation between the Lord and Nicodemus, we can understand what actually happened.

The real meaning of Jesus' meeting with Nicodemus is plain. The Lord indeed told Nicodemus that the new birth was essential in order to see the kingdom. And He told him that he should have understood this from the Old Testament.

Nicodemus came to Jesus by night (3:2; cf. 7:50; 19:39) because he did not want his interest in Jesus to be public knowledge. He knew that Jesus was "a teacher come from God" because of the signs [cf. 2:23] that He did (John 3:2).

Jesus got straight to the point: "Unless one is born again, he cannot see the kingdom of God" (3:3).[6]

---

[5] MacArthur uses the expression *obedient faith* twice (pp. 61, 113). While he doesn't come right out and define that, it is clear that he means *faith that obeys*: "Disobedience is unbelief. Real faith obeys" (p. 60, preceding the reference to "obedient faith"). "The true disciple…may occasionally turn back to his fishing nets, but ultimately…he will return to a life of service for the Savior" (p. 115, two pages after the reference to "obedient faith"). Thus obedient faith is perseverance in service for the Savior. It pictures a person who obeys God most of the time and in spite of possible falls, always returns to obedience and perseverance.

[6] Note that the Lord does not bring up the forgiveness of sins, a topic totally absent in the evangelistic encounters in John. In fact, the forgiveness of sins is only mentioned twice in John, once directly, after Jesus' resurrection (John 20:23), and once indirectly, before the disciples only, when He washed their feet (John 13:1-11). In John's Gospel the issue in evangelism is everlasting life (or not being eternally condemned).

Seeing the kingdom refers to entering and participating in it (cf. 3:5, 36; 8:51). Jesus has not yet told Nicodemus what he must do so that God would regenerate him (cf. vv 14-18). Jesus first shows him his need for the new birth.

Nicodemus, like the woman at the well in John 4 (cf. John 4:15) is confused about the new birth, but he does understand that Jesus is talking about a *second* birth (see John 3:4).

Nicodemus now wants to know how this new birth can be realized (3:9) and Jesus explains to him how it is possible and how to receive it (vv 10-18). This is the last mention of the name of Nicodemus until 7:51.

In John 3:14 we read about the episode in Numbers 21 of the bronze serpent. When God heard the complaints from the Israelites about the miraculous manna He provided freely while they were in the wilderness, He sent deadly serpents among them, killing many (Num 21:4-9). Directed by God, Moses lifted up a bronze serpent. Whoever looked at it was healed. The uplifted serpent was a type of Christ,[7] picturing how the Messiah, who would be *lifted up on the cross*, would save everyone who simply looked to Him. Looking to Jesus in John 3:14 is a figure for believing in Him as John 3:15-18 makes abundantly clear.

MacArthur, like some preachers, is willing to embellish God's Word if embellishing helps him make the point he wants to make. Concerning Numbers 21 and the uplifted serpent MacArthur shares insights not found there or anywhere in the Bible concerning that incident. He says that the people of Israel "turned to God in desperation and with genuine repentance" (p. 59; see also p. 58, "When they realized they were dying, they repented"). He then adds, "Jesus was demanding that Nicodemus do the same" (see also earlier on p. 59 where he says, "He was showing Nicodemus the necessity of repentance"). There is no mention of repentance in John 3 or John's Gospel or Numbers 21, but MacArthur manages to find it anyway.

In the first edition of *The Gospel According to Jesus* he boldly said, "In order to look at the bronze snake on the pole, they had to drag themselves to where they could see it" (p. 46). Drag themselves? There is no hint of that in Numbers 21 or John 3:14. Evidently

---

[7] The uplifted serpent wrapped around a pole is also the symbol of the American Medical Association.

someone convinced MacArthur that he was going too far. In the second and third editions this claim was toned down to the following: "Undoubtedly many were already sick and dying, fast losing their strength" (p. 52 [second edition], p. 59 [third edition]).

But in all three editions he then makes this statement: "They were in no position to glance flippantly at the pole and then proceed with lives of rebellion" (p. 46 [1st edition], p. 52 [2nd edition], p. 59 [third edition]).

How does he know that a special type of look was needed? And what would "glancing flippantly" at the pole even mean?

MacArthur is suggesting that those Jews of that generation who saw the uplifted serpent ceased rebelling and lived in fellowship with God after Numbers 21. But that is not supported by the remainder of Numbers or of Deuteronomy. Numbers 25:1 says that "the people began to commit harlotry with the women of Moab." The next verse adds, "They invited the people to the sacrifice of their gods, and the people ate and bowed down to their gods." Does that sound like national repentance occurred in Numbers 21 like MacArthur says? Moses had to contend with the people of Israel repeatedly, and it did not stop after the uplifted serpent incident.

In John 3:15-16, Jesus twice says directly that believing in Him is the condition of everlasting life. The moment anyone believes in Jesus he has (present tense) everlasting life (3:16). The issue is belief, not behavior (even though God wishes believers and unbelievers to obey Him).

In John 3:18 the Lord summarizes the life and death issue: "He who believes in Him is not condemned; but he who does not believe is condemned already, because he has not believed in the name of the only begotten of God." Three times in John 3:18 Jesus refers to the necessity of *believing in Him* to escape eternal condemnation. Five times in John 3:15, 16, 18 the Lord told Nicodemus that whoever believes in Him has everlasting life. John's Gospel is rightly called *The Gospel of Belief.*

Jesus didn't tell Nicodemus that he needed to repent, commit, and obey in order to be born again. He told him that he needed to believe in Him in order to have everlasting life.[8]

---

[8] In John 3:19-21 the Lord Jesus challenges Nicodemus to confess Him openly. Since the Lord did not challenge unbelievers to confess Him, it is evident that Nicodemus came to faith while hearing the Lord's words as recorded in John 3:14-18.

Conclusion

John 3:1-21 is a crucial passage for understanding how to be born again. Having carefully examined those verses, we can conclude that, contrary to MacArthur's understanding of this passage, believing in the Lord Jesus Christ is the only condition of everlasting life. The Lord said this over and over again to Nicodemus in 3:14-18.

The Savior did not talk to Nicodemus about repentance, commitment, or obedience—the three conditions of everlasting life MacArthur suggests are evident in this passage. The issue in relation to the new birth is belief, not behavior.

Nicodemus did not confess his faith in Christ, however (cf. John 7:48-52; 12:42-43; 19:38-39). In the section which follows, John 3:22-36, John gives a prime example of someone who did confess Jesus openly, John the Baptist. For more discussion of the secret believer motif in John see Bob Bryant, "The Secret Believer in the Gospel of John," *JOTGES* (Autumn 2014): 61-75.

CHAPTER 4

He Demands True Worship

Introduction

Anyone who doubts that God can use the most broken of people to become the most powerful witnesses for the gospel promise should read John 4, the story of the woman at the well.

In the fourth chapter of *TGAJ*, John MacArthur offers us his interpretation of the conversation between Jesus and the Samaritan woman. He believes the episode provides us with some critical truths that need to be emphasized when evangelizing, such as the need to confront sinners with their sin, the necessity of moral evaluation, the need for spiritual transformation, and the demand that we worship God in spirit and in truth. However, MacArthur's interpretation doesn't fit the details of the passage.

What Does Jesus Demand?

The title of this chapter is telling: "He Demands True Worship." Of all the ways you could summarize what the Lord told the woman at the well, "Jesus demands true worship" is one of the last statements that should come to mind.

True, the Lord did talk to her about true worship in John 4:21-24. But that was in response to an issue she raised about worship (John 4:20). It wasn't the main point He was communicating to her. The

Lord certainly wasn't saying that in order to be born again one had to worship God in spirit and in truth.

Just as the Lord communicated to Nicodemus that one is born again by believing in Him, the Lord's main point here is that believing in Him results in everlasting life (John 4:10-14, 25-26, 28-29).

Like a good debater, MacArthur early on addresses some possible objections to his view that the Lord was telling the woman that to be born again she must worship Him faithfully for the rest of her life. MacArthur says, "He made no mention of sin's wages, repentance, faith, atonement, His death for sin, or His resurrection" (p. 62). But he warns that we shouldn't be too quick to draw any conclusion from an argument from silence: "Are we to conclude that those are not indispensable elements of the gospel message? Certainly not" (p. 62).

Did you notice that MacArthur said, "He made no mention of... faith...."? Yet the text of John 4 shows the Lord did mention faith and that faith is at the very center of His discussion with the woman at the well.

In verses 10-14, Jesus used *drinking living water* as a metaphor for *faith*, as is clear from a comparison with John 6:35, "I am the bread of life. He who comes to Me shall never hunger, and *he who believes in Me shall never thirst*" (emphasis added).

In John 4:21, He explicitly tells the woman to believe Him: "Jesus said to her, 'Woman, *believe Me*, the hour is coming when you will neither on this mountain, nor in Jerusalem, worship the Father'" (emphasis added).

In addition, the Apostle John tells us that many Samaritans of that town "*believed in Him* because of the word of the woman" (John 4:39, emphasis added) and "many more *believed* because of His own word" (John 4:41, emphasis added).

Both the Lord Jesus and the Apostle John emphasized belief. Yet MacArthur says that faith was not brought up in this passage!

The Lesson of the Water: Everyone Who Thirsts May Come

Apparently, MacArthur disagrees that drinking is a metaphor for faith. Instead, he asserts that in this context it conveys the idea of commitment to Christ: "Can we concede that the verb *drink* conveys the idea of appropriation apart from commitment? Certainly not" (p. 66, emphasis his). As proof, he cites Matt 20:22 and John

18:11 where the Lord prophecies that He is about to drink the cup of God's wrath. He says that in those verses, "both use *drink* in a way that clearly implies full compliance and surrender" (p. 66, emphasis his).

Not quite.

MacArthur equates a sinner *drinking the wonderful living water* with the sinless Son of God *drinking the terrible cup of suffering* (also called *the cup of God's wrath*, Ps 11:6; Isa 51:17; Jer 49:12; Rev 14:10; 16:19). In John 18:11 the Lord makes it clear that the cup He was about to drink refers to the cross.

But MacArthur fails to explain what drinking the cup of suffering means. He does not discuss the cross here. And He does not discuss whether Jesus willingly going to the cross is different from a person drinking living water.

So while MacArthur is right to point out that *drinking* can sometimes be a metaphor for a painful experience, indeed, a good work (the cross of Christ is the greatest work ever done), the real question is whether *drinking living water* ever equals works, or a commitment to do works. The answer is never!

If anyone doubts that drinking living water is a metaphor for simple faith, then John 6:35, should settle the issue: "he who believes in Me shall never thirst." The Lord's point is that once someone believes in Him (i.e., drinks the living water), he will never thirst again. Drinking living water is not in any way comparable to the Lord dying on the cross.

See also Rev 22:17, "And let him who thirsts come. Whoever desires, let him take the water of life freely [= as a gift]."

Unfortunately, MacArthur fails to mention those verses.

But what's worse, MacArthur's conclusion about Matt 20:22 and John 18:11 is flawed. He says that "both [verses] use *drink* in a way that clearly implies full compliance and surrender" (p. 66). He thinks the Lord's reference to drinking the cup of suffering is a metaphor for commitment and surrender.

On the contrary, the Lord Jesus was talking about an *action*. The cup of God's wrath is the experience of crucifixion. Jesus was not saying that He was *committed* to going to the cross. He was prophesying that He would actually *die on the cross* as Matt 20:22, 28 and John 18:11 attest. Drinking that cup was the greatest good work ever done.

The Lord Jesus did not tell the woman at the well that if she drank the cup of suffering she would have everlasting life. If drinking living water had meant drinking the cup of God's wrath, as MacArthur argues, then the Lord was teaching works salvation in John 4.

Her Sinful Lifestyle

MacArthur claims that before Jesus would give her eternal life, the Samaritan woman first needed to undergo a "moral investigation and correction" (p. 68). Jesus allegedly challenged the woman to change her sinful lifestyle and alter her behavior (p. 68) before He would give her eternal life.

Now, there's no question that her sinful past was discussed. The question is, why did the Lord Jesus bring it up?

MacArthur's view is that the Lord brought up her sinful past to get her to confess that she is a sinner because such a confession is one of the many steps, along with "moral investigation and correction," to eternal salvation (p. 68). Yet that can't be right. She already knew she was a sinner. There is no evidence in this passage that she pretended not to be a sinner.

MacArthur misses the obvious reason. The Lord made His declaration about her adulterous past to prove to her that He was the Messiah. Notice that after He points out her infidelities, she says, "I know that Messiah is coming" (John 4:25a). Why would she say that? Apparently because she had been taught that the Messiah would "tell us all things" (John 4:25b). He would know things that no one else could know. Since Jesus revealed private details of her life that no stranger could have known, she wondered, *Is this the Messiah?* So when Jesus confirmed that He was, she evidently believed Him, left her water pot,[1] and went into the village and said, "Come, see a Man *who told me all things that I ever did.* Could this be the Christ?" (John 4:29, emphasis added).

So, Jesus didn't reveal the woman's sinful past because evangelism demands "moral investigation and correction." The reason the Lord revealed the woman's sinful past was to convince her that He is the Messiah. He succeeded.

---

[1] Leaving her water pot may imply that she was leaving the old water, the old religion, behind. She was taking the new water, the living water, to the village. She was the vessel that now contained the living water.

Now, if Jesus had meant to teach the necessity of moral correction for everlasting life, we would expect to see Him actually say that. But He does not. And we would expect to read that the woman indeed changed her way of life. There's nothing in the text to support MacArthur's understanding of this passage.

MacArthur's view of this passage is inconsistent with the text itself. Why? It seems that MacArthur has read his theology into the Biblical text. His Puritan theology tells him that faith alone is not sufficient to be born again, so he imports into the text repentance, commitment, obedience, and confession of past sins.[2] Are we to understand that the Lord Jesus, the perfect evangelist, failed to properly inform the woman of what she needed to do to have everlasting life?

The Lesson of True Worship: Now Is the Acceptable Time

During their talk, the Samaritan woman asked Jesus about the correct place to worship God. The Lord told her that where we worship is not important. What matters is whether we are worshipping in spirit and in truth.

MacArthur believes the Lord gave this answer because He was leading the woman to see that in order to be born again He must "transform her into a true worshiper of the living God!" (p. 70). He adds, "The hour of salvation had come for her. She would willingly become a true worshiper" (p. 70). In other words, for MacArthur, Jesus' answer shows that the condition of everlasting life—or one of the conditions, since he believes there are many—is becoming a true worshiper of God.

Is it possible to worship God and not do work? The answer is obviously no. If worship is a condition for everlasting life, then work is required to be born again.

The only way one could come to such a conclusion is by having a theological predisposition. The text itself does not in any way

---

[2] Why did she only have to confess (implicitly) that she was living with a man she was not married to? Didn't she have to confess *all her sins*? Why only that one sin? Surely she sinned in many ways every day as even believers indwelt by the Holy Spirit do (Rom 3:23; 1 John 1:8, 10). Shouldn't she have to confess all of the sins she had committed up to that point in her life? If so, wouldn't that take more than a few seconds? I would think it would take her days or weeks to even scratch the surface on all the sins she had committed up to that point.

suggest that the Lord told the woman that the condition of ever-lasting life is to become a true worshiper of God.

The Lesson of the Witness: This Man Receives Sinners

After Jesus revealed Himself to be the Messiah, the woman left her water pot, went into town, and told the men what had just happened. The first thing she declared was, "Come, see a Man who told me all things that I ever did. *Could this be the Christ?*" (John 4:29, emphasis added). Notice the question which she asked. That is the question which MacArthur fails to mention at this point. He somehow separates the question from the appeal by several paragraphs. Why? Possibly because he does not see the condition of everlasting life as believing that Jesus is the Christ (John 20:31; 1 John 5:1). MacArthur implies the reason He revealed her sinful past was to convince her that she was a guilty sinner who needed forgiveness. Of course, neither the word *forgiveness* nor the concept of forgiveness (or release from shame and liberation from guilt, as MacArthur says) is anywhere in the account. MacArthur imports those ideas into the passage.

Yet the woman's message to the men is clear. She is saying: *I know this Man is the Christ because He did what we know Messiah would do. He told me all things I ever did.*

MacArthur does get around to mentioning her question to the men. When he does, he is correct that the reason the woman asked a question ("Could this be the Christ?"), rather than asserted directly that Jesus is the Messiah, is because she had a low reputation and she was convinced a more subtle approach would have a better effect.

Instead of saying what the text says, that the men of the village *believed in Jesus*, MacArthur says they "responded to Jesus with zeal" (p. 71) and they had "a zealous reaction" (p. 72). But the Apostle John twice says that they *believed* in Jesus, in verses 39 and 41. The emphasis is the response of faith. Why, then, does MacArthur keep on emphasizing zeal, which is not mentioned in the text?

The reason he mentions zeal and not faith is because that's what his theology demands. Talking about zeal gives the impression of repentance, confession of sins, commitment, obedience, and everything else MacArthur believes one must do to be born again. So instead of emphasizing what the text actually emphasizes, *faith*, he offers up *zeal*.

Conclusion

So what should we learn from the encounter of the Lord Jesus with the woman at the well and later with the men of Sychar? MacArthur says that the lesson of this encounter is that to be born again people must "confess and forsake their sin" and must "submit themselves to worship Him in Spirit and truth" (p. 72).

What MacArthur's interpretation illustrates is the stark difference between his gospel and Jesus' gospel. It's a prime example of how MacArthur reads his theology into God's Word, rather than simply trying to understand what the text means.

The point of Jesus' conversation with the woman at the well is this: Anyone can believe that Jesus is the Messiah who guarantees everlasting life to all who believe in Him. Even an immoral woman who had not changed her ways and who was not seeking after God could believe in the Messiah upon hearing His promise. The "whoever" of John 3:16 is powerfully illustrated by the Samaritan woman in John 4.

CHAPTER 5

He Receives Sinners, But Refuses the Righteous

Introduction

Imagine someone too terrible to be a Christian. I mean someone so awful, horrible, and wicked that no one in his right mind could ever think he was a believer. Who would that be? What would he do?

Frankly, I can't think of such a person. The blood of Christ atones for the sins of the whole world. So no one is too evil to be born again by faith in Christ.

However, MacArthur has an example of such a person. He heard about this vile fellow from his pastor friend, who said this fellow was a member of his Sunday school class. What did this awful man do?

He owned a chain of liquor stores.

Oh, the horror!

Now, you might not be too disturbed, dear reader, by this tale, but apparently MacArthur was. In fact, he was so shocked at the idea of a Christian owning liquor stores that he "wondered aloud how such a thing could be" (p. 73). How could someone who sells liquor be born again? Isn't it obvious that man is headed straight to hell?

Well, it certainly isn't obvious to me. And I come out of an alcoholic family. I know what alcohol can lead to. I don't drink at all. Not even a drop. However, it is clear that the Bible doesn't forbid the drinking of wine, beer, and other distilled drinks. After all, Jesus' first miracle was turning water into real wine. And it wasn't just any type of wine, but the very best wine (John 2:10). Paul told Timothy to drink some wine for his stomach and other ailments (1 Tim 5:23). And the Psalmist said that wine gladdens the heart (Ps 104:15). So while we are commanded not to get drunk (Eph 5:18), contrary to what MacArthur would have us believe, we are not forbidden from drinking or even from selling liquor.

Though I don't drink and would be glad if no one in the world drank, I am unwilling to go beyond what Scripture says on this or any other matter. Sometimes one of my friends has a glass of wine or a beer while I am with him. I never take offense or ask him to stop. That would be intruding on his personal freedom when I am not tempted to drink or offended by his action.

MacArthur assumes that if a man makes a living by selling liquor, then he must be morally bankrupt. As it happens, MacArthur finds out some other unsavory details about the liquor store owner's life. Specifically, we are told the man has been divorced. However, this isn't necessarily an example of his sin. The Lord allowed for divorce and remarriage in one case only, sexual infidelity (Matt 5:31-32; 19:9). But even if he was guilty of breaking up his marriage, are we to believe that divorced people are condemned to hell?

We are also told that the liquor store owner was "living with a young girl" (p. 73)—the implication being they weren't married and that she was younger than he was. If so, yes, it is sinful to have marital relations with someone and not be married to that person.

So the "false professor" in MacArthur's story owns some liquor stores, is divorced, and is living with a younger woman. The first action is not a sin. The second action isn't necessarily a sin. But the third action is sinful (assuming they are not married). So the man is a sinner, though, of course, we already knew that (Rom 3:23).

But MacArthur wants us to take this man as an example of "wanton rebellion against God's standards" (p. 73). Wanton rebellion? And more than that, he wants us to agree that this is the example of someone who is *clearly* not born again.

But isn't the illustration a bit weak? If that's the worst example MacArthur can present, then it's no wonder why so many Lordship Salvation people lack assurance. Can any of us really say that we're much better than this man, in the eyes of God?

Think of what that would mean for the rest of us. If MacArthur is correct, then anyone who sells beer or other alcohol is probably not born again. This would include not only those who *own* liquor stores, bars, restaurants, grocery stores, convenience stores, and all other places that sell beer, wine, and spirits, *but also anyone who works in a place that sells beer, wine, or liquor.* Let me list some people who fit this profile:

- waiters and waitresses,
- bartenders,
- beer, wine, and liquor distributors,
- grocery store clerks,
- anyone who works at Walmart (which sells wine),
- people who work in breweries and wineries and distilleries,
- importers who import beer, wine, and spirits,
- those who own vineyards,
- those who make cans and bottles for alcohol,
- those who make labels for alcohol,
- those who drive beer and wine trucks,
- caterers, and
- people who run wedding chapels.

But it gets worse. MacArthur also implies that divorced people aren't born again. Nor are people who are living together. But why stop there? Why not include alcoholics and drug addicts? Oh, wait a minute. MacArthur *does* include those people, because he says that in order to experience "justification by faith" one must "let go of sin" (p. 247).

What kind of sin does he have in mind? Later in the book he mentions three vice lists (1 Cor 6:9-11; Gal 5:19-21; Eph 5:5) which he says refers to people whose sins show they are going to hell (p. 247). Those vice lists include the sins of covetousness, outbursts of anger, jealousy, and envy. Does he really mean to say that believers who struggle with jealousy prove they are unregenerate? Yes, he does.

Immediately after quoting these vice lists MacArthur then says that we must persevere or else we won't make it to the kingdom: "For Paul, perseverance in the faith is essential evidence that faith is real. If a person ultimately and finally falls away from the faith, it proves that person never was redeemed to begin with" (p. 248).

Is it true that owning liquor stores or struggling with jealousy disqualifies a person from spending eternity with the Lord? No.

Please don't misunderstand. Sin is serious business. We do need to call for believers and unbelievers to turn from sin. We should be deeply concerned that believers live righteous lives that honor God. It should grieve us whenever we hear of a pastor or church leader or believer who has a moral fall. But to link the eternal destiny of people with their behavior is to pervert the gospel of Christ (Gal 1:6-9).

Over thirty years ago during a chapel message at Dallas Theological Seminary one of my seminary professors, Dr. Howard Hendricks, who recently went to be with the Lord, said that we must not "front-load the gospel" in order to improve the quality of people in the church. He is right.

Nominalism and carnality are problems in churches, but the solution isn't to compromise the freeness of the gospel promise by making it depend upon works. If we want people to grow spiritually, we must call them to follow Christ, and teach them about such things as grace, belief, everlasting life, God's discipline, the blessing and cursing motif, eternal rewards, and the possible approval and praise at the Judgment Seat of Christ. But we dare not tweak the message of everlasting life in a misguided effort to improve the quality of people in our churches (Gal 1:6-9).

Coming to Grips with Sin

When MacArthur speaks of *salvation*, he means regeneration, or salvation from eternal condemnation. He condemns the belief that regeneration "is only the granting of eternal life, not necessarily the liberation of a sinner from the bondage of his iniquity" (pp. 73-74). In other words, MacArthur is implying that true regeneration includes liberating the sinner from sin *in one's experience*.

Of course, everyone should know that Paul taught that believers have been liberated from sin's bondage. For example, Paul said, "And having been set free from sin, you became slaves of righteousness" (Rom 6:18). That is true *in our position*.

However, we should also know that Paul also taught that born-again believers are *not necessarily liberated in our experience*.

Notice that in Romans 6 Paul also says,

> Therefore do not let sin reign in your mortal body, that you should obey it in its lusts. And do not present your members as instruments of unrighteousness to sin, but present yourselves to God as being alive from the dead, and your members as instruments of righteousness (Rom 6:12-13).

By urging Christians, people who have everlasting life, not to let sin dominate their experience, Paul was showing that they might allow that to happen (cf. John 8:30-32).

MacArthur says that God has set believers free from sin's bondage *in our experience*. If so, then why would any believer ever sin *at all*? Will we sin in eternity future when we have glorified bodies? Of course not. Then we will be free from sin's bondage in our experience (1 John 3:2). But now we are still in our mortal bodies and we still fall short of the glory of God every day (Rom 3:23; 1 John 1:8, 10).

If God's intention were to keep believers in this life from sinning, then believers in this life would never sin. God does not tell us why He allows believers to sin or why He even allows believers to be enslaved to sin in their experience. The implication from various texts of Scripture is that He keeps us in flawed bodies for now because this life is a test to determine our position in the Lord's coming kingdom (Luke 19:16-26). We will be judged for "the things done in the body" (2 Cor 5:10), that is, in our fallen bodies (2 Cor 5:1-8).

I long for the day when I will sin no more at all. I'm sure MacArthur does as well. But the fact that we long for that day shows that there is no guarantee that in this life as believers we will never fall.

How much unrighteousness does it take to call our eternal destiny into question? Following MacArthur's logic, any sin in our life should lead us to have doubts about whether we are born again.

Is Sin the Issue?

Sin is serious business. Sin destroys, which is why the Bible warns against it. But in the grand scheme of things, how central should sin be *in an evangelistic presentation*? MacArthur says, "Sin is no peripheral issue as far as salvation is concerned; it *is* the issue" (p. 74, italics his). What, then, does MacArthur think was the point of Jesus' shed blood? Did Jesus not take away the sins of the world when He died on the cross as the substitute for all of mankind (John 1:29)? Is He not the propitiation not only for our sins, but also for the sins of the whole world (1 John 2:2)?

The atonement guarantees that sin isn't the issue anymore *in terms of regeneration*. As Lewis Sperry Chafer, founder of Dallas Theological Seminary, said, because of the cross of Christ people no longer have *a sin problem*, they have *a Son problem*.

Do you see the difference between the views of Chafer and MacArthur?

MacArthur says the issue in salvation is our sin. Thus MacArthur points people to themselves. The solution, MacArthur implies, is for us to deal with our own sins by turning from them and determining not to live that way any longer. We must have a "longing to turn from it" (p. 74).

By contrast, Chafer pointed people to Jesus. Jesus took sin away. He reconciled the world to God. He paid for our sin by dying on the cross for us. So sin is not the issue anymore. Faith in Jesus for everlasting life is the issue. Do you believe in Him for the promise of everlasting life?

In order to make his point that people can't be saved without "coming to grips with the heinousness of sin," MacArthur gives a number of examples of people who repented or had some sort of conviction of sin (p. 74). Interestingly, although MacArthur is trying to argue that this experience of turning from sin is necessary to be born again, many of his examples are of people who were already born again at the time they repented. Peter was already born again when he lamented his sinfulness in Luke 5:8. Job was as well when he repented (Job 42:6). So was Isaiah when he said he was a man of unclean lips (Isa 6:5). Where are the examples of people who had to turn from their sins *in order to be born again*?

More to the point, why doesn't MacArthur deal with the fact that repentance is not even mentioned in John's Gospel, which is the only evangelistic book in the Bible (John 20:30-31)? When the Lord evangelized Nicodemus (John 3:1-18), He didn't even mention sins or turning from sins. If sin is the main issue in evangelism, then why didn't the Lord Jesus mention sin to Nicodemus?

Why isn't repentance found in some of the most beloved evangelistic verses in the Bible like John 1:12; 3:16; 5:24; 6:35, 47; 11:25-27;

20:21; Acts 16:30-31; Rom 4:4-5; Gal 2:16; Eph 2:8-9; Titus 3:5; Rev 22:17?[1] Why isn't repentance found in Paul's defense of the gospel in Galatians? Why doesn't Paul mention repentance when he answers the question, "What must I do to be saved?" (Acts 16:30-31)?

MacArthur's position is inconsistent with Scripture.

Receiving Sinners

MacArthur goes on to appeal to the example of Matthew, the tax collector. Since the passage doesn't mention repentance, MacArthur naturally has to speculate, so he imagines the following scenario: "Deep down in his heart he [Matthew the tax collector] must have longed to be free from his life of sin, and that must have been why he virtually ran to join Christ" (p. 77). Nothing in Matt 9:9-13 implies any of this.

The truth is, we really don't know what motivated Matthew or the other disciples to follow Jesus. So why does MacArthur imagine that Matthew must have wanted to follow Jesus in order to be free from his life of sin? The reason is because in the previous section he claimed that one must long to be free from sin's bondage in order to be born again. He needed evidence to support his position. But instead of finding actual evidence for his view, he speculated.

Jesus invited Matthew to follow Him. Matthew followed Him. MacArthur understands the call to follow Jesus as a call to everlasting life. And yet we know from John 6 that *some unbelievers followed Jesus* (John 6:64). Is MacArthur suggesting that all who followed Jesus were born again? No. Is he suggesting that anyone who follows Him today is born again? No, he is not saying that either. What he is saying is that following Jesus is one of many conditions necessary to spend eternity with the Lord.

That Matthew, as a tax collector, was regarded by the Pharisees of his day as one of the worst of sinners is certainly true. But MacArthur builds an entire section about Matthew's supposed repentance when turning from sins is not mentioned in any of the texts he cites.

---

[1] It should be noted that Rom 4:4-5; Gal 2:16; Eph 2:8-9; and Titus 3:5 are not strictly speaking evangelistic verses. They are written to believers reminding them of what the evangelistic message is. However, I include them here since they do explain that the sole condition of regeneration and justification is faith in Christ.

Refusing the Righteous

In his final section, MacArthur brings in repentance once again: "The gospel according to Jesus is first of all a mandate for repentance" (p. 79).

MacArthur rightly says that Jesus began His preaching with a call to repent. But he fails to give the entire quote. Jesus, like His forerunner, said to Israel, "Repent, *for the kingdom of heaven is at hand*" (Matt 3:2; 4:17, emphasis added). This call is not evangelistic.

Jesus preached repentance. The issue He was discussing was not individual salvation from hell, but the coming of the kingdom for the nation of Israel. In order for the kingdom to come for Israel, the entire nation must both believe in Jesus for everlasting life and be repentant. That will be true at the end of the Tribulation (Rom 11:26). But neither the Lord nor John the Baptist were evangelizing when they said, "Repent, for the kingdom of heaven is at hand." They were inviting the nation to prepare to receive the kingdom (cf. Lev 26:40-45; Isa 40:3; 59:20; Jer 4:14; Mal 3:1-3; 4:5-6).

Of course, if the nation had repented, it would have also come to faith in Jesus for the promise of everlasting life. And then the Lord Jesus would have died on the cross, risen from the dead, ascended to heaven, and returned to establish His kingdom seven years later (i.e., after the Tribulation, which would have ended in AD 40).

But to see in this call to repentance the offer of everlasting life to people in the Church Age—or in any age—is to misunderstand Scripture.

Conclusion

MacArthur argues that repentance—turning from sin— is an essential condition for being born again.

The truth is there are many people who will only believe in Jesus' promise of everlasting life after repenting. But that isn't true of everyone. And it isn't absolutely necessary. There are thousands of different ways of coming to the point of believing in Jesus for eternal life. How we arrive at the point of believing in Jesus isn't the key. The key is that we come to believe His promise.

But MacArthur won't have that. He believes that there are multiple conditions for the new birth, not just believing in Jesus Christ (contra John 3:16; Gal 2:16; Eph 2:8-9; etc.). One of those conditions is turning from sins. And there are many other conditions which he lays out in *TGAJ*—submission, confession, obedience, and perseverance.[2]

Remember the liquor store owner? MacArthur did not discuss whether the man repented, submitted, confessed, and obeyed *in the past*. That wasn't MacArthur's concern. His issue with the man was that he was *currently* sinning. The liquor store owner illustrated the need for perseverance. One must continue to repent and obey and submit and confess in order to be able to enter into the coming kingdom.

If MacArthur really knew you, would he conclude you were born again? Maybe. But know this. If you were to backslide, he would surely doubt your salvation, not because of what you believe, but because the quality of your life had dipped below the standard he sees as necessary. MacArthur's view begs the question, *how good is good enough*?[3]

As a senior in college I first heard about the free gift of everlasting life to all who simply believe in Him. It was at a Campus Crusade for Christ meeting, called College Life.

I initially rejected the idea as silly. That would mean that sinners could be saved just as they were.

Yet I heard enough Scripture that night that I began to worry. What if this is correct? I had turned from my sins. I had committed my entire life to God. I was obeying Him as best I could. But I did not believe this faith-alone message. If it is required to believe that, then I was unsaved no matter my works.

I met with a Campus Crusade for Christ staff member, Warren Wilke, for four weeks running. I can't remember much of what he said then. That was over forty years ago. But I remember he quoted Eph 2:8-9 over and over again every time we met: "For by grace you have been saved through faith, and that not of yourselves; it is the gift of God, not of works, lest anyone should boast." I'd ask him about difficult verses that seemed to teach that we could lose everlasting life and he'd give me a brief explanation and then he'd quote Eph 2:8-9 again.

---

[2] See footnote 3 in chapter 3 for a list of places in which he says that these things are conditions of everlasting life.

[3] That question was the title of a fine book by Andy Stanley, *How Good Is Good Enough*? (Sisters, OR: Multnomah Publishers, 2003).

By the end of a month I was convinced. I became sure of my eternal destiny. That was the fall of 1972. I came to believe that I had been saved by grace through faith and apart from works. There is no ground for boasting.

I have not doubted my eternal destiny since. The reason is simple. Jesus is trustworthy. He promises everlasting life to all who believe in Him. I believe in Him. Therefore, I am secure in His love.

How about you?

CHAPTER 6

He Opens Blind Eyes

Introduction

Does the new birth always lead to noticeable and lifelong changes in someone's behavior? MacArthur thinks it does. As he writes,

> If…salvation is truly a work of God, it cannot be deficient. It cannot fail to impact an individual's behavior. It cannot leave his desires unchanged or his conduct unaltered. It cannot result in a fruitless life. It is the work of God and will continue steadfastly from its inception to ultimate perfection (p. 86).

What Biblical proof does MacArthur cite in defense of his thesis? He selected John 9, the account of Jesus healing the blind man. Yet John 9 doesn't support his claim that the new birth guarantees a life of holiness.

The Problem with Appealing to John 9

There are four reasons why John 9 does not prove that saving faith always leads to noticeable and permanent changes in one's behavior.

First, there is no mention of everlasting life or salvation in this entire chapter. There are scores of texts in John's Gospel which specifically say that Jesus promises everlasting life to all who believe in Him. This is not one of them.

Second, we don't know *when* the blind man became born again. It is impossible to know if he was born again (a) before he was healed, (b) after he was healed but before he saw Jesus, or (c) when he believed that Jesus is the Messiah (John 9:38). If he was an Old Testament saint like John the Baptist or Simeon or Anna, then he was born again before he knew that Jesus is the Messiah/Son of God.

Third and most significantly, the chapter gives no indication that the man's behavior changed. Let me say that again. There is no indication what the man born blind did after he worshipped Jesus. Did he become a follower of Christ? Did he confess Christ? Did he live a godly life? Did he marry and have kids? How did he handle his finances? Did he persevere in faith and good works? The Apostle John does not tell us.

Fourth, even if John 9 had taught that the man born blind became an Apostle and wrote half of the New Testament and died for his faith, that would still not prove that every believer perseveres in holiness.

John 9 isn't addressing the question of whether regeneration always produces a life of holiness.

The ninth chapter of John shows the reader that the Lord Jesus is willing and ready to heal spiritual blindness. Anyone who wishes to know if Jesus is the Messiah will receive spiritual sight (cf. John 5:39-40; 9:32-33; Isa 35:5-6[1]).

Reading into the Text

MacArthur speculates when he says that the blind man initially "was unregenerate, having not yet come to full faith in Christ" (p. 81). What indications are there in the chapter that the man was unregenerate? We are not told. And what does "full faith in Christ" mean? Did the man have "*partial* faith in Christ"? What is *partial faith in Christ*? Does partial faith in Christ lead to partial regeneration and partial changes in behavior?

---

[1] Isaiah 35:5-6 concerns physical miracles that the Messiah would do. Thus when Jesus opened the eyes of the blind, unstopped the ears of the deaf, and healed the lame, He was proving that He is the promised Messiah.

MacArthur is surely correct that the man believed certain things about Jesus between the time he was healed and before he worshipped Him. For example, the blind man believed that Jesus was a prophet (John 9:17) and that He was sent from God (John 9:30-33). Evidently MacArthur considers this to be faith in Christ, but not "full faith in Christ."

What MacArthur probably means is that it is possible to believe some correct truths about Jesus and yet not believe in Him in the Biblical sense.[2] He accuses his critics of having "a tendency to identify the object of faith as a basic set of biblical facts…about Christ's death, burial, and resurrection" (p. 80). Yet those of us in the Free Grace camp would actually agree with MacArthur that believing in "Christ's death, burial, and resurrection" does not necessarily mean one believes in Him in the Biblical sense. Most people in Christianity believe those truths and yet are not born again because they believe in works salvation, not salvation by grace through faith apart from works (John 6:28-29; Gal 2:16; Eph 2:8-9).

MacArthur defines "full faith," which he also calls "true faith" (p. 81), in this way: "True faith embraces not only the data of the gospel, but the Person of Christ as well…The gospel…calls not simply for the acquiescence of the mind, *but for the full surrender of the heart, soul, mind, and strength*" (p. 81, emphasis added). Elsewhere in *TGAJ* MacArthur indicates that faith includes repentance, commitment, submission, obedience, and perseverance.[3]

In reality the object of saving faith is Jesus' promise that whoever believes in Him has everlasting life (John 3:16). Knowing Biblical facts about Jesus (e.g., His death on the cross for our sins and His bodily resurrection from the dead) might lead you to believe the promise of life, but believing those facts does not save anyone

---

[2] Biblically to believe in Him is to believe in Him *for everlasting life* (John 3:16; 5:24; 11:25-27; 20:30-31; Gal 2:16; Eph 2:8-9; 1 Tim 1:16). That is, when we are convinced that He guarantees the eternal destiny of all who simply believe in Him, then we believe in Him in the Biblical sense. Yet in MacArthur's view to believe in Him is not about belief, but behavior. Believing in Jesus in his understanding means turning from sins, submission, commitment of life, and obedience that perseveres until death.

[3] See footnotes 2 and 3 in chapter 3 of this book for details regarding MacArthur's equating of faith with submission, commitment, obedience, and perseverance. Regarding repentance as a part of "full faith," see *TGAJ*, pp. 11, 37, 47 ("repentance is at the core of saving faith"), 57, 151. He even coins the expression *repentant faith* (pp. 162, 195).

unless he also believes the promise of everlasting life to the one who simply believes in Jesus.

However, contrary to MacArthur, there is insufficient evidence in the text of John 9 to conclude that the blind man was not yet born again. That is, we do not know whether he believed in the Messiah for everlasting life when he was blind, when he was healed, or when Jesus identified Himself as the Messiah. What is certain is that the man born blind expressed belief in Jesus as Messiah (John 9:38).

Do We Need to Be Theologians to Be Regenerate?

MacArthur ends the introduction to this chapter with these telling words:

> But when Jesus finished opening his [the man born blind] spiritual eyes, he worshipped Christ as Lord (v. 38). It was not a theology lesson that brought about this transformation, but a miracle of divine grace (p. 81).

Is evangelism in some sense "a theology lesson"? Think about that before answering. What is theology? What is a theology lesson?

When you share your faith, are you trying to communicate truth about God? If so, is that not a theology lesson?

Sure it is. Theology is the study of God and of His Word (*Theos* means *God*, from which we get *theology*). Thus when we evangelize someone, we tell them about God and what He has said in His Word. While evangelism is not rocket science, it does involve clearly communicating the truth of John 3:16 or John 5:24 or Eph 2:8-9. *There is content to be communicated.*[4]

MacArthur assumes the blind man was not born again. How does he know that? Based on what he writes here, it's because John tells us that it is only later that the man fell down before Jesus and worshipped Him. He worshipped Jesus, and that was evidence of his transformation.

---

[4] In the conclusion to this chapter MacArthur returns to this theme: "Those who would be saved do not require in-depth theological instruction to know that Christ is Lord and that they should obey Him" (p. 88). Notice here he admits that some theological instruction is indeed needed. But the instruction MacArthur believes must be given concerns the Lordship of Christ and the need to obey Him in order to gain everlasting life. The issue in this theological lesson, according to MacArthur, is that you must obey Christ sufficiently your whole life in order to make it into Christ's kingdom. In his understanding the words "whoever believes in Him" in John 3:16 mean "whoever obeys Him."

But even according to MacArthur's own theology, that can't be right. In MacArthur's view born again people are known by their lifelong faith and obedience. We cannot be sure of the eternal destiny of anyone prior to death because it is always possible that their worship/commitment/obedience will not last. If a person worships and obeys Jesus *for a time*, and then in time of temptation falls away (Luke 8:13), according to MacArthur he proves he was never really born again in the first place (see pp. 132-33, commenting on the parallel discussion of the second soil in the parable of the four soils in Matt 13:20-21).

So, it's terrific that the blind man worshipped Jesus. It's a good thing. But it's not proof that "a miracle of divine grace" happened. If MacArthur's Lordship Salvation is correct, then it remains to be seen whether anyone who is still living is born again or not. According to MacArthur one must persevere in faith and good works until death in order to prove that he is truly regenerate. The man of John 9 had certainly not done that yet.[5]

The Physical Miracle

MacArthur believes the blind man was unregenerate up until Jesus spoke with him and asked if he believed in the Son of God (John 9:35). He is not alone in his view. Many commentators say the same thing.

But is that true? For one thing, unlike every other evangelistic encounter in John's Gospel, the Lord never once mentions the promise of everlasting life to those who believe in Him. Why would Jesus leave out that crucial message?

The Lord would do so if the man was an Old Testament saint who was already born again before he saw Him.

It is most likely that the man either was born again before his healing, or sometime between his healing and the end of his questioning by the Pharisees. An Old Testament believer was one who

---

[5] One would think that evangelism must be especially difficult for one holding to MacArthur's view of the gospel. What do you say to people? At the least you need to tell them about hell (chapters 1-24), the Lordship of Jesus Christ (esp. chapter 23), final judgment (chapter 21), and the fact that the ones who will finally be saved are those who have repented, submitted, confessed, obeyed, and persevered until death (chapters 1-24). Certainty of one's eternal destiny under this system is not possible until death. Essentially one is telling a prospect, *I'm not sure where I will spend eternity and I can tell you how you can be uncertain too.*

believed in the coming Messiah for everlasting life, but who did not yet know who He was. John the Baptist, for example, was born again before he knew that Jesus was the Messiah (cf. John 1:31-33).

MacArthur's view is that the man was born again *because* at the end of this encounter he became committed to Christ and determined to follow Him (pp. 81, 86, 87, 88). There are two problems with this view.

First, the Lord repeatedly taught that the sole condition of the new birth is faith in Him (e.g., John 3:16; 4:10-14; 5:24; 6:35, 37, 39-40, 47; 11:25-26). Regeneration cannot be both by faith alone and by faith plus repentance, submission, worship, obedience, dedication, and perseverance.

Second, John does not indicate that the man born blind pledged to follow Jesus. Possibly after he worshipped Him he did make such a commitment. But it is not stated in the passage. Indeed, there is no record in John, the Synoptic Gospels, or anywhere in the New Testament that the man born blind followed Jesus for the rest of his life.

The Inquisition

In this section, MacArthur marvels that the blind man boldly stood up for Jesus in front of a very hostile crowd of religious leaders (pp. 83-85), and makes this poignant comment about the Pharisees:

> The Pharisees…had heard the testimony, they had seen the miracle, and still they were not swayed. Theirs was hardened, vicious, determined unbelief (p. 85).

MacArthur is correct. Any reasonable person should have come to faith in Jesus Christ from this one miracle alone, let alone all of His miracles. Yet the Pharisees were hardened in unbelief. While we can't be sure, it appears the man born blind at least by this point believes in Jesus.[6]

---

[6] The man who was healed is doing what Jesus had commanded Nicodemus to do in John 3:19-21. He was out in the open confessing Jesus. While he did not yet know that Jesus is the Son of God (= Messiah), his confession angered the religious authorities because they realized his confession was essentially that Jesus is the Messiah. In Matt 10:32 Jesus said, "Therefore whoever confesses Me before men, him I will also confess before My Father who is in heaven." While an unbeliever who was open and seeking might confess Christ to be a prophet or someone sent from God (cf. John 3:2; 4:19), this man's boldness and willingness to suffer for Christ implies he is

The Spiritual Miracle

MacArthur correctly says that God is sovereign in regeneration: "Salvation always results because God first pursues sinners, not because sinners first seek God" (p. 86). However, the Biblical presentation of God's pursuit of sinners is somewhat different from what MacArthur proposes. No doubt, he is thinking along predestinarian lines. He cites John 15:16 in support of the principle of God's pursuit, but since that statement is about the Lord choosing the twelve to be His disciples, including one, Judas, who never believed and never was born again,[7] that probably wasn't the best verse to choose. Luke 19:10 is more to the point. Even better is Rom 3:11 which MacArthur cites, but does not quote.

It is true that no one seeks God unless God first seeks him. However, contrary to MacArthur's view, God is seeking everyone, not just a chosen few. That is what the Lord said in John 12:32, "And I, if I am lifted up from the earth, will draw all peoples to Myself." The Lord is drawing *all*. (The word *peoples* is not in the Greek.) Likewise, the Apostle John in his prologue said, "That was the true Light which gives light to every man coming into the world" (John 1:9). *Every man* is given light.

MacArthur goes a bit too far in pressing the illustration of physical and spiritual blindness: "This blind man in John 9 did not gain his sight because he was exposed to the light. No amount of light affects blindness" (p. 86).

The narrative shows that MacArthur has read this theology into the passage. It was precisely because the blind man was exposed to *the Light*, that is, the Light of the world, that He gained physical and spiritual sight. Light in John's Gospel clearly "affects blindness," despite MacArthur's claim. That is one of the puzzling aspects of his book. Wonderful observations and interpretations are followed by non-sequitur pronouncements.

---

an Old Testament saint already. Lacking direct statements, we can only speculate as to when this man was born again.

[7] It is hypothetically possible, of course, that Judas came to faith after he betrayed Jesus. However, that is extremely unlikely for three reasons. First, if he had come to faith, why would he kill himself? In that case, like Saul of Tarsus, he would have every reason to become a mighty witness for Jesus. Second, if he did come to faith, surely the Gospel writers would tell us. Third, Jesus called him "the son of perdition" (John 17:12).

In addition to John 1:9, cited above, note the following statements in John about the light:

> Then Jesus spoke to them again, saying, "I am the light of the world. He who follows Me shall not walk in darkness, but have the light of life" (John 8:12).

> "As long as I am in the world, I am the light of the world" (John 9:5).

> "I have come as a light into the world, that whoever believes in Me should not abide in darkness" (John 12:46).

As you can see, one of those "I am the light of the world" statements comes right from John 9. Yet MacArthur not only does not mention that, He denies that exposure to Jesus and His word is what leads to the new birth (or to additional spiritual insight for one who is already born again).

MacArthur's Calvinism seems to have led him to deny one aspect of what the text is highlighting. In this passage Jesus is revealing Himself to be the Light of the world. He not only opens eyes *physically*, but also *spiritually* (cf. John 9:40-41). Exposure to the Light is indeed the cure for spiritual blindness.

This is why it is wise to encourage unbelievers to read the Gospel of John. While all Scripture is inspired and profitable (2 Tim 3:16-17), John's Gospel is uniquely suited for evangelism since that is its purpose (John 20:30-31).

I encourage those who lack assurance of everlasting life to read a chapter a day of John's Gospel, and to do so prayerfully. Ask God to show you the truth about assurance. *Can I be sure that all who simply believe in the Lord Jesus have everlasting life that can never be lost? Please show me, Lord, as I read.*

In three weeks a person can read the entire Gospel of John. I encourage people to read it as many times as it takes to gain assurance. But it is God's Word, not our works (repentance, submission, confession of sins, commitment, obedience, and perseverance), that leads to the miracle of spiritual sight and the new birth.

Conclusion

John 9 does not support Lordship Salvation. It does not show that worshipping the Lord is a condition for receiving eternal life.

It does not show that believers will manifest changed lives from the moment of their new birth until they die or are raptured. More generally, there is no indication in John 9 (or in all of John's Gospel) that one must turn from his sins, submit to the Lordship of Christ, and persevere in obedience until death in order to be born again.

CHAPTER 7

He Challenges an Eager Seeker

Introduction

If you were on an airplane, and someone next to you asked how to have a relationship with Jesus, what would you say? What Scripture would you go to? MacArthur thinks the story of the rich young ruler would help.

That story is a good litmus test for telling if someone believes in salvation by faith or if they believe in salvation by faith plus works.

Leaving on a Jet Plane

MacArthur opens chapter 7 with an illustration of what he now thinks is the wrong way to do evangelism. One day he was on a plane when the man next to him asked how to have a relationship with Jesus. MacArthur told the man to "simply believe in the Lord Jesus Christ and accept Him as your Savior" (p. 89). He did not tell the man to turn from his sins or submit to Christ. He only needed to believe. Later that month MacArthur baptized the man, and soon after, MacArthur "discovered that he had no continuing interest in the things of Christ" (p. 89).

MacArthur became convinced that the problem is that he had shared the wrong message on the plane. MacArthur never asked the man "to acknowledge his sinfulness" (p. 95). He went on,

As I think back to my conversation with the man on the airplane, I realize that this is where I failed. Too hastily I offered him Christ for his psychological needs without compelling him to acknowledge his sinfulness. The salvation I described to him had a manward focus, rather than a Godward focus (p. 95).

There is certainly a problem with converts who do not continue in discipleship. Anyone who has been in ministry for any length of time has seen people drop out of church, stop reading their Bibles, and even stop following Christ. One solution is to dismiss everyone who falls away as a false professor, as MacArthur does.

But that "solution" creates an even bigger problem. It means that no one, not even MacArthur himself, can be sure of his eternal destiny. Since no one can be sure he will persevere in faith and good works (cf. 1 Cor 9:27), no one can be sure he will make it into God's presence if perseverance is required.

In the introduction to this chapter MacArthur suggests that the story of the rich young ruler is one of the most "straightforward presentation[s] of the gospel according to Jesus" (p. 89). Yet the rich young ruler passage has long been regarded as a tough text for those who believe in justification by faith alone, apart from works.

To say that the rich young ruler passage is one of the most "straightforward presentation[s] of the gospel according to Jesus" is troubling. One wonders if the reason MacArthur says this is because he has found in this text one that is easily adaptable to his Lordship Salvation teaching.

He goes on to say, "The term [sic] *eternal life* is used about fifty times in Scripture" (p. 90). Actually the expression *eternal life/everlasting life* occurs 98 times in the New Testament. Yet the statement which follows is far more inaccurate: "It always refers to conversion, evangelism, the new birth—the entire salvation experience (p. 90)." He does not offer any evidence to support his statement. It is merely an unsupported claim.

The evidence contradicts that claim. One of the uses of the expression *eternal life* occurs at the end of this passage, in Matt 19:29. There the Lord promises the eleven believing disciples that they would "inherit eternal life" as a result of their service to Him. But the eleven already had eternal life in the sense of the new birth (cf. John 2:11; 3:16; 13:10). The Lord was not saying that if the disciples persevered in service then they would in the future be born again. That makes no sense.

Everlasting life is sometimes presented in the New Testament *as a possible future reward for work done.* It is popularly believed that the afterlife will be the same for all Christians. But that isn't true. Jesus said He came that we might have life, and that we might have it more abundantly (John 10:10). The believer who perseveres will inherit a fuller life forever than the believer who does not. Compare Gal 6:8-9,

> For he who sows to his flesh will of the flesh reap corruption, but he who sows to the Spirit will of the Spirit reap everlasting life. And let us not grow weary while doing good, for in due season we shall reap if we do not lose heart.

Paul is talking to people who already have everlasting life (Gal 1:9; 3:3, 5, 26; 4:31). Yet he says that they—and he himself (note the "we" in v 9)—can reap everlasting life, that is, they can *earn it by work done*, if they continue doing good. This is not the message of the new birth described in Eph 2:8-9 or John 3:16. This is the message of the potential fullness of life that awaits the believer who perseveres in doing good works.

Before leaving the introduction to chapter 7, MacArthur offers his conclusions about the rich young ruler. First he says, "There was no way he [the rich young ruler] would get away without receiving eternal life" (p. 90). Then MacArthur reverses course and says, "But he did. He left [without receiving eternal life] not because he heard the wrong message, *not even because he did not believe*, but because he was unwilling to forsake what he loved most in this world and commit himself to Christ as Lord" (p. 90, emphasis added). Notice the words "not even because he did not believe."

According to MacArthur the rich young ruler believed in Christ and yet he left without everlasting life! That is a contradiction. Many times in *TGAJ* MacArthur says that anyone who has faith in Christ has everlasting life (pp. 34, 86, 133, 176, 223, 274). Here MacArthur indicates that the man believed in Christ and yet he was not born again.

Of course, it is true that MacArthur indicates in many places that it takes a special type of faith in Christ to be born again. He calls this special type of faith in Christ "true faith" (pp. 7, 36, 44, 48, 60,

66, 81, 98, 107, 149, 191, 211, 215, 246, 250, 257, 258), "genuine faith" (pp. 44, 48, 99, 115, 133, 252), "authentic faith" (pp. 3, 4, 51), "full faith" (p. 81), "repentant faith" (pp. 162, 195), and "obedient faith" (pp. 61, 113).

He calls what he considers faith in Christ that will not save "spurious faith" (pp. 52, 186), "false belief" (pp. 133, 267 [favorably citing Spurgeon]), "false faith" (p. 51), "false professions of faith" (p. 213), and "false assurance" (pp. 93, 213, 214, 279, 281).

According to MacArthur, good works are the difference between faith in Christ that saves and faith in Christ that does not save. MacArthur is convinced that faith in Christ by itself will not save anyone. Faith in Christ must be joined with a lifetime of good works in order for someone to be born again. Faith in Christ plus a life of good works equal salvation. Faith in Christ without a lifetime of good works equals eternal condemnation.

Here is a place where MacArthur slipped. He said the rich young ruler had "faith in Christ." He did not say he had "spurious faith," "false faith," or the like.

MacArthur is correct when he then says, "Our ideas of evangelism cannot indict Jesus; rather, He must judge contemporary methods of evangelism" (p. 91). That is true, for all believers must stand before the Judgment Seat of Christ. There He will evaluate our entire lives, including how we evangelized (1 Cor 4:1-5; 2 Cor 5:9-10). Yet one wonders why MacArthur chose a non-evangelistic text to discuss Jesus' method of evangelism. In this text the Lord does not even mention believing in Him. Instead, He points the young rich man to the Law of Moses! That is something that MacArthur, by his own admission "a leaky Dispensationalist," does not do.

Why didn't MacArthur choose an evangelistic text like John 5:24; 6:35-40; or 11:25-27[1]? Probably he bypassed texts like that because those texts only call for belief in Christ. This text calls for the listener to do good works (though it does not mention faith in Christ).

He Had the Right Motive

MacArthur summarizes the rich young ruler's right motive as follows: "This man came seeking eternal life. He knew what he

---

[1] While John 11:25-27 is not evangelistic *for Martha*, who was already a believer, it was used by John as an evangelistic text *for his unbelieving readers* (John 20:30-31).

wanted, and he knew he did not have it" (p. 91). What in the text leads to these conclusions? MacArthur does not say. Evidently he bases these conclusions on the question the man asks, "'Good Teacher, what good thing shall I do that I may have eternal life?'" (Matt 19:16). While it is possible he wanted the present possession of eternal life and knew he did not have it, it is likely that something else is going on here.

Jews of the first century thought in terms of a physical earthly kingdom in which Messiah would reign. It is likely that the man did not believe that eternal life was a present possession. He seems to think that good Jews, those who keep the Law of Moses faithfully, would enter into everlasting life, that is, into the kingdom, when the kingdom began (after the resurrection).

MacArthur is writing with a twenty-first century Church-Age mindset. But is that the way the rich young ruler was thinking? Was he thinking of being born again? That seems unlikely. He was not seeking to gain eternal life right now. He wanted Jesus' confirmation that he was well on his way into the kingdom because of his good works.

Even MacArthur's later suggestion that what he was seeking was "being alive to the realm where God dwells…walking with the living God in unending communion…that caliber of life" (p. 92) seems to be reading later New Testament theology into the man's thinking. Yes, believers have the potential to experience life in close communion with God. But there is no indication that is what the rich young ruler is seeking either.

Is the rich young ruler's motive right? Is he really seeking the Lord? Based on the entire conversation between him and Jesus, it seems the young ruler doesn't really want to hear what the Lord has to say unless what He says confirms his standing.

MacArthur also says, "All his religion and wealth had not given him confidence, peace, joy, or settled hope" (p. 91). Possibly. But the text gives indication that he was quite confident—until He hears the Lord's final answer. He claims to have kept the entire Law of Moses from his youth up! He certainly acts like he sees his wealth as a sign that God is pleased with him and with his works.[2]

---

[2] Wealth was widely regarded by Jews as a sign of divine blessing. Of course it often was (e.g., Abraham, David, Solomon). However, the mere experience of wealth did not at all guarantee that the person was pleasing God (e.g., Nabal, Zacchaeus).

The text does not give sufficient indications to show that this young man had the right motive.

He Had the Right Attitude

If the man's motive was suspect, so was his attitude. There is good reason to question MacArthur's suggestion that the rich young ruler "was not haughty or presumptuous" (p. 92).

For evidence MacArthur turns to Mark's report of this incident, who tells us that the young man knelt before Jesus (Mark 10:17). That is a sign of respect at the least. Possibly that suggests he is not haughty.

However, neither Matthew nor Mark is presenting this man as one whom anyone should emulate. It is hard to see evidence that his motive or his attitude is right. He seems to want Jesus to validate his legalistic thinking.

He Came to the Right Source

MacArthur is correct when he says, "But the young ruler had not come to just an evangelist—this was the Source of eternal life Himself" (p. 93). The Lord Jesus is indeed the Source of everlasting life (John 3:16; 5:24, 39-40; 6:35, 47; 11:25-27; 20:30-31).

MacArthur continues with this excellent observation: "Most people never find eternal life because they spend their entire lives looking in the wrong places" (p. 93).

The Lord Himself said so on many occasions. He said, "I am the way, the truth, and the life" (John 14:6). He said, "I am the resurrection and the life" (John 11:25). Likewise He said, "he who believes in Me has everlasting life" (John 6:47).

One of His statements to a legalistic Jewish audience fits this encounter as well: "You search the Scriptures, for in them you think you have eternal life; and these are they which testify of Me. But you are not willing to come to Me that you may have life" (John 5:39-40).

Yes, the Lord Jesus is indeed the source of eternal life. The rich young ruler came to the right source.

He Asked the Right Question

In this section MacArthur says that the one thing we must do to have eternal life is this: "we have to believe [in Christ]" (p. 94). Amen. That is true, as long as it is belief, understood as persuasion, alone. Jesus was not telling the man what he needed to do to be born again. He was showing him the impossibility of obtaining everlasting life by good works. This is why the young man went away grieved.

However, why in this statement does MacArthur make belief the condition of receiving eternal life, while elsewhere in the chapter (and book) he makes the condition confession of sin and submission to Christ? It is because for MacArthur belief alone is not enough, despite the Biblical evidence to the contrary (e.g., John 3:16; 5:24, 39-40; 6:35, 47; 11:25-27; Gal 2:16; Eph 2:8-9).

This comment by MacArthur is excellent:

> Strictly speaking, Jesus' answer was correct. If a person could keep the law all his life and never violate a single jot or tittle, he would be perfect, sinless (cf. James 2:10). But no one except the Savior alone is like that; we are born in sin (Ps. 51:5). To suggest that the law is a means to eternal life clouds the issue of faith (p. 90).

Unfortunately, this excellent statement is followed by contradictory teaching about the same passage. The issue moves from simply believing in Jesus to "obey[ing] the Lord," "be[ing] willing to forsake all for Him," and being "willing to turn from sin, possessions, false religion, or selfishness" (pp. 98-99). For MacArthur faith alone is not enough to obtain everlasting life.

He Was Filled with Pride

How is it that the man was humble and not haughty, as MacArthur has already said, and yet "he was filled with pride" (p. 94)? Those are contradictory statements. How can both be true at the same time?

This comment is worth additional consideration: "Much of contemporary evangelism is woefully deficient when it comes to confronting people with the reality of their sin" (p. 95). I suppose that would also be true—if you held MacArthur's view—of the evangelistic conversation that the Lord had with Nicodemus in John 3 and with the woman at the well in John 4. It would also be true of Jesus' comments to Martha in John 11:25-27. Even the Lord's conversation with the rich young ruler is not the type of confrontation that MacArthur and others (e.g., the Way of the Master) promote.

Notice that the Lord does not ask the man if he ever told a lie, cheated, or stole something. He just points him to the second half of the ten commandments, the commands related to our treatment of our fellow man.

This is pre-evangelism and not evangelism. The Lord is indeed showing the man that he is not sinless, though in an admittedly roundabout way. He does not directly say, "You have lied many times in your life" or "You have stolen things that did not belong to you." Instead, the Lord simply mentions the commandments and lets them convict the man.

Do all people need such confrontation? Evidently not, for the Lord rarely did this. Nor do we see the Apostles routinely doing this in their evangelistic sermons in Acts. While this is a fine tool to have in our evangelistic tool belts, it's wrong to think that most people fail to recognize their own sinfulness. The Holy Spirit convicts the world of sin (John 16:7-11).

Of course, MacArthur is absolutely correct when he later says, "The pattern of divine revelation confirms the importance of comprehending one's sinfulness" (p. 96). But most people are quite aware of their own sinfulness. Only those who harden themselves to the work of the Spirit actually fail to comprehend that they are sinful.[3]

Expanding on that point MacArthur says, "In Romans Paul spends three full chapters declaring the sinfulness of humanity before he begins to discuss the way of salvation" (p. 96). Let's see whether this is true. In the first place, what Paul discusses in Rom 3:21–4:25 is not "the way of salvation," but *the way of justification.* The words *save* and *salvation* are not found in the justification

---

[3] In an odd twist, Lordship Salvation has a tendency to blunt people's comprehension of their own sinfulness. Lordship Salvation tells professing believers to look at their good works and their bad works to see if they give evidence of being born again. There is a tendency for people like that to downplay their own sins so that they feel better about their chances of making it into the kingdom. If Lordship Salvation people were especially sensitive to their own sinfulness, then they would realize that they had no hope of making it into the kingdom based on anything other than faith in Christ.

section of Romans. In Paul's letter to the believers in Rome every use of the words *save* (*sōzō*) and *salvation* (*sōtēria*) refer to deliverance from God's temporal wrath (Rom 1:16-32), not salvation from hell.

In the second place, the reason Paul describes sin so much in Rom 1:18–3:20 is because sin brings about God's wrath here and now. The legalist cannot escape the wrath of God because he is a sinner and he can only be set free from bondage to sin through justification (Rom 3:21–4:25; 5:1–8:39). It is that bondage to sin that brings about God's temporal wrath.

It is going beyond Scripture to say, "It is meaningless to expound on grace to someone who does not know the divine demand for righteousness" (p. 96). Everyone knows of the divine demand for righteousness because of the convicting work of the Spirit (John 16:7-11). Even people who have never heard about the Bible know of the Creator, of coming judgment, and of their own sinfulness. What they do not know is that God became a man and dealt with our sin problem by dying for our sins on the cross and rising from the dead so that all who believe in the God-Man, the Lord Jesus, have everlasting life that can never be lost.

Neither the Lord nor His Apostles routinely mentioned *the divine demand for righteousness* in their evangelistic preaching. Were their efforts "meaningless"?

When we proclaim the message of John 3:16 or John 6:28-29 or Eph 2:8-9, it is clear that apart from faith in Christ we cannot have everlasting life. It is clear that everlasting life is a gift and that it is not of works. There is no ground for boasting. So the message of grace has within it the idea that our best works are as filthy rags (Isa 64:6). Whether mentioned or not, once we say that everlasting life is a gift and that it is only for those who believe in Christ, claims of works righteousness are invalidated.

He Did Not Confess His Guilt

While it is true the rich young ruler did not confess his guilt, his problem was much bigger. The young ruler said, "All these things I have kept from my youth. What do I still lack?" (Matt 19:20). So not only does he fail to confess his guilt, he actually affirms his view that his works are sufficient to warrant kingdom entrance. He sounds like the people of Matt 7:22.

MacArthur comments, "Salvation is not for people who want an emotional lift; it is for sinners who come to God for forgiveness. Those who are not ashamed of their sin cannot receive salvation" (p. 97). That first sentence is certainly true, though it is more accurate to say that we come to God *for everlasting life*, not *for forgiveness* per se. While it is true that when we believe we receive total (positional) forgiveness of all sins, including all future ones (Acts 26:18; Eph 1:7; Col 1:14; 2:13; Heb 10:17), that is not the theme we typically find in evangelistic encounters recorded in Scripture.[4]

The second sentence is not quite true. There is no condition that people must be "ashamed of their sin" to be born again. What one must do is believe in the Lord Jesus Christ for the everlasting life He promises (John 3:16; 5:24; 6:35). Nowhere in all of Scripture is anyone told that he must be ashamed of his sin to be born again.

Of course, shame over one's sin may lead a person to church and to hearing the message of everlasting life. Thus shame might result in one hearing the message and then believing it. But shame is not a requirement. One need not "hit bottom" to be born again. How could children be born again if shame over their sin is required? What of adults who, like the rich young ruler, are fairly good people in the eyes of the world?

The rich young ruler did not need to feel shame about his *bad* works. He needed to know that his *very best* works are as filthy rags before God (Isa 64:6). Clearly if one's best works are not enough to grant one everlasting life, then the only way to life is faith in Christ, which is what the Lord said again and again in His public ministry.

MacArthur says, "The Lord Jesus does not take sinners on their own terms" (p. 97). Amen. They must come to Him *on His terms*. And what are His terms? Faith in Him. That is the only way to be

---

[4] The only evangelistic book in the Bible, John's Gospel, only mentions forgiveness of sins directly one time (John 20:23; see also John 13:6-11), and never in an evangelistic context. Never in the Fourth Gospel do we read, *the one who believes in Him has the forgiveness of sins*, or anything close to that. It is true that in Acts 10:43 Peter said, "whoever believes in Him will receive remission of sins." And at that point Cornelius and his household believed and were forgiven and born again. However, even there, more is in view. Compare Acts 11:14. Cornelius had been told in advance by an angel that Peter would tell him words by which his and he household *would be saved*. Thus when Cornelius heard Peter speak of forgiveness, he understood that salvation was in view. That helps explain the abrupt ending of Peter's sermon. He surely intended to say more. But the Holy Spirit fell on Peter's audience at that point and thus he stopped his evangelistic message (Acts 10:44-48).

born again. Works will not do. Works don't work when it comes to the new birth (John 6:28-29).

He Would Not Submit to Christ

MacArthur's final section of the chapter is a bit speculative. The rich young ruler does not immediately do what the Lord tells him to do. He goes away. However, the text does not tell us what happened later. He might have come to faith and even followed the Lord later.

The bigger point, of course, is that the issue here is "treasure in heaven," not regeneration and future entrance into the kingdom. Treasure in heaven is a rewards concept (cf. Matt 6:19-21).

MacArthur reverses himself momentarily when he says, "He [Jesus] was not saying that it is possible to buy eternal life with charity" (p. 98). Why not? If MacArthur is right and "treasure in heaven" refers to regeneration and spending eternity with the Lord, then the Lord was indeed telling him he could buy everlasting life by obeying His command to give everything away.

MacArthur claims, "In effect, He [the Lord Jesus] was saying, 'Here is the test of true faith: Are you willing to do what I want you to do?'" (p. 98). That's not true. It is quite possible to believe something and yet not live in light of what you believe. How many pastors believe that they are to love their wives and yet they end up committing adultery? Does that mean that they didn't really believe that they should love their wives? Does that mean that they didn't really believe in Christ? Is it not conceivable that a believer in Christ might find it difficult to give away his cars, his computers, his boat, his home(s), his furniture, his extra clothing, his golf clubs, his televisions, his savings, his retirement accounts, and everything he has?

The essential mistake that MacArthur makes is that he merges the call of discipleship with the promise of everlasting life. For him, justification and sanctification are intertwined, and faith becomes works of obedience.

MacArthur says that Zacchaeus (cf. Luke 19:1-10) "was willing to do anything—including getting rid of all his wealth—to come to Jesus on His terms" (p. 98). That is not what Luke reports in Luke 19. Luke quotes Zacchaeus as saying, "Look, Lord, I give *half of my goods* to the poor; and if I have taken anything from anyone by false accusation, I restore fourfold" (Luke 19:8, emphasis added). "Half of [his] goods" is not "all of his wealth."

More importantly, Zacchaeus did not do this giving to gain everlasting life—which is what MacArthur suggests ("to come to Jesus on His terms"). He did it out of thanks for already having everlasting life. Zacchaeus was born again when he heard the Lord Jesus speak and then came to faith in Him: "Today salvation has come to this house, because he also is a son of Abraham" (Luke 19:9).[5] Zacchaeus became a son of Abraham spiritually that very day. Thus he gave half of his goods out of joy and gratitude. He did not do so in order to buy everlasting life.

The last four paragraphs in this chapter are filled with contradictions. MacArthur says here that everlasting life is a free gift received purely by faith in Christ. Yet he also says that

> Christ will not give it to one whose hands are filled with other things. Those who are not willing to turn from sins, possessions, false religion, or selfishness will find they cannot turn to Christ in faith (p. 99).

Conclusion

Readers of *TGAJ* should believe what MacArthur says about the freeness of everlasting life and the sole condition for receiving it: faith alone in Christ alone. If they do, they will be certain of their eternal destiny.

But, those who read *TGAJ* should reject MacArthur's contradictory claims that in order to obtain everlasting life one must also turn from sins, yield everything to Christ, and obey Him. If readers fail to reject those contradictory claims, they will lack assurance of everlasting life and will be trapped in a gospel of doubt.

MacArthur merges justification and sanctification, discipleship and the promise of life; and that has confused many people.

---

[5] Admittedly, Luke does not specifically tell us that Zacchaeus came to faith that day. However, he does tell us that he gained salvation that day. And since Luke knew that salvation is by faith in Christ, apart from works (Acts 10:43; 15:7-11; 16:30-31), he expected his readers to conclude that Zacchaeus came to faith in Jesus then.

CHAPTER 8

He Seeks and Saves the Lost (Luke 19:1-10)

Introduction

Is a dramatic change in our life and our desires proof that genuine salvation has taken place? Is that how we have assurance of our eternal destiny? MacArthur thinks so and he appeals to the story of Zacchaeus to prove it.

Search and Rescue

"The nature of God is to seek and to save sinners" (p. 101), says MacArthur, and he's right. That certainly is the point of Luke 19:1-10 and Luke 15. Of course the *saving* of sinners is not limited to their regeneration. It also includes rescuing born-again people who have strayed, as the three parables of Luke 15:1-32 show.

MacArthur quickly follows up this correct statement with an unsupported claim: "The unequivocal teaching of Jesus is that those who will not acknowledge and repent of their sin are beyond the reach of saving grace" (p. 101). What is his evidence for that claim? MacArthur says that "Jesus' parable in Luke 18:10-13 under-scores this truth" (p. 101).[1] There's only one problem. The Parable of the Pharisee and the Tax Collector *does not mention repentance or*

---

[1] Actually, the parable runs from Luke 18:9 through 18:14, not just verses 10-13.

turning from sins. So how does it prove that one must acknowledge and turn from his sin to be born again?[2]

MacArthur's position is even more untenable when we look at the Gospel of John. Not once in the entire book do we find the words *repent* or *repentance.* We are never told that the one who repents has everlasting life. Instead, over and over again the Lord says that the one *who believes in Him* has everlasting life. Faith in Christ is the one and only condition of regeneration in John. And, of course, faith in Christ is the one and only condition of justification in Romans and Galatians as well.[3]

If, as MacArthur claims, we must acknowledge and repent of our sin in order to be saved, what about the woman at the well in John 4? She never acknowledged her sins to the Lord or indicated that she would turn from them. And Jesus didn't ask her to. Instead, she came to faith in Christ and was born again, without repentance being mentioned.

The same is true with what the Lord told Nicodemus in John 3:1-18 and Martha in John 11:25-26.

And if repentance and acknowledgement of sins were necessary to be in reach of "saving grace," you would expect Paul to have mentioned it in Eph 2:8-9, where he famously speaks of those who have been saved by grace through faith. But repentance is not mentioned there either.

MacArthur compounds the confusion when he writes: "Humble repentance is the *only* acceptable response to the gospel according to Jesus" (p. 102). This contradicts what he has said up till now. He has maintained that the acceptable *responses* to Jesus' gospel include repentance, confession, submission, obedience, and perseverance. Thus a more accurate statement of his view would be: *The only acceptable responses to the gospel according to Jesus are*

---

[2] MacArthur appears to see the actions of Zacchaeus as reported in Luke 19:8 as referring to an earlier repentance. Luke 19:8 is where Zacchaeus pledged to give up to half his goods to the poor and to restore fourfold to anyone he may have defrauded. I say *appears to see* because later in the chapter when he discusses what Zacchaeus did, he does not call that repentance, but "important evidence that his faith was real" (p. 106). He does imply, however, at the very end of the chapter that these actions by Zacchaeus represent "fruits in keeping with repentance" (p. 106). Thus he appears to believe that Zacchaeus first turned from his sins of taking too much in taxes, then submitted himself to Christ and then pledged to do works of charity and restitution.

[3] In fact, belief in the Messiah for everlasting life is the only condition for regeneration listed in the Bible.

recognition of and turning from sin, submission to Jesus' Lordship, confession of Christ, a firm commitment to obey Him in all areas of life, and perseverance in obedience until death.

The only saving response to the gospel according to Jesus is faith in His promise to give the believer everlasting life. There is no other object of saving faith. Humble repentance may be a part of pre-evangelism. It might lead a person to church, to seek God, or to read the Bible; but repentance gives no one everlasting life. Only faith in Jesus does that.

Seeking the Savior

MacArthur opens his discussion of Zacchaeus with the claim that "Zaccheus [sic][4] was seeking Jesus," although not "on his own initiative" (p. 103). MacArthur speculates that being in the crowd meant that Zacchaeus was in danger of "a well-placed elbow in the jaw, a heavy boot on the big toe, or even a knife in the back" (p. 104).

MacArthur continues to speculate, saying that "Jesus had never met him [Zacchaeus] before" (p. 104). The text doesn't say that. Indeed, Jesus looks up and calls him by name, "Zacchaeus, make haste and come down, for today I must stay at your house" (Luke 19:5). Did Jesus know Zacchaeus from an earlier encounter?[5] Or is that a demonstration of Jesus' omniscience, as with the woman at the well in John 4:17-19? In any case, the text does not warrant a dogmatic assertion that Jesus had never met Zacchaeus before.

MacArthur is more cautious when he admits that we do not know what the Lord said to Zacchaeus when He evangelized him (p. 105), though we do know that the Lord said, "Today salvation has come to this house, because he too is a son of Abraham" (Luke 19:9). MacArthur now proposes several applications about evangelism from Luke 19:1-10.

One application suggested by MacArthur is that there is no "pre-fabricated prayer that can guarantee the salvation of a soul" (p. 105). That is certainly true. But that isn't the point of this text. (He

---

[4] MacArthur uses the spelling of the NASB translation, Zaccheus. Nearly all other English translations have a second "a" in the spelling of his name: Zacchaeus (KJV, NKJV, NIV, HCSB, NET).

[5] It is possible that Zacchaeus was a friend of Matthew and might have met Jesus at the feast Matthew held for Jesus in his house (Luke 5:27-31).

should have appealed to verses like John 3:16; 5:24; 6:35; 11:25-26; Eph 2:8-9, and Rom 4:4-5 to prove his point.)

Another application he makes is that "there is no four- or five-step plan of salvation" (p. 105). That is true; however, it is also not something that we learn from Luke 19:1-10. Jesus told people that whoever believes in Him has everlasting life (John 3:16; 5:24; 6:35, 47; 11:26). It is that simple.

The Fruit of Salvation

MacArthur makes a clear and simple statement about salvation in this section that contradicts the rest of what he says in his book: "Zaccheus [sic] was a son of Abraham not because he was Jewish, *but because he believed*" (p. 106, emphasis added).

Yes! He is a son of Abraham *because he believed*. There's no mention of confession of sins. There is no indication of turning from them. There is no commitment of life, no submitting to Christ's Lordship, and no obedience until death. There are no works at all; only faith. True, MacArthur talks about those things in preceding paragraphs, but here at least we find some precious gospel clarity that is sorely lacking in the rest of *TGAJ*: salvation comes by faith alone in Christ alone. No works are required to be born again since the Lord Jesus already did all the work that needs to be done for us. If a person believes what MacArthur says in this paragraph, then he is certain that he will be spending eternity with the Lord based on faith in Christ, apart from works.

Then MacArthur offers a contradictory and inconsistent patchwork of requirements for one to obtain everlasting life. On the one hand, he says that regeneration is by faith apart from works. But on the other hand, he claims that the new birth is by works. For example, MacArthur makes this terrific observation: "Salvation did not come to Zaccheus [sic] because he gave his money away, but because he became…a believer." So true! However, MacArthur immediately contradicts himself by once again imposing his theology on the text. After citing 2 Cor 5:17 about the new creation, he says,

> Zaccheus's [sic] response to Christ confirms the truth of
> that verse. He would have had a hard time understanding

contemporary people who claim to be born again but whose lives challenge everything Christ stands for (p. 106).

In the first place 2 Cor 5:17 does not say "*he is* a new creation." The Greek just says, "If anyone is in Christ, new creation." This isn't a verse that promises that all who come to faith in Christ experience a radical change in lifestyle. (There is no such verse.) In light of the context, Paul's point is that believers are part of a new world in which there are those who have everlasting life and those who do not. We no longer should recognize people according to fleshly distinctions. The only distinction that ultimately matters is who has everlasting life and who does not. Indeed, the *New Geneva Study Bible*, a Calvinist work, says concerning 2 Cor 5:17, "The believer's union with Christ is nothing less than participation in the 'new creation.' Translating 'there is a new creation' instead of 'he is a new creation' draws this conclusion more clearly…" (p. 1835). That translation fits the context.

When MacArthur says that Zacchaeus would have had a hard time understanding "contemporary people who claim to be born again but whose lives challenge *everything* Christ stands for," it is not clear who he has in mind. It is doubtful that anyone, believer or unbeliever, has led a life that challenges everything Christ stands for (p. 106, emphasis added), unless MacArthur is thinking of someone like Jeffrey Dahmer or Adolph Hitler. But he's probably thinking of allegedly horrible people like the Christian liquor store owner from chapter 5. If so, his audience must be left wondering about their own salvation. If MacArthur had railed against "people who claim to be born again *but whose lives are quite similar to nice unbelievers*," he surely would have disturbed the readers. But isn't that the logical conclusion of his position? If regeneration guarantees transformation, then believers will not only be different from serial killers (most people are), they will also be different from really nice unbelievers like Catholic or Buddhist priests, doctors who work with AIDS or Ebola patients, philanthropists, etc.

But if that is true, if that is the standard by which we determine if we are born again or not, then who can have assurance? Are any of us radically better than our nice unbelieving neighbors, let alone someone like Gandhi or Mother Theresa?

MacArthur says, "If such a change does not occur, there is no reason to think genuine salvation has taken place" (p. 107).[6] How radical and complete must the change be? Is it MacArthur's view that the moment one is born again that all of his sinful actions and cravings instantly vanish? Is he saying that the alcoholic who comes to Christ need not go through rehab of some sort? Do the cravings for liquor immediately disappear? Is the college student who had been sleeping with a different girl each night suddenly free from lust? Is the jealous person suddenly no longer jealous? Does the angry person become as peaceful as a lamb?

If Christians are set free from all sinful actions and desires, do they still need to grow? If his understanding of 2 Cor 5:17 is true, then would not a brand-new Christian be just as spiritually mature as the person who had walked with Christ for eighty years? And would it not be true that if anyone ever again felt a desire to sin then he would prove that he had never been born again?[7]

Coming back to Zacchaeus, is there anything in this text that indicates that his life was radically transformed to that extent? Not at all. We don't even know if Zacchaeus ever gave away his money or restored anyone fourfold. All we have is a statement of intent to change in one area of his life, not a report that his entire life was transformed. Does MacArthur think a statement of intent to give away half his money means that Zacchaeus was suddenly a great husband, father, neighbor, evangelist, prayer warrior, etc.? Is there any indication that he stopped living a life that challenged what Jesus stood for? We don't know. We can hope so, but we can't know for sure. There is no indication of that in this passage.

---

[6] MacArthur gives no support for this statement other than pointing to the experience of Zacchaeus in Luke 19. He assumes that the life of Zacchaeus radically changed after this encounter with Jesus. Then he further assumes that the Lord was teaching that radical change of lifestyle is something everyone experiences when he is born again.

[7] Those in Scripture who did not end well contradict MacArthur's statement. Solomon wrote several books of Scripture. Yet he died as an idolater (1 Kings 11:1-13). Demas was one of Paul's trusted fellow workers in gospel ministry (Col 4:14; Philem 24). Yet Paul's last words about him are these: "Demas has forsaken me, having loved this present world" (2 Tim 4:10). Speaking of believers in Corinth who abused the Lord's Supper, Paul says, "For this reason many are weak and sick among you, and many sleep" (1 Cor 11:30). Many of the believers in Corinth were carnal and died as a result of their carnal attitudes and actions. Yet Paul says they *sleep*, an expression Paul and all New Testament writers reserve for believers.

Conclusion

Christians are commanded to grow in maturity precisely because we are not immediately transformed the moment we believe in Jesus for everlasting life (Heb 5:12-14). The old habits and thinking don't get thrown off in a night. Our minds don't get renewed all at once (Rom 12:1-2; 1 Cor 2:14–3:4). The seed gets implanted, but it needs to grow. It takes time for the acorn of faith to mature into a towering oak.[8]

---

[8]And there is no guarantee that every believer will maximize his or her life for Christ. Compare the first and second servants in the Parable of the Minas. Servant one maximizes his opportunities, turning one mina into ten. Servant two does not. He turns one into only five. The result is that servant one hears, "Well done, good servant…have authority over ten cities" (Luke 19:17), but servant two hears, "You also be over five cities" (Luke 19:19). The second servant is not commended. He receives half as many cities to rule over. The third servant is actually called a wicked servant and receives no cities to rule over, though he does get into the kingdom (compare Luke 19:20-26 with Luke 19:27).

He Condemns a Hardened Heart

Introduction

How are spies unmasked? What gives them away?

Something in their behavior gives them away. Maybe they are overheard speaking to their handler. Possibly someone sees them meeting with a government official. Maybe they just appear jumpy. Spies must be very cool customers in order to fool the groups they are infiltrating.

Is it possible that a person who calls himself a Christian might not be one? If so, what gives him away? Is it his behavior or what he professes to believe?

In chapter 9, MacArthur uses the example of Judas to try to prove that the difference between a genuine believer and a false professor is that the genuine believer will never finally fall away and betray Christ.[1]

True Believers Don't Persist in Disobedience

MacArthur begins by discussing carnality and false professions of faith. He chastises "opponents of lordship salvation" and "one

---

[1] Of course, if this is true, then certainty that one has everlasting life is impossible prior to death since no one can be sure he will not fall in the future (1 Cor 9:27).

antilordship[2] writer" who "define the terms of salvation so loosely that virtually every profession of faith in Christ is regarded as the real thing" (p. 108).

The problem, as MacArthur sees it, is that these "antilordship" people "exclude obedience from their concept of saving faith" in order "to make room in the kingdom for professing believers whose lives are filled with sin" (p. 108). For MacArthur obedience (i.e., good works) is part of what saving faith is. Hence anyone who says that saving faith is simply believing in Jesus for everlasting life, apart from obedience, is *antilordship*.

By professing believers "whose lives are filled with sin," MacArthur does not mean someone who falls short of the glory of God. All fall short, including believers (Rom 3:23). Even believers sin so much that there is no point in our lives where we can honestly say, "We have no sin" (1 John 1:8).

What MacArthur means by professing believers "whose lives are filled with sin" is that they exhibit "a persistent pattern of disobedience, gross sin" (p. 108). Note the words *persistent pattern* and *gross sin*. In his view such people prove over time by their pattern of disobedience that they are not actually born again, regardless of what they profess to believe.

According to MacArthur "Christians can and do behave in carnal ways" (p. 138; see also p. 279). But he sees behaving in carnal ways as something Christians can only do for a time (pp. 11, 39-48, 113, 138): "Carnality is never spoken of by Scripture as a perpetual state for believers" (p. 279).

Paul said in 1 Cor 3:1-4 that the born-again people in Corinth were carnal. They were not merely behaving in carnal ways: "And I, brethren, could not speak to you as spiritual people but as to carnal, as to babes in Christ" (1 Cor 3:1). Paul wrote First Corinthians four to five years after the church in Corinth was founded. These people had been believers long enough to be spiritual people. Note the word *still* in verse 3: "for still you are carnal." This was the state they were in.

Yet MacArthur denies that they were carnal:

---

[2] *Antilordship* (which is not a recognized word in dictionaries) is an exceedingly offensive term. For a response to this canard see above on pp. 20-22 under "The Problem with a Feel-Good Gospel." There I discuss MacArthur's use of the synonymous expression: "no-lordship.".

These were not people living in static disobedience. Paul does not suggest that carnality and rebellion were the rule in their lives (p. 108, footnote 2).

MacArthur does not quote or explain 1 Cor 3:1 or 3:3. In 1 Cor 3:1 Paul says that the believers in Corinth were "babes in Christ," baby Christians, immature believers. In 1 Cor 3:3 he asks rhetorically, "are you not carnal and behaving like mere [i.e., unregenerate] men?"

MacArthur suggests that carnal means "living in static disobedience" or being in rebellion against God. But Paul does not say that. He says that to be carnal is to be an immature believer who still thinks and acts like unbelievers do.

So while it is true that the believers in Corinth were not rebelling against God, they clearly were "carnal and behaving like mere men." They were "babes in Christ," that is, immature Christians. MacArthur's definition of carnality contradicts that of Paul.

MacArthur attempts to prove that the Corinthians were not really carnal, but were merely behaving in some carnal ways, by pointing out they did not lack any spiritual gift and that they were eagerly awaiting the soon return of Christ (p. 108, footnote 2). But having spiritual gifts and eagerly awaiting Christ's soon return does not equate to being spiritual, as 1 Cor 3:1-3 makes clear. Twice Paul said that the believers in Corinth were carnal, not spiritual.

Since the Apostle Paul is the only Biblical author to speak of carnal people, shouldn't we define carnality the way he does? Paul says that believers who think and act like unbelievers are *carnal* and *babes in Christ* even if they have been believers for a long time.

Baby Christians behave like natural men unless and until they are transformed *by the renewing of their minds* (Rom 12:2; 1 Cor 2:14-16; 2 Cor 3:18).[3] Any believer who is still a babe in Christ is carnal even if chronologically he is no longer a new believer. The problem in Corinth is that they had been believers for four or five years and yet they were still babes in Christ. That shouldn't happen.

---

[3] A brand-new Christian has *some* renewal of his mind simply by virtue of coming to faith in Christ. And if immediate follow up is done, he might experience more change of mindset. So some change of thinking and behavior can and often does occur in the first few days of new life. But the type of radical changes that occur when one becomes spiritually minded take time. That is why a new believer cannot be made an elder even if he is older in terms of physical age (1 Tim 3:6). Growth takes time.

While no timetable is given, Paul starts 1 Cor 3:3 with the word *still* (*eti* in Greek). Apparently, Paul believed that five years was more than enough time to become mature believers. Note the same idea in Heb 5:12: "For though by this time you ought to be teachers, you need someone to teach you again the first principles of the oracles of God; and you have come to need milk and not solid food."

True Believers Persist in Holiness

The second issue MacArthur discusses is perseverance. The Reformed doctrine of the perseverance of the saints is not the same as the Biblical doctrine of eternal security:

> I am committed to the biblical truth that salvation is forever. Contemporary Christians have come to refer to this as the doctrine of *eternal security*. Perhaps the Reformers' terminology is more appropriate; they spoke of *the perseverance of the saints* (p. 109, emphasis his).

What's the difference?

According to the doctrine of eternal security, once you believe in Jesus for eternal life you have that life as a present possession and can never lose it, no matter what you do or believe afterwards (John 5:24; 10:28-29; 11:26; Eph 2:8-9). In this view you are certain of your eternally secure position as long as you believe the promise.

But according to the Calvinistic doctrine of perseverance, it is impossible to know if you believe in Christ. Faith in this understanding is unknowable. So Calvinists like MacArthur look for signs that indicate it is likely that belief has occurred.

The signs they need to prove their eternal destiny are a lifetime of good works, of orthodox theology, and of special feelings that God has been working within you. But even if a person is fairly confident that he has had all those things for decades, he cannot be sure he is a believer. MacArthur says concerning those who are true believers, "They will persevere in grace unto the very end" (p. 109). A bit later he adds, "True believers *will* persevere. Professing Christians who turn against the Lord only prove that they were never truly saved" (p. 109, emphasis his).

This teaching, if true, destroys the possibility of assurance of salvation. And assurance is vital to Christian growth, for just as a human parent does not want his children to doubt their secure family relationship, neither does God. Growth occurs within a context of love and security. Insecurity and doubt is not conducive to maturation.

If the Apostle Paul was not sure he would persevere (1 Cor 9:27), then we can't be sure either.

God calls for believers to persevere. He warns of judgment now and at the Judgment Seat of Christ for believers who fail to persevere. But He does not link eternal destiny to perseverance. Our assurance is found in the promise of "whoever believes in Him has everlasting life," not in our perseverance.

Of what practical value is belief that salvation is secure forever *for those who persevere in faith and good works until death* if we can't be sure we will do that? Practically speaking, Calvinists like MacArthur live like Arminians. Neither knows where they will spend eternity. Both believe they must persevere until death in order to make it into the kingdom.

The Question of Judas

After discussing these two introductory issues, MacArthur gets to the heart of the chapter's message. He uses Judas as the prime example of a professing believer who fails to persevere and shows he was never truly born again to begin with.

Notice his first words about the betrayer: "Judas is a prime example of a professing believer who fell into absolute apostasy" (p. 110). MacArthur assumes that Judas professed to believe in Jesus. Since there is nowhere in the Gospels or anywhere in the Bible which indicates that Judas professed to believe in Christ for eternal life, it's unclear on what basis MacArthur makes that claim. Clearly, Judas followed Jesus around. He was one of the disciples who walked and talked with Jesus, and participated in His ministry. But where do we ever read that Judas professed to believe in Jesus?

In point of fact, MacArthur doesn't try to prove that Judas was a professing believer. He just presumes it is true: "*Presumably* he thought of himself as a believer, at least at the outset" (p. 110, emphasis added).

There is no Biblical evidence that Judas ever believed that Jesus is the Christ, the Son of God. Martha did (John 11:27). The other Apostles did (John 2:11; 13:10). If Judas believed that, why would he have betrayed Jesus? And if he believed that, why would Jesus say that he was not yet spiritually clean (John 13:10)? Of course, what MacArthur may mean is that Judas thought of himself as one who believed *something about Jesus.* Judas probably believed that Jesus was a miracle worker, a prophet, and a good man. But there is no evidence that he ever believed in Jesus in the Johannine sense, that is, believing that He is the Messiah who guarantees everlasting life to all who believe in Him (John 3:14-18; 5:24; 6:35, 47; 11:25-27; 1 John 5:1, 9-13).

MacArthur puts himself in the difficult position of arguing that a person is not truly a believer unless he perseveres in faith and good works until death. In his view anyone who departs from the faith before death is an unbeliever, regardless of whether he once believed or not. Thus for MacArthur being a believer is not something that occurs at a point in time, an absolute passing from death into life (John 5:24). MacArthur holds to a linear view of regeneration.

Biblically a false professor is far different than what MacArthur teaches. A false professor is one who professes to believe in Christ, but who does not believe in Him *in the Biblical sense.* Biblically to believe in Jesus is to believe in Him *for everlasting life*—or for the equivalent[4] (John 3:16; 5:24; 6:35, 47; 11:25-27; Gal 2:16; Eph 2:8-9; 1 Tim 1:16; 2 Tim 1:1; Rev 22:17). The issue is the root (i.e., what one believes), not the fruit (i.e., what one does).

If someone believes in Jesus for something other than his eternal destiny, then he is not born again. Piper, who himself holds to Lordship Salvation, nonetheless says that one cannot be born again simply by believing that Jesus died on the cross for our sins and rose from the dead.[5] He says we must believe in Him for justification, regeneration, or forgiveness.[6] To believe in Jesus for "prosperity or health or a better marriage," Piper says, will not result in the new birth.[7]

---

[4] A person might not have heard the words *everlasting life* and yet still might have believed in the equivalent concept, like justification that is once for all, a guaranteed home in heaven, a secure relationship with God, once-saved, always-saved, etc. The point is, one must believe that his eternal destiny is secure not because of his works, but because he has believed the promise of the Lord Jesus Christ.

[5] John Piper, *The Future of Justification* (Wheaton, IL: Crossway Books, 2007), pp. 20, 85-86.

[6] Ibid.

[7] Ibid.

The point Piper is making is that we must believe in Jesus *for our eternal destiny.*[8] Believing in Him for well-being here and now is not saving faith.

We might take Piper's point in a slightly different direction. Someone may have orthodox beliefs about the person and work of Christ, and yet believe in salvation by works. If that's the case, he doesn't have saving faith. To be born again one must believe that he has everlasting life (or the equivalent) that can never be lost simply because he believes in Jesus for that life, not because of any works he has done or will do. The root is faith, believing the promise of life that Jesus makes to the believer. The root is not a lifetime of good works.

Is that what Judas believed? Did he believe in Jesus Christ *for everlasting life*? The Scriptures never indicate that he did. We know from John 13:10 ("you are clean, but not all of you") that Judas had not yet believed in Christ by the Last Supper, for he was not clean, though the other disciples were. And there is no indication that he came to faith after the Last Supper either.

One of You Will Betray Me[9]

According to MacArthur, in order to be eternally saved, Judas would have had to repent: "At every opportunity, Jesus warned Judas and entreated him to repent and be saved…yet he refused to turn from his sin and selfishness" (p. 111). MacArthur adds that Judas' decision to betray Christ was "a decision that would condemn him to eternal torment" (p. 111). Hypothetically, could not Judas have come to faith (or repentance, submission, confession,

---

[8] This is a bit confusing because, like MacArthur, Piper does not believe it is possible to be certain that you believe in Jesus. He too believes that one must persevere in faith and good works in order to prove that he actually believes. Note that on p. 20 where he says, "If we are going to help people believe the gospel in a saving way," he immediately adds, "not the way demons believe, and not the way Simon the magician believed, James 2:19; Acts 8:13, 21-23." But in a sense that makes this observation by him even more telling. For MacArthur we do not need to believe in Jesus for anything. There are no statements like these by Piper in *TGAJ*. According to MacArthur the issue is that we need to turn from our sins, submit to Jesus, obey Him, and persevere in faith and good works until death. The issue for him is not believing in Jesus for our eternal destiny.

[9] This is the first subheading in chapter 9 of *TGAJ*. I placed several subheadings before this since MacArthur covered a lot of material in the first three pages of this chapter, all without headings.

obedience, and perseverance, to use MacArthur's terms) *after* he betrayed Christ? There is no evidence that he did. In fact, Jesus called him "the son of perdition" in John 17:12. That seems to indicate that Judas was not going to come to faith even after he returned the blood money. MacArthur evidently believes that once Judas left the supper to betray Jesus, God hardened his heart so that belief was impossible (p. 111). That could well be true, but we have no indication in Scripture that that happened. It's conjecture.

Who Is It?[10]

It is surely correct for MacArthur to suggest that the disciples did not know that Judas was the betrayer (John 13:28). Each in turn wondered if it might be him. And MacArthur is also right to say that Jesus must have treated Judas just like He did the other disciples. (Of course, Peter, James, and John were the inner three who had special access to Jesus. But of the other nine, Judas Iscariot was surely treated the same.)

MacArthur suggests that Judas hated Jesus: "Contrast the hatred Judas harbored for Jesus with the love John had for the Savior" (p. 112). The love that Jesus had for John is well established in John's Gospel. It may be reasonable to conclude that John loved Jesus as well, especially since he was one of the inner three. But where do we find even a hint that Judas hated Jesus?

MacArthur finds what he thinks is proof of hatred in the fact that Judas betrayed Jesus. However, underlying hatred is not at all obvious. Judas later returned the money and committed suicide because he regretted that he had betrayed Jesus: "Then Judas, His betrayer, seeing that He had been condemned, was remorseful and brought back the thirty pieces of silver to the chief priests and elders, saying, "I have sinned by betraying innocent blood… Then he threw down the pieces of silver in the temple and departed, and went and hanged himself" (Matt 27:3, 5).

---

[10] This subheading is the second one in *TGAJ*. Since the one which follows, "The Guest of Honor," covers essentially the same content, I've combined those two subheadings into one.

Do It Quickly

The Bible does not teach that all believers always follow Christ. Believers may or may not follow Christ. If a believer stops going to church, he is not following Christ. If a believer backslides, he is not following Christ. Yet he remains a child of God.

Believing is not the same as following. Judas proves that. He followed but did not believe. Compare John 6:64-66,

> "But there are *some* of you who do not believe." For Jesus knew from the beginning who they were who did not believe, and who would betray Him…From that time *many* of His disciples went back and walked with Him no more" (emphasis added).

Some of Jesus' disciples did not believe in Him. *Many* of His disciples departed that day, suggesting that some of those who departed were believing disciples.

Into the Night[11]

Once again MacArthur refers to Judas's purported profession of faith: "his faith was never genuine" (p. 113). He says that from the start Judas lacked "sincere, obedient[12] faith." What is *sincere faith*? Evidently it is *obedient faith*. But isn't the only condition of everlasting life *faith* in Christ? Why bring in obedience? The reason is because for MacArthur the primary condition[13] of everlasting life is obedience. Obedience, not faith, is the key for MacArthur. He does of course mention faith quite a few times in his book.[14] But when he does so he routinely qualifies it with words that relate to one's

---

[11] The material under this subheading and the one which follows it, "Kiss of Death," in *TGAJ* is very brief. Thus I discussed both under this one heading.

[12] In the second edition of *TGAJ* the expression used was "sincere, penitent faith." Why was this changed to *sincere, obedient faith* in the third edition? I assume because *penitent faith* sounds Roman Catholic, that is, related to penance.

[13] Though MacArthur lists numerous conditions of everlasting life in this book (e.g., repentance, submission, confession, obedience, and perseverance), obedience seems to be the leading term he uses. He refers to obeying or obedience 75 times (28 and 45, respectively), to repentance and repent 64 times (47 and 17, respectively), to submission and submit 32 times (24 and 8, respectively), to confession and confess 29 times (19 and 10, respectively), and to perseverance and persevere 6 times (5 and 1, respectively).

[14] He mentions faith 86 times and believing 49 times.

works. Thus he speaks of things like *obedient faith* (pp. 61, 113), *repentant faith* (pp. 162, 195), the submissive response of personal faith (p. 87), faith that is *submissive obedience* (pp. 37, 149, 238), faith that is *submissive surrender* (p. 11), etc.

The Lordship Salvation agenda once again comes into focus as MacArthur ends this section with the words, "That frightening potential [discovering you were never truly born again] exists for every person who comes to Christ without a committed heart" (p. 113).

Notice that *commitment of the heart* is also required to be born again. Faith in Christ is not enough. Nor is obedience enough. Faith and obedience must be wedded to repentance and lifelong commitment of heart. But how much commitment is needed? How do we know if we were or are or will be committed sufficiently? No wonder MacArthur speaks of the "frightening potential" of his theology. One wonders how anyone who listens to this sort of teaching could avoid being afraid for his salvation. MacArthur absolutely undermines the possibility of having assurance of everlasting life.

Does God want His children to have assurance, that is certainty, about their relationship with Him and hence about their eternal destiny? Or does God want His children to live in fear of "the frightening potential" that their destiny might be the lake of fire?

They All Forsook Him and Fled

A bit of explanation is needed as to how born again people might stop following Christ. Earlier MacArthur had indicated that a believer is a disciple and that all believers follow Christ until death. But now he finds people whom he knows are genuine believers, the eleven disciples, who stop following. How does he explain that?

> The mark of a true disciple is not that he never sins, but rather that when he does sin he inevitably returns to the Lord to receive cleansing and forgiveness. Unlike a false disciple, the true disciple will never turn away completely...
> He will return to a life of service for the Savior (pp. 114-15).

Notice how this impacts one's assurance. Say you know you are capable of falling away, as MacArthur says we all are. And you know it is possible you may "turn away completely" and might not "return to a life of service for the Savior." If so, what does that mean? That means you might not be born again.

How will you find out if you are born again? The proof is in your works. Will you persevere in your service for Christ? Only time will tell.

And what is your motivation to serve Christ? Gratitude? Love? A desire to please the Lord? MacArthur says that we should be motivated to serve Christ so that we can avoid spending eternity in the lake of fire.

MacArthur's position, although well-intentioned, has the effect of stripping believers of assurance of their eternal destiny (or of keeping unbelievers from believing in Jesus *for everlasting life*) and of giving them an improper motivation for service (i.e., fear that if they do not do enough good works then they will be eternally condemned).

Assurance is a great help in perseverance.[15] Knowing that I am secure in Christ motivates me to keep on serving Him. If I doubted my standing with Him, I would be in despair all the time.

The Marks of a False Disciple

This chapter ends with the application for the reader, which has been touched on earlier in the chapter, but which will now be addressed head on.

Do you want "temporal gain more than eternal riches"? Do you want "glory...success...earthly treasures" (p. 115)? Are you "in it for what [you] receive" (p. 115)?

Evidently there are a lot of people in today's churches like that, for MacArthur says,

> I fear there are multitudes like Judas in the contemporary church. They are friendly to Jesus. They look and talk like disciples. But they are not committed to him and are therefore capable of the worst kind of betrayal (p. 115).

---

[15] Indeed, it is hard to see how anyone could persevere in faith and good works unless he was certain of his eternal destiny. Doubt may produce legalistic strivings (e.g., the Pharisees and the Judaizers) and "an appearance of wisdom in self-imposed religion, false humility, and neglect of the body" (Col 2:23a,b). But those things "are of no value against the indulgence of the flesh" (Col 2:23c). We are to live by faith (Gal 2:20), not by doubt.

If believing in Jesus for everlasting life must be supplemented with repentance, obedience, commitment of life, and perseverance in service, then assurance of salvation is impossible prior to death. MacArthur's Lordship Salvation theology makes assurance impossible.

Of course, some see this as a good thing. They see fear of hell as a powerful motivation to live for God. But fear of hell should be a thing of the past for the believer (John 3:16; 5:24; 11:26). God wants His children to remember that they have everlasting life right now, that they will never come into judgment concerning their eternal destiny, and that they have already passed from death into life (John 5:24). Such assurance is powerful.

Conclusion

There are many false professors out there, as MacArthur says. But they are not false professors for the reason he suggests. MacArthur thinks that a person is a false professor if he does not persevere in good works until death. That is not what the Bible says.

The truth is, false profession is about what you believe, not about what you do. If someone claims to be a Christian, yet believes in salvation by works, then no matter what else he says or does, he is a false professor. But if someone believes in Jesus for everlasting life, he is what he professes to be, a believer in Jesus Christ. Whether or not he perseveres in good works is a question of discipleship, not salvation (2 Tim 2:11-13; 1 Thess 5:10).

You can be sure you have everlasting life and that you will never be eternally condemned (John 5:24). Just believe the promise of the Lord Jesus Christ, the One who cannot lie. But if you think you must persevere in faith and good works in order to prove you are a true believer, then you will live daily with the frightening possibility that you will spend eternity in the lake of fire. MacArthur's Lordship Salvation produces doubt, not assurance.

CHAPTER 10

He Offers a Yoke of Rest

In chapter 10, MacArthur discusses the Lord's famous teaching on coming to Him and learning from Him to gain rest (Matt 11:28-30). In the introduction he says, "Jesus' offer of rest for the weary is a call to conversion. It is a masterpiece of redemptive truth—a synopsis of the gospel according to Jesus" (p. 118).

And MacArthur couldn't be more wrong.

The Yoke of Rest

MacArthur entitles this chapter "He Offers a Yoke of Rest" (p. 116).

In our stress-filled age, nearly everyone wants rest for their souls. We need it. The Lord Jesus gave a very well-known promise about rest when He said:

> "Come to Me, all you who labor and are heavy laden, and I will give you rest. Take My yoke upon you and learn from Me, for I am gentle and lowly in heart, and you will find rest for your souls. For My yoke is easy and My burden is light" (Matt 11:28-30).

What type of rest is the Lord talking about? MacArthur says, "This is an invitation to salvation, not just an appeal for believers to move into a deeper experience of discipleship" (p. 117). Further he says, "It is...a synopsis of the gospel according to Jesus" (p. 118).

Then he brings up the essentials, "It outlines *five essential elements of genuine conversion*, all so inextricably linked that it is impossible to eliminate any one of them from the biblical concept of saving faith" (p. 118, emphasis added). Those five essential elements of genuine conversion are the five other subheadings for the chapter: humility, revelation, repentance, faith, and submission.

For MacArthur to say there are "five essential elements of genuine conversion" is especially surprising since just two chapters earlier, in chapter 8, he said, "there is no four- or five-step plan of salvation" (p. 105). Isn't "five essential elements of genuine conversion" the same idea as a "five-step plan of salvation"? This looks like a contradiction.

But more importantly, where does the Bible list these five elements as conditions for receiving everlasting life? The five elements are not found in the text MacArthur cites, Matt 11:28-30, nor are they found together anywhere in the Bible.[1]

Matthew 11:28-30 says nothing about repentance, humility, or revelation, though it certainly speaks of faith as a condition of regeneration ("Come to Me," compare John 6:35) and of submission as a condition of discipleship ("Take My yoke upon you and learn from Me").

Before we examine MacArthur's five essential elements for salvation, notice that the Lord mentions *rest* twice (Matt 11:28, 29), and with two different conditions for having rest.

The first *rest*, mentioned in verse 28, is conditioned upon *coming to Jesus*.

Verse 29 speaks of a second rest, conditioned upon *taking up Jesus' yoke and learning from Him*.

Is *coming to Jesus* the same as taking up His yoke and learning from Him? That is the position MacArthur advocates. Yet the Biblical text does not support MacArthur's claim.

In the Fourth Gospel *coming to Jesus* is a metaphor for believing in Him. The Lord said, "You are not willing to come to Me that you may have [everlasting] life" (John 5:40). A bit later He said, "He who

---

[1] In addition, other than faith in God's revelation concerning Christ (John 3:16; 5:24), none of the other things which MacArthur says are essential conditions for receiving everlasting life are said to be conditions of the new birth or of justification in the Bible. Even if all five elements were found together, they would need to be listed *as conditions for regeneration or justification*. They are not.

comes to Me shall never hunger, and he who believes in Me shall never thirst" (John 6:35). "All that the Father gives Me will come to Me, and the one who comes to Me I will by no means cast out" (John 6:37). Coming to Jesus is believing in Him.

Yet where in John's Gospel or the entire Bible do we find *taking up Jesus' yoke* as a metaphor for believing? A yoke was a wooden implement which had openings for the heads of two oxen to be placed so that they could pull a plow or a cart. *A yoke is a symbol of hard labor*, not a symbol of faith.

In addition, learning [*manthanō/mathētēs* in Greek, the noun form being the word translated *disciple(s)* in the New Testament] from Jesus is a discipleship concept. It is not a picture of believing in Him.

The Lord Jesus is saying in Matt 11:28-30 that the first *rest*, the one for those who come to Him, pictures everlasting life for the believer. The second *rest*, the one for those who take His yoke and learn from Him, pictures a life of discipleship, which is a life of such fulfillment and joy that it can be said to be rest from the aimlessness and discontentment that characterizes a life without eternal significance.[2]

Humility

The first of MacArthur's "five essential elements of genuine conversion" is humility. He finds this in a verse that precedes Matt 11:28-30. In verse 25 the Lord says, "You have hidden these things from the wise and prudent and have revealed them to babes." The wise and prudent are "the Pharisees, the rabbis, and the scribes" (p. 118). "Their sin is not their intellect; it is their intellectual pride."

MacArthur continues:

> Who can enter into salvation? Those who, like children, are dependent, not independent. Those who are humble, not proud. Those who recognize that they are helpless and empty. Aware that they are nothing, they turn in utter dependency to Christ (p. 119).

Doesn't this statement contradict the main point of *TGAJ* and of this chapter? MacArthur has been arguing that everlasting life

---

[2] It is possible that this second *rest* (*anapausis*) is the same *rest* spoken of by the author of Hebrews (using the related word *katapausis* in Heb 3:11, 18; 4:1-11).

is only for those who deny themselves, take up their crosses, and follow Christ till they die. But why would someone who recognizes that they are "helpless and empty" and "aware that they are nothing" ever presume to save themselves by works? Working for Christ (taking His yoke upon you) is not dependency, humility, and helplessness. It is sweating, working, and helping.[3]

This section on humility illustrates the inconsistency of MacArthur's position, an inconsistency born of his days before he studied the Puritans in 1980. He often makes comments that make it seem like he believes in salvation by faith alone, but just as quickly contradicts himself and teaches salvation by works.

Revelation

The other four items in MacArthur's list (humility, repentance, faith, submission) are all conditions placed upon the person who wishes to be born again. This lone item is not, at least in the way it is stated.

Possibly what MacArthur means here is that in order to be born again *a person must be open to Divine revelation* (see his comments on the need to be open on pp. 71, 87, 105, 119).

However, MacArthur does say, "The only people who receive it [personal knowledge of the Father and the Son] are those who are sovereignly chosen" (p. 120), which obviously reflects his commitment to Calvinism and unconditional election.

Only by special revelation from God—that is, only from Scripture—can a person come to faith. Paul said that in Rom 10:14. However, contra MacArthur, *anyone*, not just the so-called *elect*,[4] can receive revelation from God through His Word and believe and be born again.

---

[3] MacArthur believes that "not of works" in Eph 2:9 refers to works humans do *independent of God's enablement* (see p. 189). However, Paul does not make that distinction in Eph 2:9 or anywhere. The Lord in John 6:28-29 also ruled out works that people do and He too did not qualify His remarks. Though God gives believers *the power we need to obey Him* so that He might give us eternal rewards, that is not the same as saying that He does the work without our involvement. We must run, fight, and keep the faith (2 Tim 4:6-8).

[4] I believed in election *to everlasting life* for 25 years (1980-2005). I no longer do. I've come to see that the Scriptures do not teach that. What they teach is election *to service*. For explanation see my book *The Ten Most Misunderstood Words in the Bible*, pp. 182-86.

Repentance

MacArthur himself notes, "the word *repentance* is not specifically used here" (p. 121, emphasis his). Yet he says, "that [repentance] is what our Lord is calling for." He says, "'Come to Me' demands a complete turnaround, a full change of direction" (p. 121).

MacArthur makes this claim without providing any support. He does not mention or explain New Testament passages in which the expression *coming to Jesus* occurs. He fails to demonstrate that Jesus' use of the exhortation "Come to Me" in Matt 11:28 or elsewhere is a demand for "a complete turnaround, a full change of direction."

While the English expression *come to Me* is found in many places in the New Testament, the exact Greek expression in Matt 11:28 (*deute pros Me*) is only found here.[5] Thus we need to look at uses of this same idea using a different but synonymous Greek verb (*erchomai*).

In John 6:35 the Lord said, "He who comes to Me [*ho erchomenos pros Me*] shall never hunger, and he who believes in Me shall never thirst." *Coming to Jesus* there is a synonym for believing in Him, not a synonym for repentance (see also John 5:39-40; 6:37, 44, 45, 65). That is, *coming to Him* in the first half of the verse is synthetically parallel with *believing in Him* in the second half.

Three texts speak about allowing children to come to Jesus (Matt 19:14; Mark 10:14; Luke 18:16). They either refer to people of that day literally allowing children to approach and listen to Jesus, or else they refer to allowing children to believe in Him. Either way the Lord meant that children should be evangelized.

If MacArthur could show a text in which *coming to Jesus* refers to repentance, then that might support his interpretation here. But he can't do that, and he doesn't even try to show that. There is no verse anywhere in the Bible which indicates that *coming to Jesus* refers to turning from one's sins.

MacArthur goes on to define *repentance* as "turn[ing] from self and sin to the Savior. This is not an invitation to people to enjoy their sin" (p. 121). So one must turn from his sins, reject his sins,

---

[5] There are two uses of *duete* (from *duerō*) *opisō mou*, come *after* Me (Matt 4:19; Mark 1:17). However, coming *after* Jesus is a much different idea than coming *to* Jesus. Indeed *deute opisō mou* is almost always translated as "Follow Me" (KJV, NKJV, NASB, NET, HCSB; ESV; NIV has "Come, follow me").

and turn to Christ and follow Him in order to be born again. How he gets that from this passage, or from the New Testament concept of coming to Jesus, is impossible to see.

Faith

Having identified *coming to Jesus* as repentance, how will MacArthur find faith in this passage?

Amazingly, having just said that the call to "Come to Me" is a call to repentance, he now says,

> "Come to Me" is tantamount to saying "Believe in Me." In John 6:35…to come to Jesus is to believe in Him (p. 121).

Apparently it can mean both. How? Because, "Faith is the flip side of repentance" (p. 121).

So here is what MacArthur expects the reader to understand: any time the word *repentance* or a synonym occurs, faith and repentance are both meant. Likewise, any time *faith* or a synonym occurs, faith and repentance are both meant.

However, there is not a shred of evidence that supports the idea that faith is the flip side of repentance. Nor does MacArthur try to provide such evidence.

Have you ever seen a coin that was cut in half and then put back together? I have. You can separate the face of the coin from the back of it. You end up not with one coin, but two half coins.

Well, if the front half of the coin is faith and the back half is repentance, then justification is by faith plus repentance, not by faith alone. You can't have it both ways.

Notice how short this section is in relation to the other sections, especially the section on submission which follows. Nine lines on faith.[6] Fifty-three lines on submission. Thirty-four lines on repentance.

The tiny amount of space MacArthur devotes to faith speaks volumes. Faith clearly is not very important to MacArthur. If it were, he wouldn't have only given it a handful of lines. Submission and repentance, however, are vital based on the fact that he gives ten times as much material discussing those issues than he does discussing faith.

---

[6] Actually five of those nine lines deal with repentance, not faith. Thus he really only has four lines on faith.

Tenney famously called John's Gospel *The Gospel of Belief.* The reason he did so is because the verb *believe* (*pisteuō*) occurs 99 times in John. Over and over again the Lord says that the one who believes in Him has everlasting life, shall not come into judgment, shall never hunger or thirst, and shall never die (John 1:12-13; 3:14-18; 5:24; 6:35, 37, 39, 45; 11:26).

Nor was this merely the teaching of the Lord Jesus, although that would be enough since He is, after all, the Lord. But His Apostles followed their Lord and also taught that justification and regeneration are by faith alone. The Apostle Paul famously said, "Believe on the Lord Jesus Christ and you shall be saved…" (Acts 16:31). Paul said that he was "a pattern to those who are going to believe on Him [Jesus] for everlasting life" (1 Tim 1:16). He said that salvation, that is, the new birth (Eph 2:5) is "by grace…through faith…not of works" (Eph 2:8-9). He said three times in one verse that "a man is not justified by the works of the law but by faith in Jesus Christ" (Gal 2:16). Over and over again in Gal 3:6-14 he said that justification is by faith alone.

The Jerusalem Council was a meeting of the early church to settle the issue of whether Gentiles had to be circumcised and keep the Law of Moses in order to be born again (Acts 15:1) and even in order to be sanctified (Acts 15:5). At that meeting the Apostle Peter, speaking of his ministry to Cornelius and his household (Acts 10:34-48), the first Gentile converts,[7] said,

> "God chose among us, that by my mouth the Gentiles should hear the word of the gospel and believe. So God, who knows the heart, acknowledged them by giving them the Holy Spirit, just as He did to us…purifying their hearts by faith" (Acts 15:7-9).

Peter spoke of faith and believing. He did not mention repentance or submission.

James said God "brought us forth by the word of truth" (1:18), that is, by believing the message of everlasting life sourced in Jesus Christ. He too did not mention repentance or submission.

---

[7] The Ethiopian eunuch of Acts 8 may well have been a Jew. However, if he was a Gentile, he is generally considered as an individual (though possibly some of his servants came to faith as well), not as a group as in the case of Cornelius, his family, and his household (which would include servants and possibly friends and neighbors who came to hear this important message).

I love the old Baptist hymn "Whosoever Surely Meaneth Me." That song is based on John 3:16 and Rev 22:17 (from the KJV). The Lord Jesus said that "whosoever believeth in Him should not perish, but have everlasting life" (John 3:16, KJV). The issue was and remains belief in Jesus or lack thereof.

Submission

Often an author saves the best for last. That is certainly MacArthur's view in this chapter. He thinks the key element in the new birth is submission.

The first lines are telling: "Salvation does not end there. Another element of genuine conversion is submission" (p. 122). The word *there* refers back to the preceding section on faith. Thus when he says, "Salvation does not end there" (p. 122) he means *salvation does not end with faith in Christ*. He then adds, "Another element of genuine conversion is submission" (p. 122). That is an amazing statement. Submission (and repentance, pp. 120-21) must be *added* to faith in order for a person to have salvation:

> The call to surrender to Jesus' lordship is part and parcel of His invitation to salvation. Those unwilling to take on His yoke cannot enter into the saving rest He offers (p. 122).

MacArthur's discussion of the yoke (pp. 122-23) is very helpful. He clearly shows that it is an implement for work.

He is also correct that the "the imagery [of learning from Jesus]... [is reminiscent of] a pupil who submitted himself to a teacher [and] was said to take the teacher's yoke" (p. 122).

The problem is that MacArthur equates the call to discipleship with the call to everlasting life. For him *following Jesus* is required to be born again as this section and the title of the book's first chapter show.

Notice that we find no discussion of the difference between coming to Christ and taking His yoke upon us and learning from Him. How anyone could think those two things are identical is hard to fathom, unless, of course, his theology demands it.

In this section on submission MacArthur is teaching works salvation. He is saying we must work for Christ to be born again. This is Nike evangelism: *Just do it.*

MacArthur says that "the yoke of the law, the yoke of human effort, the yoke of works, and the yoke of sin are all heavy, chafing, galling yokes...The yoke He [Jesus] offers is easy, and the burden He gives is light..." (pp. 122-23). His point seems to be this work is easy. It is not difficult.

Regardless of how hard or easy Jesus' yoke is, His yoke is a yoke. It is an implement of work.

MacArthur may be hinting at what we see in 1 John 5:3, "His commandments are not burdensome." True. But they are still commands and effort is still necessary. Work is to be done. The point made by the Lord and the Apostle John is that the born again person is well fitted to the task of working for Christ because of the power of the Spirit in his life.

MacArthur pictures a form of works salvation that isn't heavy, chafing, or galling. This is work we can do and enjoy. And if we do, then we will gain everlasting life for the work we've done for Christ. This idea that everlasting life is by works—whether easy or difficult—cannot possibly be harmonized with texts like John 3:16; 5:24; 6:28-29; Rom 4:4-5; Gal 2:15-16; Eph 2:8-9; or Titus 3:5.

The only "submission" that is a precursor to faith in Christ is a willingness to do what God says we must do:

> [Jesus said,] "You search the Scriptures, for in them you think you have eternal life; and these are they which testify of Me. But you are not willing to come to Me that you may have life" (John 5:39-40).

Here is another use of *coming to Jesus*. Again, that expression is a synonym for believing in Him. The vast majority of Jews were unwilling to believe in Jesus for the everlasting life He promised because in their minds that was too easy. That contradicted their tradition, just as justification by faith alone contradicts MacArthur's theological tradition.

Conclusion

Like Naaman, who initially chafed at the condition of healing that Elisha gave him as being too easy (2 Kings 5:9-13), MacArthur is unwilling to submit to the simple condition of coming to Jesus for the rest that is everlasting life. Hence he gives the reader a harder way of deliverance. Yet since it isn't God's way, the gospel according to MacArthur is a message that is not true.

Naaman ended up submitting to the condition God gave him through Elisha for healing (2 Kings 5:14), a condition that initially offended him. Have you submitted to the only way for everlasting life given by God? That is, have you come to Jesus, have you believed in Him for everlasting life? I hope you have. I hope your assurance is based solely on the promise of God to the believer and not at all on your works. I have written this book so you can be sure that you have everlasting life which can never be lost no matter what.

CHAPTER 11

The Soils (Matthew 13:1-23)

Introduction

The Parable of the Four Soils is one of the most popular passages used to teach that genuine saving faith is characterized by fruitfulness and longevity, and that is how MacArthur interprets it. But even though many people agree with the way MacArthur interprets this parable, the Berean (Acts 17:11) asks if that interpretation is really the correct interpretation of the parable.

The Kingdom and Parable

The Parable of the Four Soils, also called The *Parable of the Sower*, is found in all three of the Synoptic Gospels (Matt 13:1-23; Mark 4:1-20; Luke 8:1-15). MacArthur chooses the passage from Matthew to discuss the parable.

It is not uncommon for Dispensationalists to say what MacArthur says here, that there is *a mystery form of the kingdom* operating on earth today: "The kingdom—God's rule over the earth and in the hearts of people—exists now in mystery form" (p. 128). MacArthur does not cite any evidence for this.

While the Lord did use the word *mysteries* (*mysteria*) when discussing the kingdom, He did not speak of "a mystery form of the kingdom." Instead He spoke of "mysteries of [or about] the kingdom" (Matt 13:11; Mark 4:11; Luke 8:10).

The kingdom is not yet. It is future only (Matt 6:10; Acts 1:6; Rev 12:10). There is no sense in which Jesus is ruling on earth as the King of Israel today. He is not "ruling in the hearts of people" today in any kingdom sense. Instead, Satan is "the god of this age" (2 Cor 4:4). While Jesus is sovereign and in ultimate control, He allows Satan his day (with restraint)[1] and the Lord Jesus is not ruling as King today.

The Wayside Soil

MacArthur says that the first soil is "the hard-packed dirt of the road bordering the field" (p. 129). Most commentators disagree, suggesting that this soil represented the walking path between the rows of grain. The one sowing the seed needed someplace to walk. In any case, some of the seed fell on the hard ground and the birds ate it. While MacArthur does not say anything about the spiritual condition represented by this soil at this point, a few pages later he calls this type of person "unresponsive, unconcerned, inattentive, indifferent, negligent, and often hostile" (p. 132).

The Shallow Soil

In Matthew's version there is no explicit indication that any of the four soils believed. In Luke's reporting of the parable, the Lord explicitly says that the first soil did not believe (Luke 8:12), but He says that the second soil represents "those who believe for a while and in time of temptation fall away" (Luke 8:13).

The idea of believing is conveyed in Matthew's version with the words, "he who hears the word and immediately receives it with joy" (Matt 13:20). The words "they immediately sprang up" (Matt 13:5) shows that the seed (the word) had germinated. Life had begun. Clearly germination must occur before any sprig can spring up out of the soil. So regeneration, the new birth, has occurred in the second soil.

---

[1]Paul said that, "He who now restrains will do so until He is taken out of the way" (2 Thess 2:7). The Holy Spirit restrains sin in the world today. When the Rapture occurs, He will allow sin to flourish even more than it does in our age. Thus Satan's rule on earth today is not unchecked. But that is not at all the same as saying that the kingdom of God is operating on earth today. Didn't the Lord teach us to pray, "Your kingdom come, Your will be done on earth as it is in heaven (Matt 6:10)"?

MacArthur does not agree that germination equates to the new birth, but he does say that here. Later in this chapter he specifically rejects that idea (p. 136). At this point he explains the second soil's response to God's Word in his discussion of verse 5 (pp. 129). He says that the seed germinated and that due to a shallow root "those plants would be the first to die" (p. 129). He says nothing in this initial discussion about whether this soil represents regenerate people or not.

The Weedy Soil

MacArthur basically recites verse 7, and while offering little explanation at this juncture, he does point out that the plant is damaged by the fast growing weeds: "In the end, the good plants are choked out" (p. 130). While MacArthur calls these "the good plants," suggesting they represent regenerate people, he actually thinks otherwise as he later indicates (p. 134).[2]

The Good Soil

Very little is said here about verse 8. We are just told that this is the best of the four soils and as a result the seed "brings forth a tremendous harvest" (p. 130). While MacArthur does not yet say so specifically, it is clear he takes this soil as referring to regenerate people.

The Condition of the Soil

MacArthur's main point in this section is excellent. There is nothing wrong with the seed or the soil per se: "The difference in the soils has to do with how they have been conditioned" (p. 131). He rightly sees the condition of each soil as illustrative of the preparation of one's heart: "a person's response to the gospel depends primarily on the preparation of his or her heart. A heart not properly prepared will never bear spiritual fruit" (p. 128).

MacArthur is laying the groundwork here for the idea that the Lord's whole point is whether one believes *the gospel* and is born

---

[2] MacArthur asks, "Has such a person [the third soil person] lost his salvation?" (p. 134). He answers, "No, he never had it…The gospel germinated but was choked out before it could come to fruition. The person with the weedy heart was never saved in the first place" (p. 134).

again or not. Where he is headed is that the first three soils all do not believe and are not regenerated.

Notice that MacArthur speaks of "a person's response *to the gospel*" (emphasis added), whereas the Lord spoke of a person's response to "the word of the kingdom" (Matt 13:19) and to "the word" (Matt 13:20, 22, 23). In Luke the Lord says the seed is "the word of God" (Luke 8:11). In Mark He calls the seed "the word" (Mark 4:14, 15, 16, 17, 18, 19, 20).

The gospel and the word of the kingdom/the word of God/the word are not the same thing.[3] In the application section of the Parable of the Sower in Luke the Lord said, "Therefore take heed how you hear. For whoever has, to him more will be given; and whoever does not have, even what he seems to have will be taken from him" (Luke 8:18). That sure sounds like He is instructing believers to be attentive to the teaching of His Word.

The Unresponsive Heart

Here we find MacArthur's explanation of soil one, which he calls "the unresponsive heart" (p. 132).

The first soil represents unbelievers (compare Luke 8:12, "the devil comes and takes away the word out of their hearts, lest they should believe and be saved").

He calls this type of person "the hard-hearted individual" (p. 132). MacArthur says, "He is unresponsive, unconcerned, inattentive, indifferent, negligent, and often hostile" (p. 132). The word *unresponsive* rightly suggests that the first soil does not respond in belief to the word. But to say that the people represented by this soil are "unconcerned, inattentive, indifferent, negligent, and often hostile" is moving beyond what the Lord said. In addition, MacArthur does not mention the fact that the Lord said "the wicked one comes and

---

[3] The Word of God contains the message of everlasting life/salvation. The Lord said of the first soil that "the devil comes and takes away the word out of their hearts, lest they should believe and be saved" (Luke 8:12). Thus believing the word does result in salvation. However, the Word of God contains much more than simply the promise of life. It mostly contains instructions on how born again people are to think and act. Soils two (for a time), three, and four not only believe the word in relation to everlasting life, they accept many teachings in God's Word.

snatches away what was sown in his heart" (Matt 13:19; compare Luke 8:12 cited above).[4]

While some of the wayside soil might be inattentive, indifferent, negligent, or hostile, some might be attentive, concerned, and certainly not hostile, as MacArthur himself suggests in the last paragraph of this very section (p. 132).

MacArthur says that this type of person has "no sorrow over sin, no guilt, and no concern for the things of God" (p. 132). Yet none of that is in the text. MacArthur wants to support his claim that turning from sins, submission, and obedience are necessary to be born again. However, despite his claims, none of these things are supported by the Biblical text. Rather, the text talks about the need to respond in faith to the Word of God.

The Superficial Heart

Here is how MacArthur explains the second soil:

> It responds positively but not with saving faith. There is no thought involved, *no counting the cost*. It is quick, emotional, euphoric, instant excitement without any understanding of the actual significance of discipleship. That is not genuine faith (p. 133, emphasis added).

What cost is there to be born again? Does this passage list a cost we must pay? Didn't MacArthur himself already say that "the Savior Himself paid the ultimate price" (p. 72) and "Jesus' death [paid] the price for salvation" (p. 59)?[5] So what is this cost *we must pay*?[6] Is the blood of Christ insufficient? Must it be wedded with our own blood shed in service of Christ?

The second soil actually represents born again believers (compare Luke 8:13 with Luke 8:12) who fall away at some point and do not persevere in faith and good works: "who believe for a while and

---

[4] Compare 2 Cor 4:4. That is why before anyone believes in Christ the Holy Spirit opens his heart (Acts 16:14). In light of Acts 17:11, 27 and Heb 11:6, it seems that the Lord opens the hearts of those who respond to His drawing by seeking Him.

[5] In light of the fact that in many places in this book MacArthur says that in order to be born again we need to count the cost (pp. 12, 45, 145, 149, 150) and pay the price (pp. 143-50, esp. p. 148, "a joyous price to pay"), it is probably correct to say that he believes *both* that Jesus paid for our salvation and that we pay for our salvation too.

[6] See the discussion of chapter 13, "The Treasure of the Kingdom." There MacArthur lays out the price that a person must pay to buy the kingdom for himself.

in time of temptation fall away" (Luke 8:13). Since everlasting life cannot be lost (e.g., John 6:35), such people are and remain born again.

The Lord said that the second soil believed. Yet MacArthur says "it responds positively but not with saving faith" (p. 133). Isn't that a direct contradiction of the Biblical text?

MacArthur ends this section by stressing that the plant in the second soil *dies*. He writes, "If a profession of faith[7]...does not involve a willingness to deny self, to sacrifice, and to suffer for Christ's sake, then it is without proper root. It is only a matter of time before the flourishing growth withers and dies" (p. 133). What does he mean when he says that *flourishing growth dies*?

The parable does not specify that the plant died. When the Lord told the parable He said that the second soil "withered away" (Matt 13:6; Mark 4:6; Luke 8:6). It is quite possible that *withered away* implies that the plant both withered away *and died*. But if so, bigger questions remain.

What kind of life did this plant have and what kind of death did it suffer? Only something which is alive can die. MacArthur nowhere in this chapter or book answers either of those questions.

MacArthur does not believe that everlasting life can die (i.e., be lost). Yet he sure sounds like he believes that here. How can *an unregenerate person* experience "flourishing growth"? According to Calvinism the unregenerate cannot respond to God in any way and certainly cannot produce spiritual growth, let alone *flourishing* growth.

Of course, if the Lord intended us to understand that the plant in the second soil died, he would have been alluding to physical death[8], not to loss of everlasting life, which is impossible. If a believer falls

---

[7] MacArthur speaks of "a profession of faith." Yet the Lord says the ones on the rock "believe for a while." He says they had faith. The Lord does not indicate that they professed their faith to anyone. MacArthur changes the language for no apparent reason.

[8] Another option is that if death of the plant is in view it might refer to loss of fellowship. In the Parable of the Prodigal Son the Lord said, "But the father said to his servants, 'Bring out the best robe and put it on him, and put a ring on his hand and sandals on his feet. And bring the fatted calf here and kill it, and let us eat and be merry; for this my son was dead and is alive again; he was lost and is found.' And they began to be merry" (Luke 15:22-24).

away, there is such a thing as the sin unto death (1 John 5:16-17). While everlasting life cannot be lost, physical life can be lost.

This is a common concern in Old Testament wisdom literature, like Proverbs, and it's what Jesus is concerned about here. Believers can grow in the faith, but, if they rebel against God their lives may be cut short by an untimely (i.e., premature) death (1 Cor 11:30; Jas 5:19-20).

MacArthur posits that the plants in the second soil died; yet he gives no explanation as to what type of life and death are in view.

The Worldly Heart

Each soil is better than the one before. But you would never know that from MacArthur's explanation. As we will see in a moment, he says that the third soil is just another type of unbeliever.

Note these words: "The gospel germinated but was choked out before it could come to fruition" (p. 134)." What does MacArthur mean by *the gospel germinated*?[9] He does not mean that *the saving message* germinated (compare Luke 8:12, "lest they should believe and be saved"), since he says, "The person with the weedy heart was never saved in the first place" (p. 134).

MacArthur says the problem is the gospel which germinated "was choked out before it could come to fruition" (p. 134). In other words, the gospel initially took root, but it did not produce sufficient fruit in the life of the person over time in order for the person to be saved. MacArthur is arguing here for a linear view of conversion. That is the view that one is not born again at a point in time, but over a period of time.

MacArthur cites nothing from the passage to prove that this third soil represents unregenerate people. Instead he quotes Matt 6:24, "You cannot serve God and mammon," and 1 John 2:15, "If anyone loves the world, the love of the Father is not in him." However,

---

[9] Elsewhere in this book MacArthur uses the term *gospel* to refer to the saving message: "God hates sin and will punish unrepentant sinners with eternal torment. No gospel presentation is complete if it avoids or conceals those facts. Any message that fails to define and confront the severity of personal sin is a deficient gospel" (p. 74). MacArthur indicates that "obedience, submission, [and] Jesus' right to rule" are all part of the gospel message (p. 80). He later explains, "The gospel is not a sterile set of facts; it is the dynamic through which God redeems sinners from the bondage of sin (Rom. 1:16). It calls not simply for the acquiescence of the mind, but for full surrender of the heart, soul, mind, and strength" (cf. Mark 12:30) (p. 81).

neither of those verses says that a person who serves money or who loves the world is unregenerate. They just say that we cannot simultaneously love and serve God and love and serve money/the world. As Bob Dylan famously wrote, "You're gonna have to serve somebody."

Elsewhere in *TGAJ* MacArthur says that born again people sometimes do not serve and do not love the Lord. He says that believers can fall away from the Lord for a time:[10] "Because we are sinful creatures," MacArthur says, "we can never respond as obediently as we would like. In fact, we often experience pathetic failures and extended periods of dullness and sin" (p. 16). He also said, "Christians can be carnal. That is, they can behave in carnal ways. But 'carnal Christian' is not a plane of spiritual existence where one can remain indefinitely" (p. 279).

On the one hand, MacArthur says that believing the gospel does not result in eternal life, but that continued response to the Word of God is necessary for regeneration to occur. On the other hand, he says that believers can fall away and can experience pathetic failure and extended periods of sin. Those two views do not mesh. The second view contradicts the first. The net impact is to make assurance of one's eternal destiny impossible for the one who believes what MacArthur is saying. MacArthur's gospel is a gospel of doubt.[11]

The Enemies

Before discussing the fourth soil, the author briefly reviews the enemies that prevent bringing forth mature fruit. He identifies them as "the weeds, the sun, and the birds of this parable" (p. 134). Then he explains how they represent "'the worry of this world and the deceitfulness of riches' (Matt. 13:22)," "'affliction and persecution' (cf. vv. 6, 21)," and "'the evil one' (cf. vv. 4, 19)," that is, Satan (p. 134).

---

[10] MacArthur does say, however, that "Those whose faith is genuine will never *totally or finally fall away from Christ*" (p. 109, emphasis added).

[11] A Pastor friend, Paul Carpenter (Jansen [NE] Bible Church), who for years held to the Reformed doctrine of the perseverance of the saints, proofed this manuscript before publication. He commented at this point: "We must not forget that this is the genius of Reformed soteriology, to keep people in doubt and in fear, yet motivated by some vague sense of hope that if we just keep scratching and clawing and hanging on for dear life, perhaps somehow in the end we will wind up in eternity with God."

He fails to point out that Satan is the one who keeps people from being born again by snatching away the seed (Luke 8:12; cf. 2 Cor 4:4) and that the other two enemies are enemies of born again people. Worries of this world and the deceitfulness of riches are discipleship issues. So are affliction and persecution. MacArthur lumps all these things together as conditions of regeneration. He has supplanted what the Lord Jesus said about the various responses to God's Word and he has not offered any Biblical support for his suggestion that germination of the seed is not indicative of regeneration.

The Receptive Heart

MacArthur seems to think that we will find three different types of unbelievers in our ministries.

Some reject the gospel right away and do not have faith.

Some accept the gospel initially, believe in Christ, and have joy for a time. But because they later fall away, MacArthur considers them to be false professors.

Still others accept the gospel, have joy, accept the teaching of God's Word, believe in Christ, and don't fall away. They remain in our churches right up until they die. But MacArthur would have reason to suspect that they are not true believers because they are concerned about finances and they show a love for things like hunting, fishing, golf, and other "pleasures of life" (Luke 8:14).

But take heart. According to MacArthur's interpretation there are some in our churches who are the real deal. Though it is impossible to know for sure who the real believers are, because we all fall short of God's glory (Rom 3:23), and according to MacArthur even the truly born again sometimes fall away for a time, we should be glad to learn that some will make it.

If MacArthur is preaching at the funeral of someone who gave every indication that he loved the Lord and persevered in faith and good works, then he could indicate that the person was likely a true believer. Of course, even then he could not be sure this person is with the Lord. But he could with a great degree of confidence say that the person who died may well be with the Lord. But he could not say that with total confidence, because in MacArthur's view only God knows for sure who is His.

Isn't that a bleak perspective?

One of the lessons of this parable MacArthur wishes his read-ers to accept is that it is okay if they doubt their eternal destiny, especially if they find they are concerned about finances and espe-cially if they find themselves loving things of this world in some ways. The issue of assurance will be explicitly addressed later in this book. There MacArthur will state that doubts about one's salvation can be a good thing.

Suffice it to say, MacArthur's view of this parable is wrong. Germination means new life has begun. Thus only the first soil represents an unbeliever, because only the first soil never germi-nated. Instead of *three types of unbelievers* as MacArthur suggests, the Lord is actually telling us about *three types of believers*, some who start well but fall away, some who persevere but are not fully effective due to "cares, riches, and pleasures of life" (Luke 8:14), and some who produce mature fruit. We find examples of all three types of believers in the New Testament[12] and in our churches.[13]

The Fruit

MacArthur suggests that "Fruit, not foliage, is the mark of true salvation" (p. 135). This statement ties in with MacArthur's com-ment that the Word of God can germinate in you and you can expe-rience growth, but if the growth does not result in mature fruit, then you prove your germination was something less than the new birth.

How can that be? How can the gospel germinate in someone's life and yet the person not be born again? MacArthur is about to tell us.

In this last section we get an explanation of what germination means if it does not mean the new birth. See if you find this expla-nation convincing.

---

[12] Examples of believers who fit the pattern of the second soil, that is, who believe for a time and then later fall away, are found in Luke 19:20-26; 1 Tim 1:18-20; and 2 Tim 2:14-18. Believers who persevere (or who are persevering), but whose effectiveness is lessened by cares, riches, and the pleasures of life, are found in Luke 19:18-19; 2 Tim 4:9-10; and Rev 2:1-7, 12-17, 18-29; 3:1-6, 14-21. Good soil believers appear in Luke 19:17-18; 2 Tim 4:6-8; and Rev 3:7-13.

[13] A practical reason for this teaching was to aid churches in moving believers from soil 2 to 3 to 4. Churches need to teach believers to "take heed how you hear" (Luke 8:18, the application by the Lord of the Parable of the Four Soils in Luke 8:4-15).

After citing the argument from Zane Hodges that germination proves regeneration, MacArthur says, "That misses the point completely" (p. 136). He continues:

> The sprouting of the seed in the shallow soil and the weedy soil simply means *that the Word had been received and begun to operate*, not that eternal life had been conferred (p. 136, emphasis added).

And what is the seed again? MacArthur earlier said that the seed "is the message about the King and His kingdom" (p. 131); it is "the gospel" (p. 131). So what does the message of the gospel produce once it has "been received and begun to operate"? According to the parable in Luke, once the word is received, the person is saved: "Those by the wayside are the ones who hear; then the devil comes and takes away the word out of their hearts, lest they should believe and be saved" (Luke 8:12). The Lord there says that anyone who believes is saved. And He goes on to say that the second soil believed (Luke 8:13). MacArthur does not explain that.

Does MacArthur really believe that the gospel can be received and spiritual growth can commence and yet regeneration has not occurred? Is that the gospel according to Jesus?

And how does he prove this point? Instead of citing Scripture, he quotes Warren Wiersbe. While I appreciate Wiersbe's writings, this is not one of his better comments. Wiersbe actually says, "The proof of salvation is *fruit*, for as Christ said, 'Ye shall know them by their fruits (Matt. 7:16)'" (p. 136, emphasis his). Yet in Matt 7:16 the Lord was saying that you will know *false prophets by their fruits*. Verse 15 sets the context: "Beware of *false prophets*, who come to you in sheep's clothing, but inwardly they are ravenous wolves. You will know them by their fruits" (emphasis added).

The fruits *of false prophets* are their false teachings. They look good externally (sheep's clothing), but their words betray them. Matthew 7:16 says nothing about being able to spot a born again person by his deeds.

MacArthur then builds off Wiersbe's false statement saying, "Indeed, fruit is the ultimate test of true salvation" (p. 136). However, that is not true. The ultimate test of true salvation is *the root* (what they believe), not *the fruit* (what they do).

In the Evangelism Explosion (EE) program the first two questions concern the root, not the fruit:

> Question 1: "Have you come to the point in your religious experience where you are sure you have everlasting life?"

> Question 2: "If God were to ask you, 'Why should I let you into My heaven,' what would you say?"

While I don't agree with everything in EE, I certainly like that opening. Consider this answer to Question #2:

> "Well, I see a lot of fruit in my life. I am a loving husband and father. I give more than a tithe. I am in church every time the doors open. I love the Lord. And I have a daily quiet time in which I read the Bible and have a time of prayer."

If that is why a person thinks God should let him into heaven, then he doesn't believe that everlasting life is a free gift which is received by faith, not works (John 4:10; Eph 2:8-9). Those questions help reveal what a person believes is the condition of everlasting life.

The test of whether we are born again is *what we believe*, not *what we do*. It is believers, not doers, who are born again. Everlasting life is for "whoever believes in Him," not for "whoever behaves in Him."

MacArthur misses the point completely. His tradition has influenced him to read into the Biblical text things which are not there.

Conclusion

According to MacArthur's interpretation of the Parable of the Four Soils, the first three soils represent three different types of unbelievers, and only the fourth soil represents a regenerate person. The result of his interpretation is to make assurance of salvation impossible.[14] He leads people to look to their works in order to make a best guess at whether or not they are truly saved.

---

[14] Paul Carpenter commented at this point as he read the manuscript, "Worse, MacArthur's interpretation makes salvation impossible, for if I don't know for certain that I have eternal life based on the promise alone, then surely to work *for the knowledge of my salvation* is no different from working *for my salvation*. How could it be otherwise?"

But a careful examination of the text reveals that only the first soil represents those who are unregenerate. The other three soils all represent different types of regenerate people. We know this because we are told the seed was planted and germinated, indicating they received eternal life. Some of the people who believe later stop believing. Others who believe persevere in faith but produce no mature fruit. Only the fourth soil believes, perseveres, and produces mature fruit.

Instead of putting our regenerate status into doubt, the parable should cause us to rejoice that we are secure in Christ. And it should motivate us to allow God's Word to do an ongoing work in us for the rest of our lives (Luke 8:18; Rom 12:2; 2 Cor 3:18). It seems there will always be Christians who fail to maximize their lives in the cause of Christ. This parable challenges us to be the good soil.

Don't you want to maximize your life for Christ? If you do, then "take heed how you hear" (Luke 8:18). Ask God to give you "a noble and good heart" (Luke 8:15). Let God's Word renew your mind and thereby transform your words and deeds (Rom 12:2; 2 Cor 3:18). Take care to cultivate the soil of your heart so that you maximize your life for Him who died for you and—if you have believed in Him—has given you the free gift of everlasting life.

The Wheat and the Tares
(Matthew 13:24-30, 36-43)

Introduction

How can you tell an unbeliever from a believer? What should be done about unbelievers in churches? And how is flagrant sin related to assurance of salvation? In Chapter 12, MacArthur provides his answers to these questions through his interpretation of the Parable of the Wheat and the Tares.[1]

The Evils of Easy Believism

MacArthur says, "I am chagrined at the way Christians tolerate flagrant sin[2] in their midst" (p. 137). As mentioned several times

---

[1] All three of these questions concern assurance. In every chapter of *TGAJ* MacArthur raises doubts about the salvation of his readers. He thinks it is vital that professing believers look at their works to see if it is likely that they are really born again. He views doubts about one's salvation as a good thing. Doubts in his view spur obedience, which he believes is one of the conditions of spending eternity with the Lord.

[2] MacArthur lists three specific sins on the same page in which he discusses "flagrant sin": divorce, immorality, and homosexuality. He does not give any further description here. However, in footnote 4 on page 20 he indicates that the sins listed in 1 Cor 6:9-10 and Gal 5:19-21 are "the grossest kinds of sins." The sins listed in those two passages include fornication, idolatry, homosexuality, theft, covetousness, drunkenness, reviling, extortion, adultery, uncleanness, lewdness, sorcery, hatred,

before, MacArthur thinks one of the main culprits behind this widespread nominalism is *easy-believism*: "The notion that faith is nothing more than believing a few biblical [sic] facts caters to human depravity" (p. 137).[3] Once again we find him saying that saving faith, understood as simply believing *a few Biblical facts*, has caused tremendous moral decay in the church: "the popularized gospel of our day[4] has made all of this [flagrant sin, including divorce, adultery, homosexuality] possible—even inevitable" (p. 137).

If saving faith is not believing *a few* Biblical facts, then what is it?

MacArthur is not suggesting that saving faith is believing *a lot* of Biblical facts. In fact, MacArthur believes that saving faith is not really believing at all.[5] Throughout *TGAJ* he says that saving faith is repentance, submission, confession of sins, confession of Christ, commitment, obedience, and perseverance. If there are some facts that must be believed, MacArthur doesn't say what they are.

Never once in *TGAJ* does MacArthur indicate a single truth of Scripture that must be believed to be born again. Never.

According to MacArthur, faith is doing. Faith is repenting, submitting, obeying, and persevering until death in service for Christ. In other words, faith means obeying God's commands. If you commit a flagrant sin, you don't really have faith. Here is the logic:

---

contentions, jealousy, outbursts of wrath, selfish ambitions, heresies, envy, and murder. Most of those are sins which Catholics call *mortal sins*. In Catholicism to commit a mortal sin causes one to lose his salvation unless and until he confesses the sin to the priest and then does the required acts of penance. In MacArthur's view to commit such sins strongly suggests you are not yet born again and that you need to repent, submit, and obey in order to gain everlasting life.

[3] He does not use the expression *easy-believism* directly in this chapter. However, that is clearly what he means. He uses that expression explicitly on pages 20, 37, 52, 91, 187, 202, 205, 219, 270, 277, 279, and 281.

[4] In light of its tremendous popularity, Lordship Salvation is, in reality, "the popularized gospel of our day."

[5] Admittedly, MacArthur never directly says this. But since he never mentions anything that one must believe, and since he repeatedly defines faith as including repentance, submission, commitment, obedience, and perseverance, it is fair to conclude that MacArthur believes that saving faith is not really believing at all.

Major premise: Christians do not commit flagrant sins.[6]
Minor premise: Mr. Smith committed a flagrant sin.
Conclusion: Mr. Smith is not a Christian.

MacArthur's approach is simple. If a person who professes faith in Christ commits some sort of lesser, non-flagrant sins, then he *may* be a believer: "Christians can and do behave in carnal ways" (p. 138). However, if a person who professes to be a Christian commits major, flagrant sins, then he proves he is a false professor (cf. pp. 20, "grossest kinds of sin," 137). Of course, if a person avoids major sins but continues behaving in carnal ways for more than a short amount of time, he also proves he is not born again. Genuine believers will not persist in carnal behavior according to MacArthur (pp. 47-48, 60, 68, 73-74, 106, 109, 115, 122, 136).

In this way the true church has little need of church discipline since true Christians are obedient, godly, holy, and blameless. True sons of God obey God's commands. They do not commit flagrant sins. While local churches, even MacArthur's Grace Community Church, may have members who behave in carnal ways, they do not do so for very long. Anyone who does proves he is not actually a Christian and thus he ceases to be a member of the church.

MacArthur wants to blame carnality on those who teach that simple belief in Jesus is all that is required to be born again. He doesn't consider Paul's teaching that carnality is actually produced by preaching and focusing upon the law:

> But sin, taking opportunity by the commandment, produced in me all manner of evil desire. For apart from the law sin was dead. I was alive once without the law, but when

---

[6] As mentioned in the previous chapter, MacArthur does believe that born again people do sometimes fail to some degree: "Because we are sinful creatures we can never respond as obediently as we would like. In fact, we often experience pathetic failures and extended periods of dullness and sin" (p. 16). However, this chapter suggests that what he meant by "pathetic failures" excludes flagrant sins like "divorce and immorality" (p. 137). In the Introduction he said, "Why should we assume that people who live in an unbroken pattern of adultery, fornication, homosexuality, deceit, and every conceivable kind of flagrant excess are truly born again?" (p. 20). Presumably there he means that the pattern of flagrant sins is broken when one is born again. It is possible he thinks that born again people may continue to commit such sins after their new birth as long as the pattern is decreasing. However, he does not say that. Indeed he seems to view that sort of teaching as being a way to tolerate flagrant sin in our churches (cf. p. 137).

the commandment came, sin revived and I died. And the commandment, which was to bring life, I found to bring death. For sin, taking occasion by the commandment, deceived me, and by it killed me (Rom 7:8-10).

Preaching obedience to God's commands as a condition for everlasting life (as MacArthur does)[7] has never succeeded in producing holiness. Not only does preaching the law not bring life, it actually brings death (2 Cor 3:6-9).

MacArthur asks: "Who knows how many unregenerate persons have been lulled into a false sense of spiritual security by the suggestion that they are merely carnal?" (p. 138).[8] I have the opposite question. How many unregenerate persons have been lulled into a false sense of spiritual security by law preaching? The unregenerate man loves to think he can be saved by his works and MacArthur's preaching only reinforces that false belief.

The Players

We come to MacArthur's interpretation of the parable. The one who sows the good seed is the Lord Jesus, the Son of Man. The bad seed was sown by the devil (though MacArthur says nothing about the devil). The two resulting crops are the sons of the kingdom and the sons of the evil one. Of the former MacArthur says, "The children of His kingdom are believing people, those submissive to the King" (p. 139). Notice that he defines saving faith here as being "submissive to the King."

Why add this note about submission when the text says nothing about submission? It is because belief in Christ is not the issue,

---

[7] On the one hand, MacArthur says that no one can be saved by keeping the Law of Moses (cf. pp. 91-98). However, on the other hand, he also says that obedience to God's commands (the commands of the New Testament), which he calls "obedient faith," is an essential part of saving faith (pp. 61, 113). And it isn't just a few years of obedience that are required: "If one does not obey Christ *as a pattern of life*, then professing to know Him is an empty verbal exercise" (p. 217, emphasis added). "True faith is manifest only in obedience" (p. 191).

[8] Evidently he is speaking of Grace preachers who say that if you believe in Jesus for everlasting life then you are eternally secure no matter what you do or fail to do (John 3:16; 5:24; 6:35; 11:25-26). Those preachers do say that immature believers are babes in Christ and carnal (1 Cor 3:1-4). But since MacArthur believes that submission and ongoing obedience are required to gain everlasting life, he must find any assurance based simply on faith in Christ "a false sense of spiritual security." The only true sense of spiritual security in his mind is a pattern of holiness that perseveres to death.

according to MacArthur. He wants his readers to understand that children of Christ's kingdom are those who are submissive to Him, that is, those who obey Him as a pattern of life until death.

Of the sons of the evil one he says,

> These are unbelievers. The phrase, "Sons of the evil one" is similar to the terminology Jesus used in John 8:44, when He castigated the religious leaders: "You are of your father, the devil" (p. 139).

Of course, if the sons of the kingdom are those who persevere in obedience to Christ's commands, then sons of the evil one are those who fail to persevere in obedience.

The Plot

MacArthur seems to think this parable has something to do with freedom of religion and not using force to compel others to believe in Jesus: "God does not sanction any effort that would rid the world of unbelievers by force" (p. 140). Church-Age believers should not kill unbelievers: "We are not God's executioners" (p. 141).

It is true that we are not to kill unbelievers and force people to profess faith in Christ on penalty of death. Sadly that has been tried in Church history (and with disastrous results, too). However, the following statement is inaccurate and highly confusing: "In the final judgment God will separate the wheat from the weeds" (p. 140).

Though he does not specify here, MacArthur indicates elsewhere in *TGAJ* that by "the final judgment" he means the Great White Throne Judgment of Rev 20:11-15 (cf. pp. 60, 142, 211, 228).[9] That occurs after the Millennium (Rev 20:1-10). Thus MacArthur is saying that at the Great White Throne Judgment the separation of believers and unbelievers will occur.

That cannot be correct for several reasons.

---

[9] It should be noted that though he mentions the expression "final judgment" six times (pp. 60, 140, 142 [2x], 211, 228), and though he has an entire chapter on "the certainty of [final] judgment" (pp. 210-18), he never once uses the expression *the Great White Throne Judgment*. Nor does he ever cite Rev 20:11-15. However, it is clear by what he says that he is speaking of that judgment (see esp. pp. 211, 214, 228). For more details see MacArthur's commentary on Revelation 12-22 in the MacArthur New Testament Commentary series. Chapter 17 of that commentary is entitled, "Man's Last Day in God's Court (Revelation 20:11-15)."

First, Christians will not be judged at the Great White Throne Judgment. The Lord promised that believers "shall not come into judgment" concerning everlasting life (John 5:24). He indicated that believers will be judged *before the Millennium* to determine their eternal rewards, including whether they will rule with Him (compare Luke 19:16-26, the judgment of the servants, with Luke 19:27, the judgment of the enemies). We know from the Apostle Paul that this is called *the Judgment Seat of Christ* (Rom 14:10-12; 2 Cor 5:9-10; see also 1 Cor 9:24-27; 1 John 2:28).

Second, living Church-Age believers will be separated from unbelievers at the Rapture, not 1007 years later at the Great White Throne Judgment. If a believer is alive at the time of the Rapture, whether morally watchful or morally asleep, he will be caught up to meet the Lord in the air (1 Thess 4:16-17; 5:10). How could such a person not know that he was born again until after the Millennium and the Great White Throne Judgment? He was miraculously caught up in the Rapture and he is with the Lord and His saints in the air and then in the Millennial kingdom. And he has a glorified, pain-free body.

Third, if a Christian dies before the Rapture, he goes to be with the Lord and is separated from unbelievers right then. Paul said that "to be absent from the body [is] to be present with the Lord" (2 Cor 5:8). The Apostle, while in prison, said that he had "a desire to depart and be with Christ" (Phil 1:23). Once a Christian dies, he goes to the third heaven into the presence of God, which Paul says "is far better" (Phil 1:23) than living here on earth. Believers are conscious and enjoying their experience in heaven after they die and until the Rapture. How could such people not know that they are truly born again until after the Millennium and the Great White Throne Judgment? They are with the Lord in heaven. They are not in Hades, the place of torment.

Fourth, this parable might well refer to the end of the Tribulation when angels will separate the surviving sheep (believing Gentiles) from the surviving goats (unbelieving Gentiles).[10] The Lord spoke

---

[10] It certainly doesn't match up closely with Rev 20:9-10 and the crushing of a Satanically-inspired rebellion at the end of the Millennium. Nothing is specifically said there concerning the role of angels or of separating believers and unbelievers. It might refer to the Rapture itself, but that doesn't fit well with some of the details of Matt 13:40-43.

of the judgment of the sheep and the goats in Matt 25:31-46. The Lord does mention the angels in relation to that judgment:

> "When the Son of Man comes in His glory, and all the holy angels with Him, then He will sit on the throne of His glory. All the nations *will be gathered before Him*, and He will separate them one from another…" (Matt 25:31-32, emphasis added).

It sounds there like the angels gather the sheep and the goats, which fits with Matt 13:41. In addition, both passages refer to being cast into "the furnace of fire" and "everlasting fire" (Matt 13:42; 25:41). No Christians will be judged at the judgment of the sheep and the goats.[11] That judgment is only for Gentiles who survive the Tribulation.

To suggest that the separation of Christians and unbelievers will occur at the Great White Throne Judgment makes no sense. They will have been separated long before that.

The Plan

In this section MacArthur brings out something not stated in the parable, "How will the reapers know the wheat from the tares?" (p. 142). The parable does not even give a hint as to the answer to that question.

To find an answer one must go to other texts that shed light on it. Yet the only text MacArthur cites is Matt 7:18, which he thinks refers to how we today are able to distinguish between believers and unbelievers:

> "Beware of false prophets, who come to you in sheep's clothing, but inwardly they are ravenous wolves. You will know them [i.e., false prophets] by their fruits. Do men gather grapes from thorn-bushes or figs from thistles? Even so, every good tree bears good fruit, but a bad tree bears

---

[11] Though many Christians do not realize it, the Church will end with the Rapture. Thus believers during the Tribulation (or Millennium) will not be Christians. They will be Gentile believers and Jewish believers, just like believers before the birth of the Church at Pentecost. Christians are those who came to faith in Christ between Pentecost and the Rapture. No more people will ever be added to the Church after that.

bad fruit. A good tree cannot bear bad fruit, nor can a bad tree bear good fruit" (Matt 7:15-18).

The Lord is not teaching there how to recognize believers and unbelievers by their behavior. He is talking about how to identify "false prophets." He is saying that we can distinguish true from false prophets by their teachings. False prophets do not produce good fruit, i.e., they do not accurately proclaim God's Word, but preach a false message instead. Still less does Matt 7:18 explain how angels will separate believers from unbelievers in the future.

MacArthur says that the angels will separate the wheat and the tares in this way: "Clearly, character and behavior are what separate the wheat from the tares" (p. 142). That does fit his view that the condition of everlasting life is submitting to Christ and persevering in obedience until death. Yet that seems to be the opposite of what the Lord is teaching in Matt 7:15-20. He specifically warned that false prophets "come to you in sheep's clothing, but inwardly they are ravenous wolves" (Matt 7:15). In other words, false prophets look like sheep on the outside, when looking at their behavior. But inwardly, they are wolves. What is inside is revealed in their words (compare Matt 12:33-37).

If the angels separated the regenerate from the unregenerate based on externally observable things, they would not be able to separate the wheat and the tares because unbelievers often live morally upright lives. Gandhi was certainly an outstanding man. Many Catholic priests and nuns have done many good works. Buddhist monks are often quite moral. Every religion produces people of high character and good behavior. There are even agnostics and atheists who qualify in those regards. And from the other side, even MacArthur acknowledges that believers do not always live exemplary lives.

Notice that neither the text of Matt 13:24-30 (the telling of the parable) nor of Matt 13:36-43 (the interpreting of the parable) mentions either character or behavior. MacArthur brings these things in from somewhere, but we are not given a single text anywhere in the Bible that speaks of character and behavior as separating believers from unbelievers.

To answer MacArthur's question, there are many ways that angels could separate believers from unbelievers, apart from external behavior. People could be separated on the basis of the indwelling

Holy Spirit, belief in Jesus Christ for everlasting life, justification and regeneration, being forgiven, being found in the Book of Life, etc. But the idea that angels will separate people on the basis of externals is not something that this parable or any passage in Scripture teaches.[12]

Conclusion

MacArthur believes the Parable of the Wheat and the Tares teaches us several lessons. First, the way to distinguish the regenerate from the unregenerate is by observation of the works each does. Second, Christians will be judged at the Great White Throne to determine their eternal destiny. Third, the condition for having everlasting life is lifelong submission to Christ, not simply believing in Him.

But none of those things are taught in this parable or in the Bible. MacArthur imposes his own views on the Biblical text.

Instead of following MacArthur, or any other teacher, we should all be Bereans concerning all that we hear and read. We are to search the *Scriptures* to see if what we read and hear is true or not (Acts 17:11).

---

[12] While it is true that believers will be judged according to their works, that judgment will take place at what Paul calls "the judgment seat of Christ" (2 Cor 5:9-10), not at the Great White Throne Judgment (Rev 20:11-15). In addition, the purpose of that judgment is not to determine destiny (or to separate believers from unbelievers), but to determine eternal rewards.

CHAPTER 13

The Treasure of the Kingdom: The Parables of the Hidden Treasure & of the Pearl of Great Price (Matthew 13:44-46)

Introduction

Two of the shortest parables in the Bible are found in Matt 13:44-46.[1] The first is just one verse and twenty-five words in Greek. The second is two verses in length, but shorter. It only contains twenty-two words in Greek. Though short, both are very powerful.

What is the pearl of great price? What is the hidden treasure? Who is it that forsakes all to get them? According to MacArthur, the Parable of the Hidden Treasure and the Parable of the Pearl of Great Price show that the sinner must buy the kingdom for himself, that belief in Christ for everlasting life is not enough.

Counting the Cost?

MacArthur thinks both parables are making the same point, namely, that

---

[1] Other very short parables are also found in Matthew 13. The parable in verses 31-32 is just 33 words; the one in verse 33 is just 17 words; and the one in verse 52 is just 9 words.

a sinner who understands the priceless riches of the kingdom will gladly yield everything else he cherishes in order to obtain it (p. 144).

He goes on to say,

The corresponding truth is also clear by implication: those who cling to their earthly treasures forfeit the far greater wealth of the kingdom (p. 144).

In other words, MacArthur says that sinners buy their own salvation from eternal condemnation.

MacArthur realizes that many Evangelicals do not take the parables that way. For example, many have read the Scofield Reference Bible and its view that the Lord Jesus is the one who buys the treasure and the pearl, not the sinner, and that He does that by dying on the cross for our sins.

In his response to what Scofield said, MacArthur cleverly avoided interacting with some of Scofield's strongest arguments. Scofield made these excellent points:

1. The sinner has nothing to sell.
2. Christ is not for sale.
3. Christ is not hidden in a field.
4. The sinner does not hide Christ again in the field after buying Him.

The expression "a man" (*anthrōpos* in Greek) not only occurs in these two parables, but also in the preceding parable, the Parable of the Wheat and the Tares. This unnamed man must be the same person in all three parables. In the first parable *anthrōpos* clearly refers to the Lord Jesus, who sows the good seed. MacArthur agrees with that. But if that's the case, then *anthrōpos* in the next two parables (vv 44, 45) must also refer to Jesus. Why would the first man be Jesus, but the other two refer to sinners? If Jesus sows the seed, does He not also buy the kingdom?

Acquiring the Kingdom

MacArthur says, "The kingdom of heaven…encompasses Christ and all that He offers—eternal life and unending blessing" (p. 147). If so, then how could eternal life be something we buy, as

MacArthur understands these parables, and yet also be "the gift of God" (John 4:10; Eph 2:9)?

If we buy everlasting life as MacArthur says, then what does Rom 4:4-5 mean: "Now to him who works, the wages are not counted as grace but as debt. But to him who does not work but believes on Him who justifies the ungodly, his faith is accounted for righteousness"?

Twice in this section MacArthur indicates that the sinner *buys* everlasting life: "one must embrace the kingdom with a whole heart—with the zeal of one who gladly forsakes everything *to buy* one treasure more precious than anything else he or she could possess" (p. 147, emphasis added) and "This man is *buying* treasure" (p. 148, emphasis added). Likewise he says a sinner *pays* for everlasting life: "Relinquishing all his other possessions was a joyous *price to pay* for such an immense wealth" (p. 148, emphasis added). Another time he says the sinner realizes that the *cost* of everlasting life is worth it: "The glorious freedom from sin and the unending blessings of eternal life far *outweigh any cost*" (p. 148, emphasis added). The final two sections in this chapter are on "the cost of following Christ" and "counting the cost."

Do we *buy* everlasting life? MacArthur thinks we do. No matter how he attempts to explain it, this is salvation by works. If one could buy everlasting life, then he could boast (contra Eph 2:8-9). After all, he bought and paid for it. Others would miss out because they didn't pay the price. He gets everlasting life that never ends because he gave his all. How is that any different from the salvation by works of Roman Catholicism, Eastern Orthodoxy, Mormonism, Jehovah's Witnesses, Islam, Buddhism, Hinduism, contemporary (not Biblical) Judaism, and all the religions of the world?

Surely the Lord Jesus is offended by this interpretation. He bought the kingdom and our salvation with His shed blood, with His very life. The kingdom is hidden in the sense that we do not yet see it here (2 Cor 4:18; 5:7), but one day soon Jesus will return and reveal it.

The idea that we buy our place in the kingdom by taking up our own crosses is offensive. When a believer who is assured of his eternal destiny takes up his cross to follow Christ, he doesn't do it to buy the kingdom, as if he needed to supplement Christ's perfect

sacrifice with his pitiful works![2] Rather, he takes up his cross first
and foremost because he loves the Lord Jesus and wants to please
Him (2 Cor 5:14; 1 John 4:19). In addition he wants to gain the eternal rewards that will allow him to serve Christ more fully in the life
to come (1 Cor 9:24-27; 2 Tim 2:12; 4:6-8). The assured believer also
wants the rewards that God gives in this life to believers who walk
in fellowship with Him (Ps 16:11; Prov 10:27; 11:8, 19; 12:28). He
wants to avoid temporal judgment (1 Cor 11:30; Jas 5:19-20). One
who is assured longs to have Christ's commendation and not His
rebuke at the Judgment Seat of Christ (Luke 19:16-26).

MacArthur thinks the notion of sinners giving up everything
to buy the kingdom glorifies God. But is it not more glorifying
to God if Jesus gave up His life to buy the kingdom? The former
is an anthropocentric (man-centered) works focus. The latter is a
Theocentric (God-centered) grace focus. The sovereignty of God
demands the second member of the Trinity buy the kingdom by
dying on the cross in our place (John 1:29; 3:16; 1 Cor 6:20; 7:23;
Gal 3:13; 1 Pet 1:18-19; 1 John 2:2; Rev 5:9). We do not die on crosses
to purchase our own salvation. We were bought with a price, the
very blood of Christ.

The Cost of Following Christ

One of the hallmarks of legalism is that it always ends up by
preaching a diminished law. Instead of preaching a perfect law
that demands nothing less than Christ's perfect righteousness, the
law is molded and shaped to suit the sinner. At this point the law
becomes subjective and relative rather than objective and absolute.

After teaching that sinners must give up everything to buy the
kingdom, MacArthur starts to backtrack. We evidently buy the
kingdom at a steep discount. He asks, "Must we literally sell everything and take an oath of poverty in order to be saved?" (p. 148). He
answers, "No," but doesn't explain why. A few paragraphs later he
says, "He was calling for implicit obedience—unconditional surrender to His lordship" (p. 149).

---

[2]There are, of course, some believers, like MacArthur, who have strayed from their
earlier belief in justification by faith alone. They remain born again even though they
no longer believe that. They have lost their assurance and they think they need to buy
their way into the kingdom. But as long as a Christian still believes in the faith-alone
promise of everlasting life, he stays free of works-salvation thinking and motivations.

What is *implicit obedience*? How is it different from *explicit* obedience? Is it the difference between willing and doing? MacArthur defines implicit obedience as "unconditional surrender to His [Christ's] lordship" (p. 149). That statement begs the question whether unconditional surrender is an objective standard or a subjective one. If it is subjective, then there is no way to be certain that one has unconditionally surrendered.

What about sins of omission? Must one be willing to go to church every week, willing to give his money as the Lord prospers him, willing to remain married until death parts he and his wife, willing to raise one's children in the fear and admonition of the Lord, willing to use his spiritual gift, willing to pray without ceasing, willing to give thanks in all things, willing to forgive those who have trespassed against him, etc.? Or is willingness not enough? Must he actually obey God in all that He says in order to gain everlasting life?

What about sins of commission? Must a person be willing to stop getting drunk or high, stop sleeping around, stop cheating on his income taxes, stop lying, stop using profane language, stop watching websites and movies that are inappropriate for Christians, etc.? Or, must he actually turn from all sins?

Where does it end? If to be born again we must have "unconditional surrender to His lordship," then if there is even one area of our life that is not surrendered to His Lordship, the person would not yet be born again.

Indeed, that is exactly what one leading teacher who agrees with MacArthur wrote. In his famous book *Evangelism and the Sovereignty of God*, J. I. Packer says,

> In our own presentation of Christ's gospel, therefore, we need to lay a similar stress on the cost of following Christ, and make sinners face it soberly before we urge them to respond to the message of free forgiveness. *In common honesty, we must not conceal the fact that free forgiveness in one sense will cost everything*; or else our evangelizing becomes a sort of confidence trick. And, *where there is no clear knowledge, and hence no realistic recognition of the real claims that Christ makes, there can be no repentance, and therefore, no salvation* (pp. 71-72, emphasis added).

Similarly, James Montgomery Boice, wrote,

> I say…that the minimum amount a person must give is *all* [emphasis his]. I say, "You must give it all. You cannot hold back even a fraction of a percentage of yourself. *Every sin must be abandoned* [emphasis added]. Every false thought must be repudiated. You must be the Lord's entirely" (*Christ's Call to Discipleship*, p. 114).

A famous Christian slogan today reads, "Please be patient, God is not finished with me yet." That is not a direct quote of Scripture. But it does accurately summarize verses like Rom 3:23 and 1 John 1: 8, 10 and 1 John 3:2.

MacArthur has an answer for this too: "Obviously, a new believer does not fully understand all the ramifications of Jesus' lordship at the moment of conversion" (p. 149). Why is this obvious? If his interpretation of these two parables is correct, then a new believer must fully understand all the ramifications of Jesus' Lordship. He must not only understand them, but he must already have *unconditionally surrendered*, to use MacArthur's expression, to all aspects of Jesus' Lordship in order to be born again in the first place.

Did you notice that no Scripture is cited to prove this point? MacArthur's *TGAJ* is built upon many pronouncements by him, but it is not supported by careful exegesis of God's Word.

Counting the Cost

One would think after the pronouncement that "a new believer does not fully understand all the ramifications of Jesus' lordship" (p. 149) that there would be no cost to count. One would simply need to be *willing* to change. Yet according to MacArthur, one must actually turn from his sins and submit to and persevere in obedience to Christ in order to get into Christ's kingdom.

Assurance of everlasting life is impossible under MacArthur's theology. His gospel is a gospel of doubt. No one could know if he had paid enough to buy the kingdom for himself.

One of the two passages MacArthur cited to prove his point that we buy the kingdom is Heb 11:26. Yet that verse speaks of *wages* for work done, something we are told by the Apostle Paul that justification is not (Rom 4:4-5). Here is what Heb 11:24-26 says,

> By faith Moses, when he became of age, refused to be called the son of Pharaoh's daughter, choosing rather to suffer affliction with the people of God than to enjoy the passing pleasures of sin, esteeming the reproach of Christ greater riches than the treasures in Egypt; for he looked to the reward.

The Greek word translated as *reward* there is *misthapodosia*, which is a combination of *misthos*, wages (BDAG, p. 653), and the verb *apodidomi*, to pay (BDAG, p. 109). BDAG says the meaning of *misthapodosia* is "payment of wages" (p. 653). Paul used the word *misthos* many times and never as a reference to the new birth or kingdom entrance. Here is the word *misthos* in Rom 4:4-5:

> Now to him who works, the wages [*misthos*] are not counted as grace but as debt. But to him who does not work but believes on Him who justifies the ungodly, his faith is accounted for righteousness...

Unfortunately for MacArthur, Heb 11:26 directly contradicts his claim that sinners must purchase their entrance into the kingdom. Moses did not buy the kingdom; Moses earned eternal rewards. His life will be fuller in the kingdom of God than it would have been. But either way he was guaranteed to be in the kingdom because he believed in Christ for everlasting life.

The only other passage MacArthur cites to support his view that we must buy our way into the kingdom is Luke 14:28-31. But he only mentions those verses without quoting them. This passage does not substantiate his claim either:

> "For which of you, intending to build a tower, does not sit down first and count the cost, whether he has enough to finish it—lest, after he has laid the foundation, and is not able to finish, all who see it begin to mock him, saying, 'This man began to build and was not able to finish.' Or what king, going to make war against another king, does not sit down first and consider whether he is able with ten thousand to meet him who comes against him with twenty thousand?"

There is nothing linking paying the price to follow Christ with entrance into the kingdom. Why does MacArthur suggest that following Christ is the condition of everlasting life? Isn't *believing in Him* the only condition? What about John 3:16; 5:24; 6:35; 11:26; Rom 4:4-5; Gal 2:16; Eph 2:8-9; Titus 3:5; and Rev 22:17?

If following Christ is the condition of everlasting life, then why speak of believing in Him at all? Let's just focus on the works we need to do to buy everlasting life. Which works? How many? For how long? What must I stop doing and what must I start doing and keep on doing until death?

Conclusion

This chapter contradicts the idea that everlasting life is a free gift and that it is not of works. Even MacArthur recognizes that he is denying that. And he seems to recognize that he is fundamentally denying the key doctrine of justification by faith alone, apart from works. So he tries to reassure his readers that this outright denial is really a "paradox":

> Eternal life is indeed a free gift (Rom 6:23). Salvation cannot be earned with good deeds or secured with money. It has already been bought by Christ, who paid the ransom with His blood. He has purchased full atonement for all who believe. There is nothing left to pay, no possibility that our own works can be meritorious. *But that does not mean there is no cost in terms of salvation's impact on the sinner's life. Do not throw away this paradox just because it is difficult. Salvation is both free and costly*[3] (pp. 148-49, emphasis added).

Salvation does *have an impact on a sinner's life.*[4] However, what MacArthur really means is that in order to be saved we must buy the kingdom with good works. So MacArthur wants us to believe that

---

[3]If MacArthur meant that salvation is free *for us* and costly *only for the Lord Jesus,* he'd be right. But he means that it is both free for us and costly *for Jesus and for us.* That is nonsense. If it costs us something, then it is obviously not free for us. If it is free for us, then obviously it is not costly for us.

[4] Lewis Sperry Chafer pointed at 33 things which happen at the moment of faith, including forgiveness, freedom from the law, adoption, justification, freedom from sin in our position, heavenly citizenship, having access to God, and being heirs of God (Lewis Sperry Chafer, *Systematic Theology,* Soteriology [Dallas, TX: Dallas Seminary Press, 1948], 3:234-65). None of these changes guarantees a holy life. But they do make such a life possible and they motivate us to such a life.

both these propositions are true: everlasting life is a free gift and is not of works, and that it is an expensive item that is of works. This is a contradiction of MacArthur's own making. As Paul showed so clearly in Rom 4:4-5, we are either justified by works or by faith, not by a purportedly paradoxical mixture of both.

If someone believes what MacArthur says here, then he does not believe the saving message, the message of everlasting life found in John 3:16 and many other texts. Despite his occasional declarations that eternal life is a free gift (e.g., p. 148), MacArthur ultimately believes in salvation by works, plain and simple. Yes, we should count the cost and follow Christ in discipleship. Yes, we should deny ourselves and take up our crosses daily. But we do that to please the Lord and gain His blessings now and forever, not to buy our way into His kingdom.

CHAPTER 14

The First and Last: The Parable of the Day Laborers (Matthew 20:1-16)

Introduction

Will eternal life be the same for all? MacArthur thinks it will, and he believes the Parable of the Day Laborers proves it. Everyone will receive the same reward, no matter how long or how little they have worked. But is this view correct?[1]

The Same Eternal Life

In this chapter, MacArthur belabors a single point, hammering on it over and over again:

All of the redeemed receive the same eternal life (p. 151).

No one is ahead and no one is behind...Everyone crosses the finish line in a dead heat (p. 152).

A dying convert inherits the same glories of eternal existence as an apostle (p. 154).

---

[1] Actually in *TGAJ* Appendix 3, question 14, MacArthur contradicts what he says in this chapter, saying, "Some people's good works are cluttered with wrong motives or unbiblical methods, *so our rewards will differ*" (p. 281, emphasis added). For further analysis see my discussion of Appendix 3 in my third appendix.

The issue here is the equality of eternal life (p. 155).

In the end all enjoy the fullness of eternal life to the maximum (p. 157).

What he is denying is that some believers will have a more abundant experience of everlasting life than others in the kingdom. He is denying that some will rule with Christ and others will not. He even appears to deny that the twelve Apostles will sit on twelve thrones and rule over the twelve tribes of Israel:

The disciples were not quite clear about what their ultimate reward for following Christ would be...Perhaps they thought they would be granted special thrones to rule over the prime real estate. Even after Jesus rose from the dead, they asked Him, "Lord, is it at this time You are restoring the kingdom to Israel?" (Acts 1:6). Is now when we get our crowns and our thrones? (p. 154).

According to MacArthur, the experience of life which the Apostles will have in the kingdom will be no fuller than someone who came to faith just moments before dying: "A dying convert inherits the same glories of eternal existence as an apostle" (p. 154).

This cannot possibly be true.

If the Parable of the Day Laborers is saying that "everyone crosses the finish line in a dead heat" and "in the end all enjoy the fullness of eternal life to the maximum," as MacArthur says, then there are many other texts which are not true. For example, in the Parable of the Minas (Luke 19:11-27) one of Jesus' servants is given rulership over ten cities, one over five cities, and one over zero cities.

"Well *done*, good servant; because you were faithful in a very little, have authority over ten cities" (Luke 19:17)...

"Likewise he said to him, 'You also be over five cities'" (Luke 19:19)...

"And he said to those who stood by, 'Take the mina from him, and give *it* to him who has ten minas'" (Luke 19:24)...

Clearly those three servants did not finish in a dead heat. They will not all enjoy the fullness of eternal life to the maximum. Some will have greater authority than others. Some will have none at all.

How can the Parable of the Minas be harmonized with MacArthur's view? It can't.

Or consider 1 Cor 9:27, where Paul said that he disciplined his body and brought it into subjection lest after having preached to others (i.e., about eternal rewards) he himself might be disapproved (*adokimos*). Was Paul expressing doubt about his eternal destiny? Was he doubting his justification? Or was he concerned with eternal rewards, saying that only if he persevered would he receive the Lord's approval and His "Well done" (Luke 19:17)?

Or what did John mean in 1 John 2:28: "And now, little children, abide in Him, that when He appears, we may have confidence and not be ashamed before Him at His coming"? Is that about destiny or special rewards in the kingdom? Clearly confidence and shame are two very different experiences for one who has everlasting life.

And what did Paul mean in 1 Cor 3:15: "If anyone's work is burned, he will suffer loss; but he himself will be saved, yet so as through fire"? What kind of loss is possible if all believers will have exactly the same experience of everlasting life in eternity?

If all believers will receive exactly the same reward, then what did Paul mean when he said, "Do not be deceived, God is not mocked; for whatever a man sows, that he will also reap" (Gal 6:7)? If one believer sows half as many good works for Christ as another believer, will he not reap half as much?[2] That is what the Lord Jesus Himself specifically said in Luke 19:16-19.

MacArthur does not answer such questions. Rather, he ignores them. MacArthur quotes the Parable of the Day Laborers and then declares his interpretation without consideration of the context or of texts that contradict his interpretation of the parable.

The Rapture

There is a much more reasonable explanation of this parable, one that actually harmonizes with other texts. This parable primarily concerns the Rapture. *The end of the day* in the parable refers to the Rapture. At the time of the Rapture imagine the range of how long people have been in service for Christ. Some will be nearing death

---

[2] I'm comparing here, as the Lord did in Luke 19:16-26, believers who have the same amount of time, talent, and treasure to invest for Christ. I'm not yet considering believers who have less time, talent, or treasure to invest.

after 80 or more years of service. Others will be in their first year of service.

This explains a rather cryptic statement the Lord made: "I must work the works of Him who sent Me while it is day; the night is coming when no one can work" (John 9:4). The day is the Church Age. The night is the Rapture, "when no one can work." The work-day for the Church ends when the Rapture occurs (i.e., when the Church Age ends). That is the final hour in the Parable of the Day Laborers.

The point of this parable is that length of service does not neces-sarily determine amount of reward.[3] The key is what a person does for Christ in the time he has. To whom much time is given, much will be required (Luke 12:48). To whom less time is given, less is required.

Most of those in the NFL Hall of Fame played more than a dozen years. However, Gayle Sayers made the Hall of Fame even though he only played seven years. A major knee injury cut his career in half. But he was one of the best running backs ever in the seven years he did play.

On the other end of the spectrum is Hall of Famer George Blanda, a quarterback and kicker. He played for 27 years in the AFL and NFL.

There are 287 members of the NFL Hall of Fame. They are all highly honored. But even in this group, they did not all get paid the same and they are not equally honored or remembered. But they are all in the Hall.

The wages the Lord is talking about are nothing like that of cur-rent NFL players. Day laborers received a denarius, a silver coin about the size of a dime for one day's work, typically a twelve-hour day. In today's dollars a denarius equals about $40.

All of the laborers in this parable received the same amount. That is clear. We will discuss why in a moment. However, the pay they

---

[3] The Lord said, "The last shall be first" both in this parable (Matt 20:16) and in Matt 19:30. In both places He is discussing eternal rewards. In Matt 20:16 His point is that those who had been Christians the shortest amount of time, the last in terms of when they entered service, would be judged first at the Judgment Seat of Christ. The first, the ones who had been serving Christ the longest when the Rapture occurred, would be judged last. In Matt 19:30 His point is that many Christians who are first in honor and authority in this life will be last in honor and authority in the life to come. And many who are last in honor and authority now will be first in the life to come.

received does not represent everlasting life. Everlasting life is not pay for work done. Instead, their paychecks, their wages for service rendered, represent eternal rewards, fullness of life in the life to come.

This parable does not contradict the Parable of the Minas or the many other texts which teach accountability and reaping what we sow. Scripture cannot contradict Scripture.

The Issue of Equality

MacArthur's view of "the spiritual point" of the parable (p. 153) is flawed for several reasons.

First, as just discussed, the denarius does not represent eternal life (contra MacArthur, p. 153), but eternal rewards (i.e., wages; see vv 2, 4, 5, 7, 8 [*misthos*], 9, 10, 13) for work done.

Second, while it is true that "eternal life is not dispensed according to how faithfully we have performed here on earth" and that eternal life "is a sheer gift of God's grace" (p. 154), that is not what MacArthur says in the rest of *TGAJ* or even the rest of chapter 14. What he means, as he goes on to point out with a death-bed conversion illustration (p. 154), is that a person is only required to follow Christ faithfully from the time of his conversion until death. So if a person is born again seconds before death, only seconds of faithfulness are required. But for the person who comes to faith in Christ in his teens and lives into his nineties, then 80 years of faithful following is required. (Of course, he teaches that a person may experience minor falls *for a short amount of time*, though the whole of his life will be characterized by faithfulness.)

Third, MacArthur is incorrect when he says that the person who comes to faith on his death bed will inherit "the same glories of eternal existence as an apostle" (MacArthur, p. 154). On the contrary, no one but the Apostles will rule over the twelve tribes of Israel (Matt 19:28; Luke 22:30). It is ludicrous to think that anyone after the Apostles in the Church Age would have an eternal experience as glorious as the Apostles. They are called the foundation (Eph 2:20). We are not the foundation. We do not write books of Scripture. Few of us are martyred for Christ. None of us literally walked with Him.

Fourth, MacArthur is incorrect when he says that the Apostles were wrong when "they thought they would be granted special thrones to rule over prime real estate" (p. 154). MacArthur is discussing Matt 19:27 and the disciples's question about what they would receive in return for leaving everything to follow Jesus. MacArthur continues, "Even after Jesus rose from the dead, they asked him, 'Lord, is it at this time You are restoring the kingdom to Israel?' Is now when we get our crowns and our thrones?" (p. 154). As these citations show, MacArthur thinks the Apostles were wrong to expect "to rule over prime real estate" and to receive "crowns and thrones." Indeed, he says concerning this parable, "The issue here is the equality of eternal life" (p. 155). Yet special rewards are precisely what Jesus promised the Apostles (the Eleven, plus Matthias who took Judas's place)[4] in the very next verse after Matt 19:27, which MacArthur fails to quote:

> "Assuredly I say to you, that in the regeneration, when the Son of Man sits on the throne of His glory, you who have followed Me will also sit on twelve thrones, judging the twelve tribes of Israel" (Matt 19:28).

The Nature of Salvation

Since this parable is not about salvation (i.e., regeneration), but about eternal rewards, five of the seven applications MacArthur gives are inappropriate.

First, while it is true that "it is God who sovereignly initiates salvation" (p. 155), this parable is not about salvation.

Second, while "God establishes the terms of salvation" (p. 155), this parable is not about the term(s) of salvation. It is wrong to say, "Christ set the price for eternal life" (p. 155) when eternal life is not in view here. This is about the price of eternal rewards.[5]

Note that on the previous page (p. 154) MacArthur said, "eternal life…is the sheer gift of God's grace." But just one page later MacArthur contradicts himself and says that there is a price to be paid after all ("Christ set the price for eternal life," p. 155), and that the price is faithful service for Christ until death ("God never stops

---

[4] Though Judas was originally one of the Twelve, he forfeited his position. Peter and the rest of the Eleven chose Matthias to take the place of Judas (Acts 1:15-26). Luke says, "And they cast their lots, and the lot fell on Matthias. And he was numbered with the eleven apostles" (Acts 15:26).

[5] See the discussion above on the distinction between everlasting life and eternal rewards in the section entitled, "The Issue of Equality," point 2.

soliciting workers for the kingdom…He continues to call people to work…Everyone worked. That is the way salvation is," p. 155).

Third, while "God continues to call men and women into His kingdom" (p. 155), this parable is not about that. All of those hired in this parable represent people who were born again before they were hired and before they did any work.[6]

Fourth, it is not true that "everyone God redeems is willing to work for him" (p. 155). What evidence is there of that in Scripture? This passage is about willing workers, but it does not say that all are willing. What of the third servant in the Parable of the Minas who kept his mina hidden away in a handkerchief and did not labor for his lord (Luke 19:20-26)? The man is a servant. He is not slain (compare Luke 19:20-26 with Luke 19:27, a reference to the second death). He represents a born again person who is not faithful.

Fifth, while "God is compassionate to those who recognize their need" (p. 156), that is not the point of this parable. Did these people need work that day? Yes. But, they did not need work in order to survive another day. They needed work in order to feed their families properly, not to survive that day. James wrote concerning rich believers, "Indeed the wages of the laborers who mowed your fields, which you kept back by fraud, cry out; and the cries of the reapers have reached the ears of the Lord of Sabaoth" (Jas 5:4). Believers do not need to work to get into the kingdom (see 1 Thess 5:10). We need to work to have fullness of life now and in the life to come (see John 10:10; 2 Tim 4:6-8).

None of these first five statements is a legitimate application of the parable. But MacArthur's final two statements are correct applications.[7]

---

[6] "To hire laborers" (Matt 20:1) is clearly not the same as calling for people to believe in Jesus and receive the free gift of everlasting life (John 3:16; 5:24; 6:35; 11:25-26; Acts 16:31; Eph 2:8-9; Rev 22:17). While hypothetically this might be a parable about God hiring *the unregenerate* to work for Him for pay in this life, that does not fit the fact that this parable is talking about what "the kingdom of heaven is like" (Matt 20:1). Kingdom-related pay is not regeneration (John 6:28-29; Eph 2:8-9) or justification (Rom 4:4-5). This kingdom pay (*misthos*, Matt 20:8) represents eternal rewards for believers (cf. 1 Cor 3:8, 14; 1 Tim 5:18; 2 John 8; Rev 22:12). Besides, where in Scripture do we find God hiring the unregenerate to work for Him for temporal pay?

[7] However, MacArthur wrongly suggests that both of these applications concern eternal salvation (p. 156). God does keep His promise concerning eternal salvation (application 6). God's gift of everlasting life is indeed undeserved (application 7) but

Sixth, "God keeps His promise" (p. 156). That is, if we serve Him faithfully, He will reward us in light of what we would have with a full life to invest, even if our time of service was cut short due to the Rapture.

Seventh, "He [God] also always gives more than we deserve" (p. 156). If we serve Him faithfully and the Rapture limits our time of service, we will receive as much as if we had served faithfully our whole lives. And there will be lots of grace at the Judgment Seat of Christ, especially to those who were merciful to others in this life (Jas 2:13).

A Picture of Grace

MacArthur appeals to the thief on the cross to show that he was a picture of grace. He was only a believer for three hours, yet the Lord said he would be with Him in Paradise.

MacArthur says that the thief on the cross repented (p. 157). Yet there is no indication that he did. It is true he stopped mocking Christ and he began to confess Him. But did the man turn from stealing and from his many other sins? Maybe he was willing. Maybe not. We are not told. That isn't the point.

What's obvious from the text, but not mentioned by MacArthur, is that the thief believed in Jesus before He confessed Him to be the Messiah. The reason he confessed his own guilt and the Lord's lack of guilt is because he had believed in Jesus. Notice carefully what he said: "Lord, remember me when You come into Your kingdom" (Luke 23:42).

Jesus is about to die on the cross. Yet the man believes Jesus will come again and establish the kingdom promised to Israel ("when You come into Your kingdom"). He clearly believes that Jesus is the Messiah, the king of Israel. He also believes that he will be in that kingdom: "remember me when You come into Your kingdom."

He is not asking the Lord to let him into the kingdom, but for the Lord to remember him when He does establish His kingdom. In other words, the man wants some measure of reward. Though his service was short, he is the only person at the cross who is confessing Christ. The Apostles were not. Mary was not. Nicodemus and

---

the issue in the parable, and in its application, is eternal rewards (pay), not eternal security.

Joseph of Arimathea were not. The other followers of Christ were not.

Notice carefully Jesus' answer to him: "Assuredly, I say to you, today you will be with Me in Paradise" (Luke 23:43).[8] That is not what the man asked about. He asked the Lord to remember him *when He came into His kingdom.* The Lord answers that by saying that *that very day* he would be *with Him* in Paradise.

MacArthur concludes this section by saying, "In the end all enjoy the fullness of eternal life to the maximum" (p. 157). On the contrary, only those who faithfully serve Christ for as long as they have before the Rapture will enjoy fullness of eternal life. But not all serve Christ wholeheartedly. Some serve Him halfheartedly (Luke 19:18-19), and some barely serve Him at all (Luke 19:20-26). Although eternal life is freely given by faith in Jesus, apart from works, our enjoyment of that life in terms of fullness and rewards in the kingdom to come all depend upon our faithfulness in the here and now.

Conclusion

What MacArthur's Lordship Salvation promotes is equality in eternity for all Christians. That may sound good to some. But is that fair? Don't those who do more deserve more?

Isn't the idea that all Christians will have the fullness of life in eternity a denial of the principle taught by the Lord and His Apostles that believers will reap in the life to come what they sowed in this life (Luke 19:16-26; John 4:36-38; Gal 6:7-9; 2 Tim 4:6-8)? If all believers will receive the same fullness of eternal reward, then the Lord and His Apostles got it wrong, because they clearly said there would be degrees of rewards in the kingdom (Luke 19:17, 19, 20-26; 1 Cor 9:24-27; Gal 6:7-9; 2 Tim 2:12; 4:6-8; 1 Pet 4:13; 1 John 2:28; 4:17-19). Only God knows how much time we have on earth, whether we will die before the Rapture, or whether the Lord Jesus will come for us while we are still alive. But we should make the most of whatever time we

---

[8] For more discussion of Luke 23:39-43 and the thief on the cross see "A Lesson from a Dying Thief," by Roscoe Barnes III, *Grace in Focus* (Jan-Feb 2003), available online: www.faithalone.org/magazine/y2003/03Al.html.

have to serve the Lord, because we will reap the effects of our actions for eternity. [9]

---

[9] As the Lord said in Matt 19:30, many who are first in the Church Age will be last in the kingdom of God. To be last in the kingdom will be to be in a position that is subordinate to those who will be first in the kingdom. The Apostle Peter also indicated that only some believers will receive *a rich entrance* into the eternal kingdom (2 Pet 1:5-11). Just as in this life believers are not all equal in terms of how effectively we serve Him, so too in the life to come some will have more authority and some less. Some will do more for Him and some will do less. Those Christians who want to glorify Christ fully forever will work hard for Him in the years they have in this life. But we need not worry that if our service is cut short by the Rapture we will be penalized. All that is required of Christians is to be faithful in service for Christ for as much time as the Lord gives us. That is the point of the Parable of the Day Laborers.

CHAPTER 15

The Lost and Found: The Parables of the Lost Sheep, the Lost Coin, and the Lost Son (Luke 15:1-32)

Introduction

There are three famous parables on repentance in Luke 15. MacArthur suggests that these parables teach that repentance is a condition (along with submission, obedience, confession, and perseverance) for receiving everlasting life.

The Hundred Sheep

In the Parable of the Lost Sheep, Jesus asked, "What man of you, having a hundred sheep, if he loses one of them, does not leave the ninety-nine in the wilderness, and go after the one which is lost until he finds it?" (Luke 15:4). Let's consider some questions about that opening verse.

How many sheep did the man have?

Was the sheep that strayed one of his flock?

Did the sheep that strayed become a part of his flock after the shepherd found it and brought it back?

Notice that the shepherd had a hundred sheep, not ninety-nine. The one that strayed was already a member of the shepherd's flock.

The lost sheep did not become a part of the flock after it was found and brought back. It merely was returning to its flock.

The shepherd in the story is the Good Shepherd, the Lord Jesus (cf. John 10:11). The sheep in the story are believers, not unbelievers. The lost sheep does not represent an unregenerate person; it represents a born again person who has strayed and who returns to the flock after the shepherd seeks and finds it and brings it back.

However, MacArthur sees this parable quite differently. He understands the sheep that strayed as representing an unbeliever who repents and is born again. MacArthur believes that repentance is a necessary step in order to become part of the Lord's flock. That faith is not mentioned in any of these parables is evidently not a problem for MacArthur. That the other things he says one must do to be born again (e.g., submission, obedience, confession, buying the kingdom, and perseverance) are not mentioned either is presumably no problem either. MacArthur fails to discuss the things which in his view are missing from these parables.

So the question is, which interpretation best fits the particulars of the parable? Is this about a believer coming back into fellowship with God, or about an unregenerate person becoming born again? Let's see.

Note verse 7, which is the conclusion of the first parable, and which MacArthur quotes, but without explaining: "I say to you that likewise there will be more joy in heaven over one sinner who repents than over ninety-nine just persons who need no repentance."

Did you see what the Lord calls the ninety-nine? He calls them "just [righteous] persons who need no repentance." Who are just persons who need no repentance? The answer is crucial if we are to understand the parable.

The word translated *just* (*dikaios*) also means *righteous*. It can refer to those who are righteous *in their position*, that is, to born again people (see Luke 14:14; Rom 1:17; Gal 3:11; Heb 10:38). However, that is not the way this term is most often used. More often it refers to those who are righteous *in their experience* (see Matt 10:41; 13:17, 43; 23:35, Luke 1:6; 23:47; Heb 11:4; Jas 5:16; 1 Pet 3:12; 1 John 3:12; Rev 22:11), that is, not simply to believers, but to mature believers who are walking in fellowship with God. That is the nuance which best fits the context of this parable.

Consider what that says about the one member of the flock who strayed. Since he was a part of the flock before he strayed, he too represents one who had been a "just person who needed no repentance" prior to his departure. The issue here is *experiential righteousness*. All hundred sheep represent those who were righteous in their behavior. Then one strayed and became unrighteous in his experience. Hence, the joy in heaven is over a believer who repents and comes back to fellowship with God and to righteous living. While there is surely joy in heaven every time a person is born again, that is not what is under discussion here.

Before moving on to the next parable, please note how MacArthur's condition for everlasting life keeps changing. In some places in *TGAJ* the condition is surrender to Christ. In other places it is a willingness to follow Him. Sometimes it is actually following Him. Here and elsewhere repentance is yet another condition that MacArthur cites. Confessing one's sins and confessing Christ are also identified as conditions of eternal life in *TGAJ*. And let's not forget that, according to MacArthur, we also have to buy our own salvation by willingly giving up all that we have.

How can the condition for being eternally saved be repentance alone here when in other places, according to MacArthur, it is one or more of the following conditions: surrendering, following, obeying, confessing, persevering, and counting the cost? Is that not many different *gospels according to Jesus*?[1]

Did the Lord mislead people over and over again in John's Gospel when He said that believing in Him is the only thing required to obtain everlasting life? Was He misleading people here in Luke 15 if He was saying that repentance only is the condition of everlasting life?

To say the least, MacArthur's understanding of Luke 15 and of the condition(s) of the new birth is confusing. To say the most, this is another gospel (see Gal 1:6-9), the gospel of salvation by following a set of rules.

---

[1] An additional problem is that if all these things are required, then why didn't the Lord say so in any single text?

The Ten Coins

MacArthur is correct when he says, "The second parable (Luke 15:8-10) makes the same point with a different metaphor" (p. 160). But what is that point?[2] Is the point really that repentance is a condition of salvation from eternal condemnation?

The ten coins are thought by Bible scholars to have been part of a family heirloom passed down from mother to daughter in the form of a bracelet. That is likely the case. However, we are not told that specifically. Possibly they were just ten denarii as MacArthur suggests. In any case, the woman is grieved over the lost coin and she takes great care to find it and return it to the other nine.

Let's again consider some questions about the details of the parable.

How many coins did the woman have before one was lost?

Did the lost coin become hers only after she found it?

Obviously, the woman had ten coins before one was lost. The lost coin did not become her coin when she found it. It was not a new coin that was being added to her collection. It simply returned to the status it had before.

MacArthur mentions verse ten, but only quotes "joy in the presence of the angels" (p. 160). Here is the full verse: "Likewise, I say to you, there is joy in the presence of the angels of God over one sinner who repents." The word *likewise* looks back to the summary statement in verse 7 where the Lord was talking about a hundred righteous persons, one of which strayed and returned.

Here the Lord speaks of "one sinner who repents." Some people think the word *sinner* must refer to an unbeliever. But that is a mistake. It may come as a surprise to you, but believers who stray can rightly be called sinners too (e.g., Jas 5:20). Believers sometimes fall away from the Lord. When we do, the Holy Spirit woos us back. If we repent, then there is joy in the presence of the angels of God.

In this parable believers are viewed as treasure (silver coins) which is valuable to God. So God is pleased when someone He values returns to fellowship with Him.

---

[2] If all three parables make the same point—and they do, it is vital that one understands the first one correctly. Otherwise, if one missed the point of the first, he will misunderstand the other two as well.

The Two Sons

While two sons are indeed discussed in Luke 15:11-32, the emphasis is on the lost son. The lost son is parallel to the lost sheep and the lost coin. Likewise, the older brother is parallel to the ninety-nine righteous sheep and the nine righteous coins, neither of which needed repentance.

MacArthur sees both sons initially as representing unregenerate people ("The second son...was as lost as his younger brother had been," pp. 162-63). The younger son in his view is born again when he repents, turning away from his sins and returning to his father (pp. 162-64).

Let's consider some interpretive questions again.

When did the younger son become a son of his father?

When did the older son become a son of his father?

Both sons were sons of their father *at birth*. The younger son did not become a son of his father by repenting. He merely returned to fellowship with his father, fellowship he had enjoyed previously.

While the younger son was living in the far country, he ran out of money (v 14a). He experienced great hunger while living through "a severe famine" (v 14b). In order to survive he had to take a menial job feeding pigs (v 15). As the Lord's audience knew, that was a terrible job for a Jewish man.

We don't know how long he expected his inheritance to last. But the money ran out quickly and now he was forced into a bare subsistence job.[3]

The world is like that. It promises feasting, but gives famine instead. It promises riches, but dishes out poverty. It holds the allure of great joy, but it actually delivers prolonged pain and suffering.

When the son returned, his father ran up to him "and fell on his neck and kissed him" (v 20). He replaced his son's miserable garments with the best robe, new sandals, and a ring as well (v 22).

Then he slew the fatted calf and threw a great party saying, "For this my son was dead and is alive again; he was lost and is found" (v 24). The expression "he was lost and is found" ties this parable with the previous two (cf. Luke 15:4, 6, 8, 9).

---

[3] The author of Hebrews speaks of "the passing pleasures of sin" (Heb 11:25). The prodigal son learned that lesson, quickly realizing that fellowship with God is far better than anything this world has to offer (Luke 15:17-19).

How do the words "my son was dead and is alive again" fit MacArthur's understanding? He does not explain the expression.

If being dead refers to being unregenerate as MacArthur evidently thinks, then being alive again means the younger son had everlasting life, lost it, and then got it back again. But MacArthur does not believe that everlasting life can be lost. So in what sense was the son *alive* before he went to the far country and in what sense did he become *alive again* when he repented?

The issue here is *fellowship with God*. The son was dead to his father while in the far country.[4] That is, he was out of fellowship with his father during that time. When he repented he was alive again in the sense that he was now back in fellowship with his father. While everlasting life cannot be lost, fellowship with God can be.

Fellowship with God is good for us.[5] It gives us true riches, true feasting, and lasting joy. The believer in fellowship with God may not appear to be rich and successful in the world's eyes. But heaven knows better. And so does any believer who understands the lesson of the prodigal son.

What about the older son? He too was already a son. He did not cease to be a son because of his initial bad reaction to the party for his brother who had departed and now returned. MacArthur thinks the older son's reaction proves he was unregenerate ("he was as lost as his younger brother had been, but he was too proud to see it," p. 163).

But if the older brother was a son of his father, how can he represent an unbeliever? Does a sinful reaction to his brother's return somehow prove he was not really his father's son?

Say that one of the elders in your church committed adultery and ran off with a younger woman. Then months later he came to his

---

[4] The word *dead* is often used figuratively in Scripture (e.g., Matt 8:22; Rom 7:8; 8:10; 1 Tim 5:6; Heb 9:14; 11:12; Jas 2:17, 20, 26; Rev 3:1). When the younger son left to pursue a prodigal lifestyle, he grieved his father. On the day of his return "when he was still a great way off, his father saw him and had compassion, and ran and fell on his neck and kissed him" (Luke 15:20). It is unlikely that this was the very first day that the father had been looking for his son's return. He had been as good as dead to him the whole time he was in the far country.

[5] As all three parables of Luke 15 show, fellowship with God is also good for Him as well. He has joy when His children are in fellowship with Him. That is the point of the third parable, and the first two as well.

senses, returned to his wife (who took him back), and wanted to return to the church. If the elders of the church decided to throw a party for the former elder who had strayed and now had returned, would your initial reaction be joy? Or might your initial reaction be skepticism? And is it not possible you might feel slighted since there had never been a big party for you and yet you had remained in the church? If you did have the wrong reaction, should you doubt your own eternal destiny?

We should immediately and joyfully join in the celebration when a fellow believer who has strayed returns. Yet the parable is also telling us that we should be patient with believers who are not as quick to share our joy and the joy that God has as well.[6]

MacArthur ends this chapter saying the older brother represents one who will be "unable to share the eternal joy of a loving Father" (p. 163).[7] What in the story tells him that the issue here is "eternal joy"? The issue is fellowship with God in the present, not in the life to come. Both sons had fellowship with their father. One son strayed for a time and returned to fellowship with his father. The older son needed to get with the program and share in the joy of the father or he could well fall out of fellowship with the father. Either way, eternal destiny is not in view.

---

[6] The older son felt it unfair that his brother was receiving a party, yet his father had never given him "a young goat that [he] might make merry with [his] friends" (Luke 15:29). His perspective was way off. The older son had been enjoying daily feasting with his father at home. He had it great. The younger son had been in a place of famine and had been extremely hungry and poor. His time away had been a disaster. Even this party for the younger brother was a feast which the older brother could and should have greatly enjoyed. He needed to be reminded just how good he had it at home with his father (vv 31-32).

[7] MacArthur spoke all over the U.S. about the Parable of the Prodigal Son. I heard him give that message in a Dallas suburb. In the message he indicated that Luke's account implies what happened after the parable ends. MacArthur said that the older brother picked up a large branch and beat his younger brother, the prodigal son now returned, to death, thus foreshadowing that the Jewish religious leaders would have Jesus killed on a tree (i.e., the cross). Later MacArthur published a book on Luke 15:11-32 entitled, *The Prodigal Son* (first entitled, *A Tale of Two Sons*). Chapter 11 is called "The Shocking Real Life Ending." MacArthur's suggestion is not suggested by the parable. Indeed, his speculation is at odds with many of the details the Lord has given us.

Conclusion

So let's summarize. The lost sheep was a member of the flock before it strayed. It did not become a part of the flock by returning. The lost coin was one of the ten before it was lost. When it was found, it returned to its proper place with its owner and the other nine coins.[8] The lost son was one of the two sons before he strayed. When he returned, he did not become a son of his father. He instead returned to fellowship with his father.

Luke 15 is not giving us three evangelistic parables as MacArthur suggests. The issue in each case is that believers who are out of fellowship with God have the opportunity to return. For the believer who strays, repentance is necessary to get back in fellowship with God. And when a believer returns to fellowship with God, there is great joy in heaven.

While the incarnation and the cross show that God loves the whole world (John 3:16), these parables show His care and compassion for those who are born again and have lost their way. These parables are about *believers* who have strayed from fellowship with the Lord and need to repent to regain harmony with God.

---

[8] While coins are inanimate objects, the coins in this parable, like the sheep and the sons in the parables on either side of this parable, illustrate a believer who was in fellowship with God, then fell out of fellowship, then was found and restored to fellowship.

CHAPTER 16

The Vine and the Branches (John 15:1-6)

Introduction

Jesus is the vine and we are the branches. This is an image that has energized Christians for centuries. But what does it really mean? What did Jesus mean when He said that fruitless branches will be "taken away"? What did the Lord mean when He said that those branches which did not abide in Him would be removed and cast into a fire? MacArthur wants us to believe that Jesus was giving a warning concerning false professors, that is, concerning unregenerate people who were never really connected to Jesus at all.[1] Let's see whether the text of John 15:1-6 supports his conclusion.

Two Interpretations

John 15:1-6 has two major interpretations: either we must abide in Christ *to have everlasting life* (the evangelism view) or we must abide in Christ *to have fellowship with God* (the discipleship view). Dallas Seminary's journal *Bibliotheca Sacra* published those two views on this passage, one by Carl Laney and one by Jody Dillow.[2] Laney took the evangelism view and Dillow the discipleship view.

---

[1] Once again, MacArthur sees certainty of one's eternal destiny as impossible and he leads his readers to doubt whether they are born again.

[2] J. Carl Laney, "Abiding Is Believing: The Analogy of the Vine in John 15:1-6," *Bibliotheca Sacra* (January–March 1989): 55-66; and Joseph C. Dillow, "Abiding Is

Which of these two views best fits the context of John 15:1-6?

In the introduction to this chapter MacArthur suggests that the burning of the branches in verse 6 shows that the fruitless branches represent unbelievers. Let's examine his reasons for this interpretation.

The Cast of Characters

Was the Lord Jesus addressing believers, unbelievers, or a mixed group?

The answer is that Jesus was addressing the eleven disciples, all born again men. That Judas Iscariot was not present is mentioned in passing by MacArthur: "He must also have been grieving over Judas, who had utterly rejected His love *and set out to betray him*" (p. 167, emphasis added). The offhanded way in which MacArthur states Judas's departure makes it easy to miss that the words "set out to betray him" mean that Judas did not hear these words (cf. John 13:27, 30).

Judas was not present to hear the discourse found in John 14-16. Does that make a difference? It certainly does. However, MacArthur barely even mentions this. Indeed, in spite of the fact that all the listeners were born again, he says, "Judas (as well as all false disciples) represents barren branches" (p. 167).

We will see. Are there clues in the text that the barren branches represent "false disciples"?

The Vinedresser

MacArthur says, "Vinedressers had two chief means of maximizing the fruit that grew on the vine. One was to cut off the barren limbs. The other was to prune new shoots from the fruit-bearing branches" (p. 169).

That is not true. Gary Derickson, who holds B.S. and M.S. degrees in horticulture and who taught grape-pruning as a teaching assistant at Texas A & M University, says of that statement by

---

Remaining in Fellowship: Another Look at John 15:1-6," *Bibliotheca Sacra* (January–March 1990): 44-53.

MacArthur, "This is a nice-sounding description for the nonviti-culturalist. But is it what was actually practiced?"[3]

Derickson, who went on to receive a Th.D. (Doctor of Theology) degree in New Testament from Dallas Theological Seminary, states that there were actually two different times of pruning, one in the spring during the growing season and one in the fall "after the harvest while the vines were dormant."[4] Verse 2 looks at the spring pruning and verse 6 looks at the fall pruning.

Verse 2 says, "Every branch in Me that does not bear fruit He takes away [or lifts up]; and every branch that bears fruit He prunes, that it may bear more fruit."

The word translated "takes away" is *airei*, from *airō*. The leading Greek dictionary of the New Testament says that the primary meaning of this word is "to raise to a higher place or position, *lift up, take up, pick up*" (BDAG, p. 28). While it lists John 15:2 under the third sense, "to take away, remove" and specifically says "of branches *cut off*," there is every reason to question if verse 2 is actually saying the same thing as verse 6, especially when we know that viticulturists do *lift up* low hanging branches.

Derickson cites Pliny to prove that "nonfruiting branches were preserved and nurtured for use the following season."[5] The actual practice of Jesus' day was that "during the spring...certain non-fruiting branches were tied to the trellises [i.e., lifted up] along with the fruiting branches while the side shoots of the fruiting branches were being 'cleaned up.'"[6]

It seems most Bible translations mislead us here. God does not immediately *take away* unfruitful branches. He *lifts them up* in order to help them bear fruit.

The Fruitful Branches

MacArthur says, "The identity of the healthy, fruit-bearing branches seems clear—they represent genuine Christians" (p. 169). The problem with saying that the fruitful branches represent genuine Christians is that it implies that the unfruitful branches

---

[3] Gary Derickson, "Viticulture and John 15:1-6," *Bibliotheca Sacra* 153 (January–March 1996): 39.

[4] Ibid., 47-52.

[5] Ibid., 49.

[6] Ibid.

represent *unbelievers*, which is what MacArthur goes on to say. Why
not simply say that the fruitful branches represent *fruitful* believers and unfruitful branches represent *unfruitful* believers? Because
MacArthur thinks that all believers will inevitably be fruitful. He
cites, without explanation, Eph 2:10 in an effort to prove his point
(p. 169). But Eph 2:10 does not say what MacArthur implies it does.
Anyone reading Eph 2:8-10 should notice a change in pronoun
from the second person plural, *you*, in verses 8-9, to the first person
plural, *we*, in verse 10:

> For by grace *you* have been saved through faith, and that
> not of *yourselves*; it is the gift of God, not of works, lest
> anyone should boast. For *we* are His workmanship, created
> in Christ Jesus for good works, which God prepared before-
> hand that *we* should walk in them [emphasis added].

Why the shift from *you* to *we*? Why didn't Paul simply say in
verse 10, "For *you* are His workmanship…"? Surely this change was
intentional.

In Ephesians, Paul uses the first person plural when he speaks of
Jews and Gentiles together in one body, that is, the Church. This is
easily seen in the verses which follow Eph 2:10, such as verses 11-12
where Paul says, "Remember that *you*, once Gentiles in the flesh…
at one time were without Christ" (emphasis added). But then in
verses 14-15 we see the first person plural, "For He Himself is *our*
peace, who has made *both* one, and has broken down the middle
wall of separation…so as to create in Himself *one* new man [= the
Church]…" (emphasis added).

Thus Eph 2:10 is not talking about individual believers. Paul is
making a corporate point. He is saying that *the Church of Jesus
Christ* was created to produce good works. Of course, this is accomplished by many believers in many churches producing good works
over many centuries (cf. 1 Cor 3:10-15; Eph 2:20). But there is nothing in Eph 2:10 that hints that all believers are equally productive,
or even that all believers are necessarily productive.[7]

---

[7] Clearly a branch on the vine that still has green foliage is alive. That is proof of
life, as MacArthur will soon say. It is also proof of some measure of productivity.
But branches on grapevines are only as productive as they are designed to be if they
produce mature grapes. Grapevines are not merely ornamental plants. They are
intended to bear mature fruit.

MacArthur next quotes from the epistle of James to prove that all believers are spiritually healthy and doing an abundant amount of good works. He says, "We are not saved by works, but works are the only proof that faith is genuine, vibrant, and alive (James 2:17)" (p. 169). But that is not what Jas 2:17 says. What it actually says is, "faith without works is dead." But it is clear that James is not saying that faith without works is not faith. That is logically impossible. Faith is faith. Faith without works is faith without works. That is obvious.

James is saying that faith without works is dead in the sense of being lifeless and unproductive. Note the words that immediately precede Jas 2:17, "What does it profit?" The issue is profitability. Faith that is not meeting the needs of the hungry and cold believers around us (Jas 2:15-16) does not profit either the needy believer (v 16) or the believer who should help them (v 14 starts, "What does it profit, my brethren...?").[8]

Next, MacArthur cites Matt 7:16-17 without giving the reader the full context:

> "You will know them by their fruits. Grapes are not gathered from thorn bushes, nor figs from thistles, are they? Even so, *every* good tree bears good fruit; but the bad tree bears bad fruit" (p. 169, emphasis his).

MacArthur thinks this proves that what he repeatedly calls *true believers* (pp. 16, 20, 38, 47, 109, 133, 136, 166, 171, 182, 188, 190, 191, 217, 273) will be known by the abundance of their good works. But *false prophets*, not false believers (MacArthur's view[9]), are being discussed in Matt 7:15-20[10]:

> "Beware of *false prophets*, who come to you in sheep's clothing, but inwardly they are ravenous wolves" (Matt 7:15, emphasis added).

---

[8] For more extensive discussion see my 19-page journal article on Jas 2:14-26: http://www.faithalone.org/journal/2002ii/wilkin.pdf.

[9] Earlier in the paragraph in which he cites Matt 7:16-17 he says, "The inevitable result of genuine salvation is good works. We are not saved by works, but works are the only proof that faith is genuine, vibrant, and alive" (p. 169). He then cites Jas 2:17 and Matt 7:16-17 in an effort to prove his point.

[10] For further discussion of this passage see Chapter 11, pp. 127-28.

Next MacArthur cites John 15:3: "You are already clean because of the word which I have spoken to you." He suggests that *clean* here refers to *pruning*: "God's Word *prunes the sin* out of our lives" (p. 170, emphasis added). And what is the proof for that interpretation? Sin (*hamartia*) does not even occur in John 15:1-6. The only thing MacArthur says which could in any way validate his point is that "The word translated 'clean' is the same Greek word He uses in verse 2 to describe the pruning process" (p. 170). As we shall soon see, that statement is a bit misleading. But even if that were true, why would that prove that "God's Word prunes the sin out of our lives"? In addition, what would *pruning the sin out of our lives* mean?

Verse 2 refers to an ongoing pruning: "Every branch that bears fruit He prunes [or cleanses], that it may bear more fruit." This pruning was done in the spring each year as Derickson noted (see above). It was not once and for all. However, verse 3 refers to a once-for-all cleansing: "You are *already clean* because of the word that I have spoken to you" (emphasis added). Note the word *already*. That is a completed event never to be repeated. MacArthur suggests that verses 2 and 3 refer to the same cleansing. If so, then has God once and for all "pruned the sin out of our lives"? That would be the teaching of sinless perfection, would it not? How could we ever sin if God had *already* pruned all sin out of our lives?

MacArthur fails to mention that the word he cites from verse 3 (*katharoi*) appears earlier in John's Gospel and sheds light on this usage. When Jesus was washing the feet of the disciples and Peter objected the Lord said,

> "He who is bathed needs only to wash his feet, but is completely clean [*kataros*]; and you are clean [*katharoi*], but not all of you." For He knew who would betray Him; therefore He said, "You are not all clean [*kataroi*]."

The words "you are clean" in John 13:10 and 15:3 refers to the fact that the eleven, but not Judas, *were forgiven*. They were *clean* in the sense that all their sins were forgiven. They needed fellowship cleansing (the washing of the feet, compare 1 John 1:9), but not bathing (regeneration and positional forgiveness). The point in 13:10 and 15:3 is forgiveness, not pruning of sin out of one's life.

MacArthur confuses things when he says, "The word translated 'clean' [in John 15:3] is the same Greek word He uses in verse 2 to describe the pruning process" (p. 170). The words are *similar* in form and sound and meaning, but they do not carry the same meaning in this context. The Lord intended a word play between *kathairei* (He prunes/trims clean) in verse 2 and *katharoi este* (you are clean) in verse 3. But the words do not mean the same thing in each verse.[11] No one translates *kathairei* as *cleansing* in verse 2 and no one translates *katharoi* as *pruning* in verse 3.[12] Cleansing is positional and is once and for all. Pruning is experiential and is an ongoing process.

The final section in this chapter is MacArthur's explanation of the spiritual condition and eternal destiny of branches that fail to abide in the vine.

The Judas Branches

In the opening sentence MacArthur makes this claim: "The fruitless branches are only superficially attached to the vine" (p. 170). What does that mean? Are they attached or not? He says "There is even leafy growth and other tokens of life" (p. 170).

The expression *tokens of life* means *signs of life*, so MacArthur admits that even the branches that fail to abide are attached to the vine *and have life!*

Even when he claims, "They are not *adequately* tied into the vine's vascular system" (p. 170, emphasis added), MacArthur is still admitting that they *are* "tied into the vine's vascular system." If a branch is attached, it is already a part of the vascular system.

If Jesus is the vine and believers are the branches, then *any* branch connected to Him represents a born again person. There is no such thing as someone who has life from the vine and who is drawing nourishment from the vine and yet who is not born again. But that

---

[11] Brown suggests that *kathairei* means "[the gardener] *trims clean*" (pp. 660, 676, emphasis added), though he also says, "it has the meaning 'to prune' that is demanded by the context here" (p. 660). If it is understood as *trims clean*, there would be a verbal link in English with verse 3. But even then the sense is not at all the same. Ongoing pruning is not the same as once for all forgiveness.

[12] BDAG, the leading dictionary of the Greek NT, says that *kathairei* (from *kathairō*) means "to remove superfluous growth from a plant, clear, prune" in John 15:2 (p. 488) and that *katharoi* means "being free from moral guilt" in John 13:10 and 15:3 (p. 489).

conflicts with MacArthur's Puritan theology and thus he posits a condition in which some unregenerate people are empowered by Christ, growing, and showing signs of life.

MacArthur continues, "Every gardener understands this principle" (p. 170). Indeed they do. Every gardener knows that branches of a grapevine are alive. Gardeners know as well that not all branches are equally productive at any given time. Gardeners certainly do not know that some branches are phony, which is the non sequitur that MacArthur would have us believe: "Spiritually, the equivalent of a fruitless branch is a phony Christian" (p. 171). How can a fruitless branch represent a phony Christian if it is attached to the vine [Jesus] and has signs of life? The problem MacArthur sees is a lack of productivity, not a lack of life.

MacArthur's interpretation departs even further from the text when he says that "the classic example of a fruitless branch is Judas" (p. 171). Judas was not a fruitless branch. He was never a branch at all. And more importantly, Judas was not even present at this discourse. The Lord said in John 15:5-6,

> "I am the vine, you are the branches. He who abides in Me, and I in him, bears much fruit; for without Me you can do nothing. If anyone does not abide in Me, he is cast out as a branch and is withered; and they gather them and throw them into the fire, and they are burned."

Who does the Lord mean by *you* in "you are the branches." He means the eleven disciples, the people He's addressing. Remember, Judas is not present. He isn't part of the group being discussed.

Now, hypothetically, this might only refer to the Apostles and not to any other believers. However, we know from the theme of abiding found in the rest of John 15 and in John's first epistle that *all believers* are called to abide. But abiding is addressed to believers, not unbelievers. In John 15:7, not cited by MacArthur, the Lord says, "If you abide in Me, and My words abide in you, you will ask what you desire, and it shall be done for you." That is *conditional*. The Lord did not say that all believers will abide.

We also know from the theme verse of First John that not all believers actually do abide:

> And now, little children, abide in Him, that when He appears, we may have confidence and not be ashamed before Him at His coming (1 John 2:28).

Notice that John calls them "little children." Compare this to 1 John 2:12-14. Believers are in view. They are commanded to "abide in Him." The reason is so that when He appears (the Rapture), John, his coworkers, and the readers ("we," notice the shift from the second person imperative "abide") may have confidence (or boldness) and that they might not be ashamed before Him at His coming.

MacArthur does not cite John 13:10 or John 15:5 or 1 John 2:28. Nor does he discuss the theme of abiding in the rest of John's Gospel (there are 39 uses, including 11 uses in Chapter 15 alone) or in First John, by the same author, and in the rest of the New Testament.[13] If *believers* are often commanded to abide (*menō* in Greek) in Christ and His Word in John and First John (e.g., John 8:31; 15:4, 5, 7, 9, 10; 1 John 2:24, 28; 3:6), then in what sense can an unbeliever be faulted for not abiding, something he cannot do? Only someone connected to the vine can abide.

MacArthur's ultimate point concerning "the Judas branches" is that they represent "counterfeit disciples" who "do not abide in Christ" and hence which are "doomed to hell" (p. 172).

MacArthur does not discuss John 15:6 or its context other than saying, "The imagery of burning suggests that these fruitless branches are doomed to hell" (p. 172). MacArthur makes a

---

[13]The theme of abiding is a major one in John 15 and in John's First Epistle. The word *menō* (to abide, remain) appears five times in John 15:1-6 (15: 4 [3 times], 5, 6) and eleven total times in the chapter (the previous five plus 15: 7, 9, 10 [twice], 11, 16). It is also used a whopping 22 times in First John (2:6, 10, 14, 17, 19, 24 [3 times], 27 [twice], 28; 3:6, 9, 14, 17, 24 [twice]; 4:12, 13, 15, 16 [twice]), far more than in any other book in the New Testament other than John's Gospel (with 39 uses). MacArthur only mentions the theme of abiding four times in his book, all in this chapter. Once he simply mentions it when he quotes John 15:1-8 (p. 166). Another time he merely says that "living branches…abide in the vine" (p. 168). After quoting John 6:37 he says, "Branches that abide in the True Vine will never be removed" (p. 171). Finally, he says that "the fruitless branches represent counterfeit disciples—people who were never truly saved. They do not abide in Christ" (p. 172). Nowhere in this chapter or in the whole book does MacArthur *explain* what abiding in Christ actually means. A vine receives sustenance by remaining attached to the vine. So too, a Christian abides in Christ when He allows His words to take up residence in him (John 15:7). It means continuing to walk in the light of His revelation (1 John 1:7). This is something all Christians can and should do. It is not, however, automatic.

proclamation, yet does not offer any evidence in support of his claim. So what does the text actually suggest?

The word translated "they are burned" is *kaietai* from *kaiō*. That word is only used a dozen times in the New Testament and only one other time in John and hence it makes a relatively easy word study. How many of the other uses refer to hell? Two. And both of those occur at the end of the book of Revelation where the lake of fire is explicitly mentioned (Rev 19:20; 21:8). In no other place in the New Testament does *kaiō* refer to burning that will take place in hell. Here are each of the other eleven uses and the translations:

- "nor do men *light* a candle..." (Matt 5:5).
- "Let your lamps [be] *burning*" (Luke 12:35).
- "Did not our heart *burn* within us...?" (Luke 24:32).
- "He [John the Baptist] was the *burning* and shining lamp..." (John 5:35).
- "though I give my body *to be burned*..." (1 Cor 13:3).
- "the mountain [Mount Sinai]...*burned* with fire..." (Heb 12:18).
- "Seven lamps of fire *were burning*..." (Rev 4:5).
- "something like a great mountain *burning* with fire was thrown into the sea..." (Rev 8:8).
- "a great star fell from heaven, *burning* like a torch..." (Rev 8:10).
- "These two [the beast and the false prophet] were cast alive into the lake of fire *burning* with brimstone" (Rev 19:20).
- "the lake which *burns* with fire and brimstone, which is the second death" (Rev 21:8).

The word *kaiō* refers to burning. It is *the context* which determines what type of burning is in view. Nine of the eleven uses outside of John 15:6 are clearly temporal burnings that have nothing to do with hell or the lake of fire. The other two burnings refer to eternal condemnation because the lake of fire and the second death are mentioned in the respective contexts.

So what type of burning is the burning of branches in a fire? Barring some reference to the lake of fire or the second death, or a statement that indicates that this is an everlasting burning or something of that sort, we would lean toward the view that this refers to temporal burning.

There is another major contextual clue. The branches represent believers, those who are clean, those who may or may not abide in the vine (John 15:4, 5, 6, 7; 1 John 2:28). The branches *which do not continue to abide* (John 15:4-5)[14] are the ones thrown into the fire and burned (John 15:6).[15] Notice that in verse 6 the Lord says, "he is cast out as [or, like] a branch and is withered; they gather them and throw them into the fire." If a branch is no longer abiding, it is no longer drawing sustenance from the vine. That is why it "is cast out as a branch and is withered." The workers are gathering up from the ground those withered branches that no longer remain attached to (i.e., no longer abide in) the vine. Of course those who still abide accomplish much in prayer (John 15:7) because they remain in fellowship with the Lord.[16]

This all supports the idea that the burning is judgment in this life. Born again people will not be eternally condemned. But they may experience temporal judgment. This might refer to premature physical death. God does take believers home early (1 Cor 11:30; Jas 5:19-20; 1 John 5:16). However, the figure of the burning of branches is flexible enough that it could refer to divine discipline that might not lead to premature death if the believer repents and gets back to work for Christ.

---

[14] The words "without Me you can do nothing" (John 15:5) are immediately followed by "If anyone does not abide in Me…" This is clearly intentional. Only by abiding in Christ can a Christian bear fruit and please God.

[15] J. Ramsey Michaels says, "He is obviously speaking of literal branches, not people, yet his point is unmistakable: those who do not 'dwell' or remain in him so as to 'bear fruit' are in mortal danger. The verb 'dwells' is present, not aorist (as in v. 4, 'Make your dwelling in me'). For this reason, the verse has played a significant role in theological debates over the question of apostasy, or whether individuals can lose their salvation" (*John*, p. 807). Similarly C. K. Barrett says, "The words [they throw them into the fire and they are burned] are primarily parabolic; that is, it is unfruitful branches which are cast into the fire and burned. Yet John would probably not have denied a similar fate for faithless Christians" (*John*, p. 475).

[16] C. K. Barrett notes, "According to Brown, v. 6 is the counterpart of v. 5, not of v. 7; there seems to be no reason why it should be taken as the counterpart of both, a negative statement between two positive ones" (*John*, p. 475).

MacArthur ends this chapter with reference to Heb 10:31. He says, "It is a terrifying thing to fall into the hands of the living God." Yet a study of Heb 10:26-31 shows that it is believers who are in view there as well.

The passage starts in this way: "For if we sin willfully *after we have received the knowledge of the truth...*" (Heb 10:26, emphasis added). In verse 29 we read of one who "has trampled the Son of God underfoot, counted the blood of the covenant *by which he was sanctified* a common thing" (emphasis added). That is followed in verse 30 by two quotes from the Old Testament, the second of which says, "The LORD will judge *His people*" (Deut 32:36, emphasis added).

Simply put, the judgment in view is the judgment of believers, those who have been sanctified by the blood of Christ, those who have received the knowledge of the truth, those who are His people. Yes, it is a terrifying thing to turn our backs on Christ and offer animal sacrifices as though the blood of Christ was not sufficient for our redemption. That is what the readers of the book of Hebrews were in danger of doing. That is the willful sinning spoken of in Heb 10:26.[17] That is the trampling under foot of the Son of God and counting His blood as common in verse 29. The consequences for doing that are serious indeed. Yet none of this is discussed by MacArthur.

Conclusion

John 15:1-6 fails to support MacArthur's claim that the way to know the difference between genuine believers and phony believers lies in their works. It is an example of trying to find in the Scriptures something you think should be there, but which is not. Chapter 16 in *TGAJ* once again shows that MacArthur's gospel is a gospel of doubt.

---

[17] Lordship Salvation unintentionally commits the same type of willful sin. While Lordship Salvation does not suggest going back to animal sacrifices to atone for our sins, it does posit that the shed blood of Christ is not sufficient in itself to buy our salvation. We must buy our own salvation by taking up our own crosses and following Christ until death (see *TGAJ*, pp. 143-50).

The Call to Repentance

Introduction

As he did in chapter 15, MacArthur again argues that repentance, which he defines as "turning from sin" (p. 178), is a condition for obtaining eternal life. MacArthur is correct that repentance is turning from sin. However, repentance is not a condition for receiving everlasting life.

The Nature of Repentance[1]

Chapter 17 begins the fourth section of the book, "Jesus Explains His Gospel." In the introduction to this chapter, MacArthur makes three thought-provoking comments.

First, he made this claim: "Repentance was a recurring motif in *all* of His [Jesus'] public sermons" (p. 175, emphasis added).

Since the words *repent* and *repentance* do not occur at all in John's Gospel—and John's Gospel contains a lot of Jesus' sermons, MacArthur's claim is not true at least in terms of John's Gospel.

---

[1] My doctoral dissertation at Dallas Theological Seminary was on the issue of repentance and salvation (1985). The heart of my dissertation was published in six journal articles available at www.faithalone.org under Free Resources/Journal (1988-1991).

In the Synoptic Gospels (Matthew, Mark, and Luke), the Lord did not always preach about repentance. Actually He mentioned repentance in less than half his sermons in the Synoptics.[2]

MacArthur's claim that repentance is a motif found in all of Jesus' public sermons is not supported by the evidence from Scripture and it leaves a false impression not in accordance with the facts.

By contrast, the word *believe* occurs ninety-nine times in John's Gospel, eleven times in Matthew, fourteen times in Mark, and nine times in Luke. The theme of belief occurs much more frequently in Jesus' sermons than the theme of repentance. And if we restrict ourselves to Jesus' *evangelistic* sermons, belief is always the one and only condition of everlasting life, not repentance plus the other elements MacArthur believes are required (commitment, confession, obedience, perseverance).

Second, MacArthur says, "He [the Lord Jesus] described His own objective thus: 'to call…sinners to repentance' (Luke 5:31)" (p. 175). That was *one* objective that Jesus had. But that was not the only one. For example, John 3:17 states another of the objectives the Lord had. There Jesus says, "For God did not send His Son into the world to condemn the world, but that the world through Him might be saved." The cross was His major aim all during His earthly ministry. He had to die to give everlasting life to those who believe in Him.

Third, MacArthur ends the introduction by quoting, without explanation, one line which is repeated in Luke 13:3, 5: "Unless you repent, you will all likewise perish." MacArthur's very next sentence is a question which reads, "When was the last time you heard the gospel presented in those terms?" (p. 175). He clearly considers the word *perish* in Luke 13:3, 5 as a reference to eternal condemnation. Hence in his interpretation this saying proves that repentance is a condition for escaping eternal condemnation. Yet that does not fit the context.

The word *likewise* in "you will all likewise perish" looks back to verses 1, 2, and 4. Verses 1 and 2 speak of Galileans "whose blood Pilate had mingled with their sacrifices." Those Galileans *perished*

---

[2] For example, the verb *repent* only occurs five times in Matthew, twice in Mark, and nine times in Luke. Out of scores of sermons, clearly Jesus did not use the verb often. How about the noun, *repentance*? The noun is only found three times in Matthew, twice in Mark, and five times in Luke.

in the sense that they died at the hand of Pilate. We don't know if they were regenerate or unregenerate. All we know is that they died while offering sacrifices.

Verse 4 is where the Lord brings up the example of "those eighteen on whom the tower in Siloam fell and killed them." Once again, we don't know whether they were born again or not. We know that they *perished* in the sense that they died when a tower fell on them.

Thus in verses 3 and 5 when the Lord says, "unless you repent you will all likewise perish," He is saying that unless His listeners repented, they too *would die prematurely*. And that's what happened. Less than four decades later over one million Jews died in the Jewish War when Rome destroyed Jerusalem and the temple. That terrible destruction is what the Lord was talking about, not eternal condemnation in the lake of fire. Jesus spoke of eternal condemnation elsewhere, but not in Luke 13:1-5.

The Missing Note

The first sentence under "The Missing Note" explains what MacArthur means by that heading. He does not mean that the preaching of repentance is missing today. He means that the preaching of repentance *as a condition of everlasting life* is missing today. He asks, "When was the last time you heard the gospel presented in those terms? It is not fashionable in the twenty-first century to preach a gospel that demands repentance" (p. 175).

He does not say how he arrived at the conclusion.

I have a large collection of evangelistic tracts. Most of them say that repentance is a condition of escaping eternal condemnation. And many evangelistic sermons preached by Evangelicals mention repentance as a condition of everlasting life.

MacArthur provides only one example in this section of anyone today who is not preaching repentance as a condition of everlasting life, i.e., Lewis Sperry Chafer, the founder of Dallas Theological Seminary (DTS). Yet Chafer died in 1952. The book that MacArthur cites by Chafer was written in 1948, sixty-seven years ago! If this sort of preaching and teaching is predominant, why not list a few dozen well-known pastors or theologians who currently teach that repentance is not a condition of everlasting life? As it happens, he does mention three more in the next section (see below), but that is a small number.

It would be great if MacArthur was right in his contention that most Evangelicals today share justification by faith alone, without mixing in repentance. Yet most do not. The *real* missing note in evangelism is a call *to faith alone in the Lord Jesus Christ,* i.e., the call to simply believe in Him for everlasting life (John 3:16).

The Discarding of Repentance

In this section MacArthur cites one of my seminary professors and friends, Dr. Charles Ryrie, as agreeing with Chafer. He also cites Drs. Tom Constable and Mike Cocoris. The funny thing is that all of those men hold to the change-of-mind view of repentance. That is, they all believe that repentance is a condition for everlasting life, but that repentance is not turning from sins, but a change of mind about Christ.

Note this statement by MacArthur: "As we have seen repeatedly, the gospel according to Jesus is as much a call to forsake sin as it is a summons to faith" (p. 177). As mentioned above, the Biblical evidence does not support that claim.

The Lord Jesus taught that the sole condition is faith in Him, not repentance or repentance plus commitment, obedience, and perseverance. John 3:16 is clear on this point. So are many of the verses in John (e.g., 1:12; 5:24; 6:35, 37, 39-40, 47; 11:25-27; 20:30-31) and in Acts and the epistles (Acts 10:43; 15:7-11; 16:30-31; Rom 4:1-8; Gal 2:16; 3:6-14; 1 John 5:9-13).

What Is Repentance?

MacArthur is correct that repentance is turning from sins and not merely a change of mind about Christ. However, there are five points he makes in this section that merit consideration.

First, MacArthur does not show what repentance is *from Scripture.* Instead he makes a series of comments about it, occasionally mentioning a passage without explaining it to prove his point. He fails to mention or discuss key passages like Matt 12:41 and Rev 9:20-21. These texts actually use the word *repent* and they specifically indicate that repentance is turning from sins.

Second, the opening statement in this section, "Repentance *is* a critical element of conversion…" (emphasis his), is not true if by *conversion* he means *regeneration.* MacArthur does not explain or even cite a single verse of Scripture to support that statement. Actually, there are no verses that say repentance is a condition of eternal life. Yet there are over 100 that say that the one and only condition of everlasting life is faith in Christ.

Third, MacArthur's statement, "Nor is repentance merely a human work" (p. 178), is correct, but it is also quite telling. The word *merely* means "without admixture, purely, altogether, entirely."[3] What MacArthur is saying is that repentance is not *entirely* a human work. It is a human work, but it is a human work made possible by God giving the person the ability to do it: "It is, like every element of redemption, a sovereignly bestowed gift of God" (p. 178).

MacArthur is right in saying that repentance is *partly a human work* and wrong in saying that it is an "element of redemption." By "element of redemption" MacArthur means *one of the conditions for regeneration* ("the repentance that takes place at conversion," p. 180). That is not true. And therein lies the problem.

Thus MacArthur's point is this: salvation is not merely a human work. Salvation is partly a human work, but it is partly (or mainly) a work which is enabled by God.

Yet the Scriptures are clear that salvation *is not of works lest anyone could boast* (John 4:10; 6:28-29; Eph 2:8-9; Rev 22:17). If a person's salvation was partly due to his own works, then he would have a ground for boasting.

Fourth, the statement, "Real repentance alters the character of the whole man" (p. 180) is only partially true. The Ninevites repented (Jonah 3:1-10; Matt 12:41). That is, they "turned from their evil way" (Jonah 3:10). Their behavior was indeed altered. But MacArthur did not speak of *behavioral change*. Instead he speaks of an alteration of "the character of the whole man." Did the character of the Ninevites radically change? There is no indication in the text of Jonah (or in the Lord's comments in Matt 12:41) that their character changed or that they suddenly became godly people.

Even the new birth does not immediately (or automatically) change one's character. Growth takes time (Heb 5:12-14). The believers in Corinth certainly did not evidence radical alteration of their character (1 Cor 3:1-3; 5:1; 6:15-20; 11:30).

MacArthur gives no Scripture to support this point. He "proves" it by citing Martyn Lloyd-Jones. While Lloyd-Jones was a powerful

---

[3] Dictionary.com.

preacher and writer, he was not an Apostle and his writings do not prove anything, especially when his quote contains no Scripture either.

Fifth, MacArthur's closing statement in this section is incorrect: "Repentance is not a one-time act. The repentance that takes place at conversion begins a progressive, lifelong process of confession (1 John 1:9)" (p. 180). In the first place, repentance is a specific act (cf. Rev 9:20-21 and note the specific sins mentioned). It occurs at a point in time. If the person who repents remains in fellowship with God, then no further repentance is needed or even possible.[4] In the second place, repentance does not necessarily take place at conversion (see point two above). In the third place, confession of sins (1 John 1:9) is not repentance. Confession of sins is agreeing with God that what we have done is sin. Confession is only effective for the one who is walking in the light of God's Word (1 John 1:7). That is, confession is for the one in fellowship with God. Finally, there is no guarantee in Scripture that a believer will always repent if he ceases to walk in fellowship with God (cf. Heb 6:4-8; Jas 5:19-20).

The Fruits of Repentance

MacArthur is right that good works should follow repentance. Turning from sinful deeds should lead to the doing of good works (see Matt 3:8; Luke 3:8, 11-14).

However, in this section, MacArthur repeatedly quotes verses without explanation. He suggests that God promises that anyone who repents (and thus, in his view, is born again) will experience "an inevitable change of behavior—a new way of life" (p. 181).

For proof he begins with a reference to Matt 4:17, "Repent, for the kingdom of heaven is at hand" (p. 181). But he neglects to discuss what *the kingdom of heaven is at hand* means.

The Lord Jesus (and John the Baptist, Matt 3:2) was not delivering an evangelistic sermon, but offering the Messianic kingdom

---

[4] One who is in fellowship with God has not gone to the spiritual far country as the prodigal son did (Luke 15:11-32). Instead, such a person is seeking to please God. The words *repent* and *repentance* are not found at all in First John, a book about how to walk in fellowship with God (1 John 1:3-4). Instead, John says that walking in the light of God's Word and confessing our known sins is what is required to remain in fellowship with God (1 John 1:5-10). If we ever plan to sin (i.e., I'm going to get drunk Saturday night), then we have become the prodigal and we indeed need to repent in order to get back in fellowship with God.

to that generation of Jews. If they had repented (and believed in Him, see John 3:3, 5), then the kingdom would have been established for that generation. Of course, before the kingdom could be established, Jesus had to die on the cross and the time of Jacob's trouble (Daniel's 70th week, Dan 9:24-27) had to occur. So if that generation of Jews had repented and believed as a result of Jesus' preaching, then seven years after His resurrection He would have returned and the Millennium would have begun in AD 40. That is why at the end of Matthew 23 Jesus said that He would have *at that time* gathered the people of Jerusalem and all of Israel, "but [they] were not willing!" (Matt 23:37).

MacArthur appeals to verses that deal with national salvation from Gentile rule, not individual salvation from eternal condemnation.[5] And those verses do not say anything about the inevitability of a change of behavior and a new way of life.

Two paragraphs later he cites Ezek 33:18-19, but again fails to explain what is meant. Here are those verses:

> When the righteous turns from his righteousness and commits iniquity, he shall die because of it. But when the wicked turns from his wickedness and does what is lawful and right, he shall live because of it.

He implies that the issue here is eternal life and death (the second death of Rev 20:14). But if that is the case, then these verses teach that everlasting life can be lost: "When the righteous turns from his righteousness and commits iniquity, he shall die because of it." Clearly this refers to premature *physical* death (and all the negative events which can lead up to that).

The person who is living righteously, but who then falls away from the Lord and does not repent, will die prematurely. But MacArthur simply ignores that part of the verse and wants us to focus on the repentance of the wicked: "But when the wicked turns from his wickedness and does what is lawful and right, he shall live because of it." The expression "the wicked" does not refer to the unregenerate. It refers to Jews who were disobeying God's Law. In

---

[5] Many Old Testament texts (e.g., Lev 26:40-46) indicate that the nation of Israel had to repent before the kingdom would be established. However, MacArthur does not mention those texts or even the nation of Israel. John the Baptist and the Lord Jesus preached repentance in light of the nearness of the kingdom because of the prophetic teachings in the Old Testament about repentance and the kingdom.

the same way "the righteous" in the previous verse does not refer to the regenerate, but to Jews who were walking in obedience to the Law. Israel was a covenant nation. Within that nation were people who acted in keeping with the Law and people who did not. Ezekiel's point is that righteousness enhances and extends one's life and wickedness diminishes and shortens one's life.

John Taylor's comments on Ezek 18:13 and the expression "he shall surely die," are very helpful:

> The alternative fates of life and death refer to what will take place in the judgment which is imminent. But Muilenburg is right to suggest that "there is more than an implication that the righteous experience life and the unrighteous experience death here and now." The Hebrew concepts of life and death represent not two distinct states, but the two poles on the graduated scale of existence. At its lower end are death, suffering, illness and even weariness; at its higher end are varying degrees of prosperity, with happiness and the divine blessing as the *summum bonum*.[6]

Once a righteous person "turns from his righteousness and commits iniquity," he becomes "the wicked." Then "he shall live" only if he "turns from his wickedness and does what is lawful and right." The quality of one's life, and even the continuation of it, is at stake. The issue here is not eternal destiny, but the fullness of one's life here and now.

MacArthur ends this section with this statement: "Radical change was also what the apostle Paul considered proof of repentance" (p. 182). He cites as proof Acts 26:19-20 and Paul's assignment to call Gentiles to "do works befitting repentance." But doing works that befit repentance is not the same as "radical change." Is MacArthur saying that brand-new believers are already radically changed before any growth occurs? What about the believers in the church of Corinth? The born-again people in Corinth were still going to pagan temples and having sex with prostitutes (1 Cor 6:18-20). The Corinthian Christians were still carnal five years after their new birth (1 Cor 3:1-4). They were even getting drunk at the

---

[6] John B. Taylor, *Ezekiel: An Introduction and Commentary*, Tyndale Old Testament Commentaries (Downers Grove, IL: Inter-Varsity Press, 1969), p. 150.

Lord's Supper with the result that some of them had already died and some were sick (1 Cor 11:30). That is not "radical change."

Spiritual growth takes time (1 Cor 2:14–3:4; 1 Tim 3:6; Heb 5:12-14). It starts (if we gather with other believers and apply the Word of God which we hear taught) after one believes in Christ and is born again.

It is understandable that MacArthur is frustrated by the fact that some of those whom he discipled and mentored have fallen away from the faith. Any pastor would likewise be upset over those in their congregations who depart from the faith.

The opposite is also true. When those whom we disciple go on in effective service for Christ, we are thrilled. The Apostle John said, "I have no greater joy than to hear that my children walk in truth" (3 John 4).

But MacArthur has allowed his frustration to lead him to a conclusion that is inconsistent with Scripture. After studying the Puritans, MacArthur came to believe that if someone he discipled later fell away, then the one who fell proved he was not regenerate at all, but was a false professor. So in his current view, if a person does not quickly manifest "radical change," then he gives strong indication that he is not a *true believer*, that is, that he is a person who will likely fall away eventually.

The Apostle Paul did not take that approach in the Church of Corinth. Paul recognized that born again people might never manifest "radical change" prior to their death.

The Gospel and Repentance

MacArthur claims, "Repentance has always been the foundation of the New Testament call to salvation" (p. 182). Since the Gospel of John is the only evangelistic book in the Bible (John 20:30-31), and it doesn't mention repentance even once, MacArthur's claim is inconsistent with the Scriptures. In fact, there is not a single verse anywhere in the Bible that says that repentance is the condition of justification or everlasting life.

MacArthur first tries to prove this statement by quoting Acts 2:38.[7] However, he does not provide any explanation. Instead, he

---

[7] For a detailed discussion of Acts 2:38 and Acts 22:16, see Lanny Thomas Tanton, "The Gospel and Water Baptism: A Study of Acts 2:38," *Journal of the Grace Evangelical Society* (Spring 1990): 27-52, and "The Gospel and Water Baptism: A

repeats the claim that "no message that eliminates repentance can properly be called the gospel, for sinners cannot come to Jesus Christ apart from a radical change of heart, mind, and will" (p. 182).

Acts 10:43-48 shows that MacArthur misunderstands Acts 2:38. Cornelius and his household were forgiven and received the Holy Spirit when they believed, *before they were baptized*. Once a person simply believes in Jesus he receives not only eternal life (see Acts 11:14), but also the forgiveness of sins and the indwelling of the Holy Spirit. Clearly, Acts 10:43-48 would contradict Acts 2:38 if not for the fact that Acts 2:38 describes a situation unique to first century Jews who had approved of the crucifixion of Jesus.[8]

MacArthur's second proof text is Matt 21:28-31. Of those verses he says, "Jesus used a parable to illustrate the hypocrisy of a profession of faith without repentance" (p. 183). Yet the passage does not mention repentance (*metanoia*). Instead it speaks of regret (*metamelomai*).

MacArthur quotes the part of the story which tells of the responses of two sons to their father's command to go and work in the vineyard. One said he would go, but did not. The other said he would not go, but afterward regretted it and did go and do the work. MacArthur ends with the question, "Which of the two did the will of his father" (p. 193). Unfortunately, the key to the story is in the material which follows that question, material which MacArthur does not quote:

> "Which of the two did the will of *his* father?"
> They said to Him, "The first."
> Jesus said to them, "Assuredly, I say to you that tax collectors and harlots enter the kingdom of God before you. For John came to you in the way of righteousness, and you did not *believe* him; but tax collectors and harlots *believed*

Study of Acts 22:16," *Journal of the Grace Evangelical Society* (Spring 1991): 23-40. Both are available at www.faithalone.org under Free Resources/Journal. Tanton released a slightly updated twentieth anniversary article on Acts 2:38 in the Autumn 2012 issue.

[8] See Tanton's articles for more details. The Jews of Acts 2 came to faith in Acts 2:36. The two things promised in Acts 2:38, the baptism of the Holy Spirit and the forgiveness of sins, occurred *after regeneration* for those Jewish believers. But by Acts 10:43-48 the situation changed and both Holy Spirit baptism and forgiveness occurred at the same time as the new birth.

him; and when you saw it, you did not afterward relent and *believe* him" (Matt 21:31-32, emphasis added).

Believing is mentioned *three times* in verse 32. There is no mention of turning from sins in Jesus' telling of the story or in the conclusion. The Lord said, "You did not *believe* him," "tax collectors and harlots *believed* him," and "you did not afterward relent and *believe* him" (emphases added). The issue is belief, not turning from sins. The will of the Father is to believe in His Son as John 6:28-29 and 39-40 shows. So does Matt 7:21-23. So does this passage.[9]

We know what John the Baptist was calling on Jews to believe. He "came for a witness, to bear witness of the Light, that all through him might believe. He was not that Light, but *was sent* to bear witness of that Light" (John 1:6-8). Here is a direct quote from John the Baptist, "He who believes in the Son has everlasting life; and he who does not believe the Son shall not see life, but the wrath of God abides on him" (John 3:36). Paul said concerning John the Baptist, "John indeed baptized with a baptism of repentance, saying to the people that they should believe on Him who would come after him, that is, on Christ Jesus" (Acts 19:4).

Matthew 21:28-32 does not teach regeneration by repentance. It teaches regeneration by believing in the Lord Jesus Christ, which is exactly what the Lord said in John 6:28-29,

> Then they said to Him, "What shall we do, that we may work the works of God?" Jesus answered and said to them, "This is the work of God, that you believe in Him whom He sent."

They spoke of "the *works* of God," plural. He spoke of one singular "*work of God*," *believing in the Son*. His reference to *work* was probably ironic.[10] This "work" is not a work in the Pauline sense (cf. Rom 4:4-5; Eph 2:8-9). Some commentators note that the Lord's words here are parallel to what Paul says about justification by faith

---

[9] See Bob Wilkin, "Is 'The Will of the Father' a Life of Obedience?," *Grace in Focus Magazine* (September-October 2013), pp. 5-7. Available at www.faithalone.org under Free Resources/Grace in Focus.

[10] See Bruce Buchanan, http://www.puritanboard.com/f44/calvins-commentary-john-6-29-a-82070/. Accessed March 2, 2015.

alone (e.g., Rom 3:28).[11] Believing in Jesus is an action, but a passive one.

Conclusion

We should all be like the Bereans who searched the Scriptures to see if what they heard was true (Acts 17:11). Likewise we should all be diligent to show ourselves approved, workmen who do not need to be ashamed, who rightly divide the word of truth (2 Tim 2:15).

Belief, not repentance, is the only condition for receiving everlasting life. That is the liberating message of Jesus' amazing grace!

---

[11] See, for example, D. A. Carson, *The Gospel According to John* (Grand Rapids, MI: Eerdmans, 1991), p. 328. C. K. Barrett also sees in Jesus' words the same message as Paul's message of justification by faith alone: *The Gospel According to St. John* (Philadelphia, PA: The Westminster Press, 1978), p. 287. However, Barrett goes on to explain that he understands both Paul and the Lord to teach that "not an *act* of faith, but a *life* of faith" is required to be born again (p. 287, emphasis his).

CHAPTER 18

The Nature of True Faith[1]

Introduction

What is the nature of saving faith? Is saving faith something different than faith in general? MacArthur says that there is a difference between saving faith and non-saving faith and the difference comes down to a matter of obedience.[2]

In this chapter, MacArthur reveals his underlying reason for saying that genuine faith will always result in obedience. As a Calvinist, MacArthur believes that God has sovereignly chosen some people for eternal salvation, and only the elect receive saving faith as a gift from God. Hence, their faith will never fail. Faith will always produce works, because it is God-given, and how could God fail? Let us see whether MacArthur's arguments stand up to scrutiny.

---

[1] This chapter title is exactly the one that MacArthur used in *TGAJ*. A more appropriate title would be "The Nature of Saving Faith." *True faith* conjures up the question of whether someone really is convinced that something is true, or is just pretending to believe. Within this chapter MacArthur gives several adjectives to faith: repentant faith (p. 185), true faith (pp. 190-92), real faith (p. 192), and saving faith (p. 193).

[2] Once again, MacArthur is leading his readers toward doubting whether they are saved. He wants people to doubt their eternal destiny in order that they might be motivated to obey God.

Just As I Am?

MacArthur starts the introduction to this chapter with the words, "Just As I Am" (p. 185). In an amazing example of chutzpah, he then says that those who say we come to Christ just as we are have "given this truth an insidious twist" (p. 185). Notice what he says, "Sinners may come to Christ just as they are—solely on the basis of *repentant faith*—and He will save them" (p. 185, italics added).

The expression *repentant faith* does not occur in the Bible. It is a man-made expression. And what does MacArthur mean by *repentant faith*? He means, as we find out in the rest of his chapter, turning from one's sins and obeying God until death.

Since repentant faith means *turning from sins and persevering in obedience to Christ until death* (every single page in this chapter mentions the need for obedience and most mention the need to turn from sins), he is actually saying this: "Sinners may come to Christ just as they are—*solely on the basis of turning from their sins and persevering in obedience to Christ until death*—and He will save them." That means that we can't come to Christ *just as we are*. As we saw in the previous chapter, MacArthur really means to say that we can only come to Jesus if we have undergone a radical change in our lifestyle.

MacArthur then cites John 3:16 to prove his point even though it does not mention repentance, obedience, or repentant faith.

Without mentioning AWANA children's ministry by name, MacArthur then attacks AWANA's video *Blessed Calvary*. He says "the film instructed youth workers not to tell unsaved young people they must obey Christ, give Him their hearts, surrender their lives, repent of their sins, submit to His Lordship, [and] follow Him" (p. 185). He calls AWANA's message "a corrupted gospel" that "will not save" (p. 186).

There are six proposed conditions of everlasting life there: 1) obeying Christ, 2) giving Him your heart, 3) surrendering your life to Him, 4) repenting of your sins, 5) submitting to Christ's Lordship, and 6) following Him. AWANA says that faith alone, not those six conditions of discipleship, are required. MacArthur says those six things are precisely what one must do to obtain eternal salvation.

How could anyone ever have assurance of everlasting life if those are the conditions, especially if all of those things must continue until death? That is a gospel of doubt. That is not "Blessed Assurance, Jesus Is Mine" and it is certainly not "Just As I Am" either.

Eternal Life from Dead Faith?

MacArthur takes just one paragraph to discuss Jas 2:14-20 (p. 186). That passage deserves a lot more than a paragraph.

He starts by saying, "James 2:14-16 says faith without works is dead and cannot save" (p. 186). He does not quote any of the verses in question. Looking at the verses will help us discern the flow of thought.

Verse 14 begins the section by asking, "What does it profit, my brethren, if someone says he has faith but does not have works? Can faith save him?" MacArthur doesn't discuss any of the words or phrases in verse 14, or in the preceding or following verses. He just makes a pronouncement.

MacArthur *assumes*, without any explanation, that James is speaking of *salvation from hell*. But none of the other four uses of the verb *save* in James refer to salvation from eternal condemnation. They all refer to salvation from temporal judgment that is leading toward the premature physical death of a Christian (cf. 1:21; 4:12; 5:15, 19-20). That is what is in view here as well. Yet MacArthur does not examine *any* of the uses of *sozein* (to save) in James. He does not even mention that the word occurs four other times in the letter.

The question "what does it profit?" (*ti to ophelos* in Greek) both starts verse 14 and ends verse 16. Why would James repeat (bookend) that expression? The reason he emphasizes that question is because the issue he is discussing is profitability of one's faith. If a believer fails to meet the needs of a poor believer in his church (Jas 2:15-16), *then neither one of them will profit*. The needy brother remains hungry and cold. The well-to-do believer will fall under God's hand of discipline because of his failure to help his brother. Neither benefits.

MacArthur also fails to note that James is speaking to and about Christians. James indicates that he wants the readers to live out their "faith in Christ" (2:1). He addresses 2:14-26 to the same people, whom he calls "my brethren" (2:14). Then in the illustration of 2:15-16 he refers to "a brother or sister" who is in need and to "one of you," that is, one of the brethren in the same church who is able to meet the needs of the poor brother or sister. When we compare this with Jas 2:1-13, we find this is an extension of the discussion that it is wrong in our churches to kowtow to the rich and to look down upon the poor. If a Christian brother sees a fellow brother or sister from his own church in need of food or clothing, it is not enough to say, "I'll pray for you." He needs to give them what they need in terms of food and clothing.

MacArthur neither quotes nor discusses the illustration:

> If a brother or sister is naked and destitute of daily food, and one of you says to them, "Depart in peace, be warmed and filled," but you do not give them the things which are needed for the body, what does it profit? (Jas 2:15-16).

James said previously in 2:12, "*So speak and so do* as those who will be judged by the law of liberty" (emphasis added). The expression *the law of liberty* refers to the teachings of the Lord Jesus Christ and of His Apostles (cf. Jas 1:25).[3] Believers are under the law of liberty and we "will be judged" by Christ at the Judgment Seat of Christ both according to what *we say and do*. The person in verse 14 *says* the right thing. He professes his faith. But he does not *do* that which pleases the Lord. The problem in verses 15-16 is not what the believer *says*. "Be warmed and filled" is a nice sentiment. He is wishing the fellow believer well. The problem is that he *does not do* anything to meet the need.

MacArthur says that the faith mentioned in Jas 2:14, 16 is "spurious faith." But what is *spurious faith*? Would that not be professing to believe something that you did not actually believe? Yet that is not what James says. He says that the readers have faith in Christ (2:1). He calls them brethren (2:14). The word *spurious* is not found in verse 16 or anywhere in James. MacArthur's statement contradicts what inspired Scripture tells us.

---

[3] This exact expression *the law of liberty* occurs only in James, in 1:25 and 2:12. James was likely thinking of the teachings of the Lord Jesus when he wrote, "But he who looks into *the perfect law of liberty* and continues in it, and is not a forgetful hearer but a doer of the work, this one will be blessed in what he does" (Jas 1:25, emphasis added). But he may also have had in mind "the message contained in apostolic preaching and now embodied in the New Testament" (D. Edmond Hiebert, *James* [Chicago, IL: Moody Press, 1979], 136). Davids reflects the view of many commentators when he says that James has in mind, "Jesus' reinterpretation of the law...the OT ethic as explained and altered by Jesus" (Peter Davids, *James* [Grand Rapids, MI: Eerdmans, 1982], 100).

MacArthur also says that the faith of some of the readers is "no different from the demons' belief (v. 19)" (p. 186). Without discussing Jas 2:19, he implies that it means that neither the demons nor some of the readers really believe in monotheism. Yet that is not a reasonable conclusion.[4] James 2:19 says, "You believe that God is one. You do well. Even the demons believe [that]—and tremble!" (author's own translation). The point is not that demons (or James) have defective faith. Remember that the "you" in verse 19 refers to James himself because this is the objector speaking. Belief in monotheism is belief in something which is true. There is indeed only one God.

The point is that both James and the demons believe in monotheism; yet while James does well ("you do well"), i.e., he does good works, the demons do not. The demons's belief in God leads them to tremble (cf. Matt 8:29). But it does not lead them to doing good works (like James does). Thus the faith of demons does not benefit anyone, but the faith of James does.

If MacArthur wishes to say that whenever a born again person fails to fulfill the law of liberty, then his faith *is not productive*, there would be no grounds for objection. But that is not what MacArthur is saying.

Finally, note the reference in the section title to "dead faith" ("Eternal Life from Dead Faith?" p. 186). The expression *dead faith* does not occur in Jas 2:14-26 or anywhere in the Bible. Three times James says, "faith without works is dead" (2:17, 20, 26). But what *dead* (*nekros*) means is obvious in light of the phrase at the end of verse 16, "what does it profit?" The word *dead* in verse 17 (as well as in verses 20 and 26) is used figuratively to refer to faith that *does not profit*.

Imagine you went to your mechanic to find out what was wrong with your car and he said, "A car without gas is dead." Would you think he was saying, "You don't have a car. What you call a car is actually not a car. You are a false professor"? No. You'd understand him to be saying that your problem is that you let your car run out of gas and so it is unproductive until you put gas in it.

---

[4] Verses 18-19 are actually the words of an objector, not of James himself as verses 18 and 20 show. However, James certainly does not deny that demons believe in monotheism.

In philosophy there is the saying, "*A* cannot be *non-A*." An apple is an apple. An apple can't be something other than what it is. A car cannot be a non-car. Faith cannot be non-faith. And so on.

When James says, "faith without works is dead," he is talking about faith, not non-faith. He is saying that faith which is not applied is unprofitable, unproductive, useless to meet its intended purpose. It's like a car without gas. But James is not saying that faith without works is non-faith. MacArthur's suggestion is both illogical and inconsistent with the context.

MacArthur ends this section by quoting 2 Tim 2:12 and alluding to John 3:17-18. Again, he fails to explain either text. He assumes, but does not show, that reigning with Christ in the life to come (2 Tim 2:12) is something all believers will do. After quoting 2 Tim 2:12 he says,

> Endurance is the mark of those who will reign with Christ in His kingdom. Clearly, enduring is a characteristic of true believers, while disloyalty and defection reveal a heart of unbelief...God's faithfulness is a blessed comfort to loyal, abiding believers but a frightening warning to false professors (p. 188).

Yet what about the second half of verse 12? Does it not say, "If we deny Him, He will also deny us"? Who is the *we* and the *us*? (MacArthur paraphrases that with these words, "Those who deny Christ, He will deny," p. 188.) Is this not the same *we* in "If we endure, we shall also reign with Him"? Paul is saying that *believers* may or may not endure in their confession of Christ (cf. Matt 10:32-33) and *if* we do not endure, *then* we will not reign. Compare Luke 19:20-26. The third servant does not rule at all even though he is a servant (vv 20-26) and not one of the enemies of Christ who are slain (v 27). Compare that with Rev 2:26, where ruling with Christ also requires endurance. All Christians will enter the kingdom as 1 Thess 5:9-11 shows. But only enduring ones will rule.

Second Timothy 2:11 and 13 have been called *twin pillars of eternal security*. If we've died with Him, then we will live with Him forever (v 11). And even if we are faithless, He remains faithful to His promise of everlasting life to all who believe in Him (cf. John 3:16-18). To be unfaithful to His own promise would be to deny

Himself. Paul clearly suggests that Christians might be unfaithful to Jesus, but Jesus will never be unfaithful to Christians.

So, let's return to the section title. Can you have everlasting life if your faith is not 100% productive? Let's say you failed to meet the need of a fellow believer *one time* in your entire life (Jas 2:15-16). Are you doomed to hell? What if you met the needs of fellow believers many times, but failed *five times*? What's the threshold for proving you have what MacArthur calls *spurious faith*?

If failing to meet the needs of a brother or sister proves that someone is not born again, then the only person who has everlasting life is one who died at the moment of faith and didn't have an opportunity to sin. We know from Scripture that we all fall short of the glory of God (Rom 3:23) and if we say we have no sin we are liars and the truth is not in us (1 John 1:8, 10). No believer obeys the Lord perfectly. Every believer has failed to meet a need around him at some point. As James says earlier in chapter 2, "whoever shall keep the whole law, and yet stumble in one point, he is guilty of all" (Jas 2:10).

Is not our salvation from eternal condemnation "not of works, lest anyone should boast" (Eph 2:8-9)? And yet, under MacArthur's gospel everlasting life is a direct result of works that you do. That is not the gospel according to Jesus (cf. Gal 1:6-12; 2:16; 5:1-4).

Faith as Scripture Describes It

MacArthur pays lip service to the necessity of faith for salvation, but what he emphasizes is the necessity of works for salvation. He accomplishes this feat by redefining faith as repentance, submission, obedience, and perseverance.

Here is the logic:

Major premise: Justification is by faith.[5]
Minor premise: Faith is turning from sins, submission, obedience, and perseverance.

---

[5] MacArthur mentions justification by faith *alone* only twice in *TGAJ* (p. 14, 191; on p. 176 he renounces those who "loudly declare they are justified by faith alone"). By contrast, he speaks of "justification by faith" eight times (pp. 13, 176 [favorable citation of Ironside], 195, 210, 211 [favorable citing of Lloyd-Jones], 247, 255, 258). See the discussion of Paul in Appendix 1 for more details.

Conclusion: Justification is by turning from sins,
                     submission, obedience, confessing Christ,
                     and perseverance.

To get there MacArthur first quotes Eph 2:8-9. Instead of seeing *everlasting life* as "the gift of God" [*Theou to dōron*] which is not of works, MacArthur claims that *faith* is the gift Paul is discussing.

MacArthur rightly points out that the word *that* in Greek is neuter and the word *faith* is feminine. He suggests that the neuter demonstrative pronoun ("that") either refers to "the act of believing" or to "the entire process—grace, faith, and salvation" (p. 188). But either way, he concludes that Paul is saying that "faith is an integral part of the 'gift' His grace bestowed on us" (p. 188). Of course, this is a major tenet of Calvinism, i.e., that the new birth occurs *before* faith.

Yet Greek grammar contradicts MacArthur's conclusion. Paul would have used a feminine form of *that* if he wished to refer to faith. The neuter refers to the salvation, which verse 5—"[He] made us alive together with Christ (by grace you have been saved)"—makes clear is everlasting life. This is consistent with our Lord's own teaching in John 4:10-14 that everlasting life (v 14) is "the gift (*dōrea*) of God" (v 10). The Lord said the same thing in Rev 22:17, "And let him who thirsts come. Whoever desires, let him take the water of life freely [*dōrean*]." None of this is discussed by MacArthur.

In addition, MacArthur skips over the part about "not of works, lest anyone should boast." Of course, if justification/salvation is not of works, then he has to work around that. He does so by simply failing to discuss that part of Eph 2:8-9.

Next MacArthur cites *part* of Phil 1:29, "To you it has been granted for Christ's sake...to believe in Him" (p. 188). He implies, but does not show, that the word *granted* means that faith is a divine gift, where God first regenerates unbelievers and then gives them faith in Christ. Yet that is not what the verse says. It says, "For to you it has been granted on behalf of Christ, not only to believe in Him, *but also to suffer for His sake*" (emphasis added).

Why did MacArthur leave off the part about being granted the right to suffer for Christ? Is that also something forced on people? That is not what the Apostles said. After they were beaten for their faith Luke tells us, "So they departed from the presence of the council, rejoicing that they were counted worthy to suffer shame for His name" (Acts 5:41). Notice they were granted the right to suffer for Christ because "they were counted worthy." Not all believers were counted worthy to suffer for His name.

Against MacArthur's Calvinistic belief that no one can believe in Christ apart from the divine gift of faith, the Bible teaches that all unbelievers are capable of believing in Christ. The Lord says, "The devil comes and takes away the word out of their hearts, *lest they should believe and be saved*" (Luke 8:12, emphasis added). If all are incapable of believing in Christ until God gives them the ability to believe, then what the Lord says here does not make sense. There would be no need for the devil to come and snatch away the word.

The Lord Jesus said to self-righteous people, "You search the Scriptures, for in them you think you have eternal life; and these are they which testify of Me. *But you are not willing to come to Me that you may have life* (John 5:39-40, emphasis added). Plainly this means that if Jesus' listeners had been willing to believe in Him, then God would have shown them that Jesus is the Source of everlasting life, not their works (cf. Acts 10:4-6, 43; 11:14; 13:46; 16:14).

MacArthur's next claim is that faith "has an enduring quality that guarantees it will endure to the end" (p. 189). To prove that he uses a verse that talks about the enduring effect of the financial support of the Philippians to Paul's gospel ministry: "being confident of this very thing, that He who has begun a good work in you will complete it until the day of Jesus Christ" (p. 189). MacArthur wrongly assumes "He who has begun a good work in you" refers to God giving them faith in Christ. Yet the context makes it clear that the good work in view is their financial support[6] that will have enduring fruit until the day of Jesus Christ, that is, until the Judgment Seat of Christ: "I thank my God upon every remembrance of you, always in every prayer of mine making request for you all with joy, *for your fellowship in the gospel from the first day until now*" (Phil 1:3-5, emphasis added).

---

[6] The words, "He who has begun a good work in you" refers to God enabling and motivating the believers in Philippi to support Paul's ministry. Even that was not a gift from God in the sense that it was simply laid on them. It was an opportunity that God allowed them to have. Of course, he allows all believers the opportunity to invest in His work via our giving.

If, as MacArthur says, saving faith "has an abiding quality that guarantees it will endure to the end" (p. 189), then why are there so many examples in Scripture of born again people whose faith did not endure?

In Luke 8:13 the Lord Himself tells of someone who believed the saving message and later fell away. MacArthur does not mention or explain that verse here. In fact, he doesn't even mention or explain it *anywhere in TGAJ* (see the Scripture index), although he does discuss Matthew's version of the parable of the four soils (chapter 11, pp. 127-36, see esp. p. 133 for his explanation of Matt 13:20-21). What is interesting is that he says concerning the second soil, "It responds positively, but not with saving faith" (p. 133). Yet in Luke 8:12 the Lord says that the devil takes away the word lest they should believe *and be saved.* Then in Luke 8:13 the Lord says that the second soil "believed for a time and in time of temptation fell away." Clearly the Lord is speaking of believing *the saving message* mentioned in the prior verse.

What of 1 Tim 1:18 where the Apostle Paul says that Hymenaeus and Alexander "concerning the faith have suffered shipwreck"? And what about 2 Tim 2:17, "Hymenaeus and Philetus are of this sort, who have strayed concerning the truth, saying that the resurrection is already past; and they overthrow the faith of some"? You don't suffer shipwreck unless you are on the ship. Unbelievers cannot "suffer shipwreck" "concerning the faith" and cannot "stray concerning the truth." Notice too that these men "overthrow the faith of some." None of this is discussed by MacArthur.

If MacArthur is right, then he does not know if he is born again, for he cannot be sure he will persevere in faith or in good works (1 Cor 9:27). If he fell away either doctrinally or morally, then by his own theology he would prove he had been a false professor. Calvinist pastors and theologians have admitted this to me in discussions and even in public debates. Lordship Salvation is a gospel of doubt.

MacArthur claims, "Clearly, the biblical concept of faith is inseparable from obedience" (p. 190). So justification by faith alone equals justification by obedience alone? For support he cites John 3:36, "He who believes in the Son has everlasting life; and he who does not believe the Son shall not see life, but the wrath of God abides on him." As you can see, the NKJV translation says, "he who does not *believe* the Son," rather than the NASB's "he who does not *obey* the Son." Both are legitimate translations since the verb in question is *apeitheō*. Its basic sense refers to the act of disobeying. Since the Father sent the Son so that people would believe Him (John 6:28-29), failing to believe in the Son is an act of disobedience.[7] BAGD says of the use of *apeitheō* in John 3:36:

> Since in the view of the early Christians the supreme disobedience was a refusal to believe, *apeitheō* may be restricted in some passages to the meaning *disbelieve, be an unbeliever.* This sense, though greatly disputed (it is not found outside our literature), seems most probable in John 3:36; Acts 14:2; 19:9; Rom 15:31, and only slightly less probable in Rom 2:8; 1 Pet 2:8; 3:1 (p. 82D, italics theirs).[8]

However, MacArthur confuses things, pretending that something other than unbelief is meant in John 3:36.

If you want to know what the section title talks about, "Faith as Scripture Describes It" (p. 188), then read the Scriptures, especially the Gospel of Belief, which is how Tenney described John's Gospel.

Faith as Jesus Presented It

MacArthur ends the chapter attempting to show that the Lord Jesus taught justification by repentance, obedience, submission, confession, and perseverance. He starts with a discipleship passage, the Beatitudes in Matt 5:3-12, yet he leaves out most of the verses. He only quotes verse 3 (p. 192). Possibly the reason he quotes verse 3 is because it ends with "for theirs is the kingdom of heaven." He doesn't see that as referring to *rewards* in the kingdom (cf. Matt 5:11-12, quoted below), but as referring to who *gets into* the kingdom.

After giving short (a few words) summaries of verses 4-10, MacArthur says, "That is Jesus' description of the genuine believer. Each of the characteristics He names—starting with humility and reaching fruition in obedience—is a consequence of true faith" (p. 192).

---

[7] Other verses that use *apeitheō* in the same way, to refer to unbelief, include Acts 14:2; 17:5; 19:9; Heb 11:31; 1 Pet 2:7-8; 3:1; 4:17. Places in which Christ directly commanded people to believe in Him include John 10:37-38; 12:36.

[8] The 2000 edition of Bauer's dictionary, known as BDAG, did not include this statement from the earlier edition (known as BAGD). However, it is an outstanding observation that should have been retained.

Look at the last three verses of the Beatitudes, Matt 5:10-12,

> "Blessed are those who have been persecuted for the sake of righteousness, for theirs is the kingdom of heaven.
>
> Blessed are you when people insult you and persecute you, and falsely say all kinds of evil against you because of Me.
>
> Rejoice and be glad, for your reward in heaven is great; for in the same way they persecuted the prophets who were before you."

Is that saving faith too? Is suffering for Christ another name for believing in Him? If so, now faith has become repentance, obedience, submission, confession, perseverance, and suffering for Christ. The list just keeps on growing.

The word *believe* occurs 99 times in John's Gospel. If MacArthur is really interested in understanding what saving faith is, why not go to John and discuss what those verses mean? Jesus asked Martha, "Do you *believe* this?" (John 11:26b, emphasis added). He wasn't asking about her obedience, her repentance, her submission, her suffering, or her perseverance. He was asking whether she was convinced that He guaranteed glorified bodies and everlasting life that can never be lost to those who believe in Him (John 11:25-26a). She answered yes and stated why she was convinced that was true (John 11:27).

Conclusion

Like most who teach salvation by works, MacArthur obscures what faith is. He thinks faith is obedience. Unfortunately for MacArthur, his attempts to support his claims from the Bible do not stand up to scrutiny. In the Bible faith is being convinced that something is true.

It is easy to miss the fact that in a chapter on saving faith MacArthur never once discussed *the object of saving faith*. What is it that a person must believe to be born again? Such a question is irrelevant to him because belief is repentance, submission, obedience, and perseverance.

The Lord Jesus emphasized that He Himself is the object of faith: "He who believes in Me has everlasting life" (John 6:47). He guarantees everlasting life to the one who believes in Him for it. That is a gospel of certainty. Such a gospel causes us to praise God, to live for Him, and to fervently desire to hear Him say, "Well done, good servant." But MacArthur's gospel is one of doubt and despair.

CHAPTER 19

The Promise of Justification

Introduction

In this chapter MacArthur talks about the doctrine of justification by faith. He does not specifically mention justification by faith *alone*, which was the cry of the Reformation (*sola fide*, by faith alone).

He points out that "this doctrine of justification is most fully expounded by the apostle Paul" (p. 195). That's true. So why discuss justification in a book entitled, *The Gospel According to Jesus*? Why not discuss *everlasting life* since that is what the Lord discussed while doing evangelism?

This chapter was not in the first edition of *The Gospel According to Jesus* (1988), probably because there is little if any teaching on forensic justification (being once and for all declared righteous by God) in the Lord's teachings.[1]

---

[1] Paul taught often on forensic justification (e.g., Acts 13:39; Rom 3:20-30; 4:5; 5:1; Gal 2:16). The Lord did not. If He *ever* taught on it, Luke 8:9-14 is the only place. However, it is more likely that in Luke 18:9-14 the Lord is there talking about *vindication*, not forensic justification. The publican was vindicated by his prayer and his attitude that day. That is, God was pleased with him. There is little if any evidence that the issue there is whether he was *declared righteous* by God.

What Is Justification?

MacArthur defines justification as follows: "*Justification* may be defined as an act of God whereby He imputes to a believing sinner the full and perfect righteousness of Christ, forgiving the sinner of all *un*righteousness, declaring him or her perfectly righteous in God's sight, thus delivering the believer from all condemnation" (p. 196, emphasis his).

MacArthur acknowledges that "Jesus rarely used the word *justification*" (p. 195). The only passage which he cites as showing the Lord taught justification by faith is Luke 18:9-14. Verse 14 reads, "I tell you, this man went down to his house justified rather than the other; for everyone who exalts himself will be humbled, and he who humbles himself will be exalted."

MacArthur concludes from this that justification is instantaneous, that it requires "no works of penance, no ritual, no sacrament, no confessional exercise, no meritorious deeds" (p. 196).[2]

He continues, "Here our Lord simply states the *fact* of justification; He does not explain the *theology* of it" (p. 196, emphasis his).

Several things are missing from MacArthur's discussion. First, if Luke 18:9-14 is about forensic justification before God, this is the one and only time the Lord spoke of it. MacArthur fails to mention that.

Second, faith in Christ is not mentioned or even implied in this passage. Does that mean justification is *not* by faith in Jesus?

Third, and most importantly, justification doesn't always mean *to declare righteous*. In the teachings of Christ and His Apostles the verb *dikaioō* often refers to vindication. Here are the four other uses of that verb by the Lord:

> "Wisdom is justified [i.e., vindicated] by her children" (Matt 11:19; Luke 7:35).

---

[2] MacArthur says that "works of penance" and "meritorious deeds" are not required for justification before God. He is rejecting a Catholic view of repentance and of merit here. *He is not rejecting the necessity of good works.* That is evident throughout *TGAJ*, including the last section in this chapter, "Justification and the Life of the Believer."

"By your words you will be justified [i.e., vindicated], and by your words you will be condemned" (Matt 12:37).[3]

"You are those who justify [vindicate] yourselves before men, but God knows your hearts" (Luke 16:15).

Here are examples from Paul and James of *dikaioō* referring to vindication:

For if Abraham was *justified* [*vindicated*] *by works*, he has *something* to boast about, but not before God (Rom 4:2, emphasis added).

For I know of nothing against myself, yet I am not *justified* [*vindicated*] *by this*; but He who judges me is the Lord (1 Cor 4:4, emphasis added).

And without controversy great is the mystery of godliness:

God [the Lord Jesus] was manifested in the flesh,

Justified [*Vindicated*] *in the Spirit*,

Seen by angels... (1 Tim 3:16, emphasis added).

Was not Abraham our father *justified* [*vindicated*] *by works* when he offered Isaac his son on the altar? (Jas 2:21, emphasis added).

---

[3] Matthew 12:37 refers to being *justified*, that is, vindicated, and to being *condemned*, that is, shown guilty, by *one's words* "in the day of judgment" (Matt 12:36). The issue is not being declared righteous or being eternally condemned by the words we speak. Forensic justification and eternal condemnation are based solely on faith in Christ or the lack thereof. The issue here is a judgment of works at the Judgment Seat of Christ (for believers) and the Great White Throne Judgment (for unbelievers). Some words said will be shown to have pleased God. Some will be shown to have displeased Him. Thus eternal rewards (for believers) and degrees of torment (for unbelievers) will be based on all works done, including the words which were spoken. See *The Grace New Testament Commentary*, edited by Robert N. Wilkin, Volume 1, s.v., "Matthew," by Hal Haller (Denton, TX: Grace Evangelical Society, 2010), pp. 58-59. The verb used in Matt 12:37 to refer to being condemned is *katadikazein*. It only occurs three other times in the New Testament, Matt 12:7; Luke 7:37; and Jas 5:6. None of those uses refers to eternal condemnation. Verses in which the related verbs *katakrinein* and *krinein* occur where they clearly do not refer to eternal condemnation include John 8:10-11; Rom 14:22-23; Jas 5:9.

> You see then that a man is *justified* [*vindicated*] *by works,* and not by faith only [lit., not only by faith] (Jas 2:24, emphasis added).

> Likewise, was not Rahab the harlot also *justified* [*vindicated*] *by works* when she received the messengers and sent them out another way? (Jas 2:25, emphasis added).

You may not have known about this other meaning of justification. MacArthur does not mention it. He simply declares his interpretation and moves on. He gives no evidence that forensic justification is being discussed.

In Luke 18:14 the Lord was saying that the tax collector "went down to his house *vindicated* rather than the other; for everyone who exalts himself will be humbled, and he who humbles himself will be exalted." So, this is not a clear example of justification by faith.

MacArthur ends this section with two extremes to avoid: "First, do not confuse justification with sanctification...second...Do not separate justification and sanctification so radically that you allow for one without the other" (pp. 196-97). This is an example of theological doublespeak. We are not to mix the two doctrines, and yet somehow we must not separate them.

Two years before the first edition of *The Gospel According to Jesus* came out one of my faculty colleagues at Multnomah Bible College, Dr. Al Baylis, said this to me:

> "Bob, the difference between your view and Lordship Salvation is whether or not one sees a sharp separation between justification and sanctification. You do. But others see justification and sanctification flowing into one another with no discernible separation."

That is exactly the point MacArthur is making. He finds it vital that one not give the impression that a person can be justified by faith alone, apart from works. We must tell people, when we evangelize them, that a person can be justified by "faith" only if he subsequently produces enough good works so that his entire life at the time of his death has been characterized by righteousness. And, since "true faith" is not simply believing,[4] MacArthur ultimately is saying that a person can only be justified by *repentance, surrender, commitment, confession, obedience, and perseverance* (i.e., "true faith") if he subsequently lives out that *repentance, surrender, commitment, confession, obedience, and perseverance.*

Imputed Righteousness

At the moment of justification the righteousness of Christ is imputed to the believer. This is positional, not experiential. This is not *infused righteousness* as Catholicism teaches.

The only thing to add is that it is God the Father who imputes Christ's righteousness to us. MacArthur implies this, but never says this directly. Regeneration is a work of God the Holy Spirit. Justification is a work of God the Father.

Forgiveness of Sins

MacArthur writes, "Justification also guarantees the forgiveness and remission of sins" (p. 198). Does he mean that justification *is the forgiveness of sins*? Or does he mean that forgiveness is a separate ministry of God (the Father) which occurs simultaneously with justification (and regeneration)? He likely means the latter, but he is not crystal clear on this point. The only passage he cites, Rom 3:24-26, does not mention the forgiveness of sins, which is confusing. Verses like Acts 10:43 or Col 2:13-14, which do mention the forgiveness of sins, would be important to mention.

MacArthur also fails to point out the difference between positional forgiveness and experiential (or fellowship) forgiveness. According to the Lord's Prayer we must forgive others if God the Father is going to forgive us. That is fellowship forgiveness. Likewise, the Apostle John says that we must confess our sins in order to be forgiven of those sins (1 John 1:9). Without discussing this distinction MacArthur risks leaving people with the wrong impression that believers no longer need forgiveness. We do. We need ongoing

---

[4] Of course, all faith is faith. There is no such thing as false faith, though a person who does not believe something may falsely profess to believe it. But if a person believes something, he believes it. I am using MacArthur's language here. He says that "true faith" is not believing, but is instead doing all the things he says that a person must do to make it into Christ's kingdom (cf. pp. 36, 44, 60, 66, 98, 149, 184, 185-93, 246, 250).

forgiveness to continue to walk in fellowship with God, though not, of course, in order to remain secure in Christ.

A New Standing

MacArthur now returns to the teaching of the Lord on the subject of justification (or vindication), Luke 18:9-14. He interprets those verses as teaching that "perfect righteousness was imputed to his [the tax collector's] account" (p. 199). He continues, "Forever thereafter he stood before God fully justified" (p. 199).

However, it is quite possible, as shown above, that *vindication*, not forensic justification, is in view. The self-righteous Jews who trusted in themselves that they were righteous were not vindicated before God by their words and attitudes. The tax collector who confessed his sinfulness was.

MacArthur somehow finds repentance in Luke 18:9-14, "All he [the tax collector] could do was repent and plead for mercy" (p. 199). Yet the words *repent* and *repentance* do not occur in the passage. Does saying that the words, "God, be merciful to me, a sinner" constitute repentance? Not according to what MacArthur has said before in his book, i.e., that repentance is turning from sins. Asking God for mercy is not the same as turning from sins. There is no evidence in Luke 18:9-14 that the tax collector turned from his sins.

MacArthur tries to find Lordship Salvation in Luke 18:9-14. Yet there is no indication that the tax collector turned from his sins, submitted to Christ, obeyed Him, began a life of perseverance, or did works of any kind. The name of Jesus is not even mentioned. MacArthur latches on to the word *justified* in English (*dikaioō* in Greek) and assumes it refers to forensic justification.

Neither the Lord nor Luke gives any indication that the tax collector's life radically changed, yet radical change is something which MacArthur says must happen when justification/regeneration occurs (pp. 15, 46, 81, 88, 107, 178, 180, 183, 206, 254).

In addition, Luke leads into this account with the words, "He spoke this parable to some who trusted in themselves that they were righteous, and despised others" (Luke 18:9). Despite MacArthur's occasional statements that Lordship Salvation proponents do not trust in themselves that they are righteous, trust of self is found over and over again in this chapter and in the whole book. It appears that those who hold to Lordship Salvation look down upon those whom they charge with antinomianism (the last section of this chapter), with easy-believism, or with being halfhearted. Here are a few typical examples:

> The gospel according to Jesus explicitly and unequivocally rules out easy-believism. To make all of our Lord's difficult demands apply only to a higher class of Christians blunts the force of His entire message. It makes room for a cheap and meaningless faith—a faith that may be exercised with absolutely no impact on the fleshly life of sin. That is not saving faith (p. 46).

> We could go on and on quoting Jesus' hard sayings... Clearly He was insisting on wholehearted commitment. He did not soften His demands with words that would accommodate the halfhearted (p. 275).

> We do not gain assurance by convincing our intellect that we are saved. True assurance is not an academic issue. There are no formulas that can bring it about. It is an important part of *the lifelong growth process of the Christian life*" (p. 273, emphasis added).

Since Luke 18:9-14 is the only passage MacArthur cites from Jesus' teaching on justification, why doesn't he discuss the larger context? Jesus' encounter with the rich young ruler is an encounter with a man like the Pharisee in Luke 18:9-14. And it follows just a few verses later (Luke 18:18-30). The Lord showed the rich young ruler that he could not obtain eternal life by keeping the Law since no one can keep the Law perfectly (Luke 18:18-23). Only God is good (Luke 18:19).

Space doesn't permit an extended discussion of the rich young ruler passage, especially since MacArthur doesn't discuss it.[5] However, it can be noted that what the Lord said was pre-evangelism, not evangelism. Nowhere did Jesus call the young man to faith in Himself. While that might be *implicit* in light of the fact

---

[5] For more information see, "Did the Rich Young Ruler Hear the Gospel According to Jesus?" by Hal Haller, *Journal of the Grace Evangelical Society* (Autumn 2000): 13-41. See also *The Grace New Testament Commentary*, Volume 2, "Luke," by Al Valdes, pp. 318-20.

that the Lord said no one is good and that the rich man would have treasure in heaven if he obeyed Him, it is not explicit.

The Lord used the incident to teach the disciples about temporal and eternal rewards as Luke 18:29-30 and the parallel in Matt 19:29-30 show. In fact, even the Lord's promise to the rich young ruler of having "treasure in heaven" (Luke 18:22; Matt 19:21) concerns more than kingdom entrance. The one who was rich in this life could be rich in the life to come. But that concerns eternal rewards (compare Matt 16:19-21; 1 Tim 6:17-19).

Of course, the rich young ruler would never obey the Lord and give away all his riches unless he first believed that he had everlasting life by faith in Him. Jesus could only promise him treasure in heaven if He could guarantee his eternal destiny.

Justification and the Life of the Believer

The burden of this final section seems to be that there is no justification apart from sanctification. MacArthur says, "Antinomianism is the notion of justification apart from sanctification" (p. 199).

Doesn't MacArthur's view more closely resemble that of the Pharisee in Luke 18:9-14 than that of the tax collector? The tax man did not point to his works. The Pharisee was thankful to God that his works set him apart (i.e., sanctified him) from sinners: "God, I thank You that I am not like other men—extortioners, unjust, adulterers, or even as this tax collector. I fast twice a week; I give tithes of all that I possess" (Luke 18:11-12).

Wasn't the Pharisee claiming that he was sanctified, set apart from other men? Wasn't he thanking God for this? Isn't the underlying idea that God had enabled him to do these works? Wasn't he claiming that his works showed he was sanctified? Of course, he trusted in himself (Luke 18:9) in the sense that he felt his sanctification, if it continued, would guarantee that he would obtain everlasting life. That is what MacArthur thinks as well. That is the point of this last section of chapter 19, as well as his entire book. Without progressive sanctification, there is no justification. MacArthur's view of justification is essentially the same as that of the Pharisee.

We should call all Christians to holiness; however, that does not mean that God guarantees that all Christians will live holy lives. Failure is possible in the Christian life as the Lord and His Apostles taught (cf. Luke 8:11-15; 19:16-26; Gal 6:7-9; 2 Tim 2:12; Heb 5:12; 6:4-8; Jas 5:19-20).

MacArthur claims that "Romans 6 is Paul's rebuttal to antinomianism" (p. 200). Since by antinomianism he means "justification apart from sanctification" (p. 199), he is incorrect. The only verses he cites in Romans 6 say: "knowing this, that our old man was crucified with Him, that the body of sin might be done away with, *that we should* no longer be slaves of sin [in our experience]. For he who has died has been freed from sin [in his position]" (Rom 6:6-7, emphasis added). Notice the word *should*. This is the subjunctive mood. It expresses possibility; not what is certain. Paul is saying that Christians should no longer be slaves of sin *in our experience* because we are no longer slaves of sin *in our position*.

Notice what Paul went on to say in Romans 6:

> Therefore do not let sin reign in your mortal body, that you should obey it in its lusts. And do not present your members as instruments of unrighteousness to sin, but present yourselves to God as being alive from the dead, and your members as instruments of righteousness to God. For sin shall not have dominion over you, for you are not under law but under grace (Rom 6:12-14).

Believers are no longer under sin's dominion *in our position*. That means we are free to live righteously. But it does not mean that we automatically escape sin's dominion *in our experience*. That is why Paul says, "Do not let sin reign in your mortal [i.e., dead] bodies" and "Do not present your members as instruments of unrighteousness to God."

Why would Paul issue such an exhortation if escape from sin's bondage is automatic for Christians? Why would he say something like this if it wasn't possible for believers to fall?

Later still in Romans 6 Paul says, "For just as you presented your members as slaves of uncleanness, and of lawlessness leading to more lawlessness, so now present your members as slaves of righteousness for holiness" (Rom 6:19).

Though we are "slaves of righteousness" (Rom 6:18) in our position, we must daily present ourselves to God in order to be "slaves of righteousness for holiness" in our experience. We need the Spirit to apply the resurrection life of Christ to our experience in order to live free from sin's dominion.

You may know the story of the sea captain who was relieved of command by his first officer. The first officer was now the captain. However, being a gracious man, he did not confine the former captain to the brig. He simply announced to the men that the captain had been relieved of command and they were no longer obliged to obey him.

Yet, the old captain came up to sailors and commanded them to do things. They were under no obligation to obey him any longer. However, many did obey his commands, whether out of fear or habit. The new captain had to remind the sailors that they were no longer subject to the orders of the old captain. In the same way, we are free from sin's dominion, but we need reminders of that fact, and we need to know *how to experience that freedom*, by daily presenting ourselves to God and looking to Him to empower us.

In the last two paragraphs of chapter 19, MacArthur summarizes his view of justification. He makes two points. First, "It [justification] is not merely a one-time legal transaction"(p. 200). Second, he then says in the very next sentence, "But a one-time legal transaction—justification—is the turning point" (p. 200). If it isn't "merely a one-time legal transaction," what is it? In MacArthur's view when God declares someone righteous, a turning point occurs. The person immediately experiences radical changes in the way he thinks, talks, and acts. He is not merely declared righteous. When the turning point occurs, the new believer begins to live righteously. Justification causes us to "walk in the light as He is in the light" (pp. 200-201).

Therein is the gospel of doubt.

What if you have believed in Jesus for everlasting life but you do not yet think you are a very holy person in your thinking, speaking, and actions? What if you are bothered by your sins? Maybe you have difficulty with anger, jealousy, or even anxiety over things like finances, health, and family concerns.

If our justification is measured by our sanctification as MacArthur says, then assurance is impossible prior to death. Doubt is the legacy of MacArthur's gospel.[6]

---

[6] Paul Carpenter, who reviewed a draft of this book, commented, "Paul said in Rom 8:15, 'For you have not received a spirit of slavery leading to fear again, but

Conclusion

The Lord did talk about justification. But He didn't teach about the same kind of justification as Paul did. Paul spoke primarily about justification as being declared righteous because Christ's righteousness is imputed to the believer at the moment of faith in Christ (Rom 3:24-28; 4:4-5; 2 Cor 5:21; Gal 3:6-14). The Lord taught about justification as vindication. Both are Biblical doctrines. MacArthur does not discuss this distinction. Instead he redefines faith to include a large number of works (e.g., repentance, obedience, submission, etc.). This redefinition enables him to claim the doctrine of justification by faith. However, as one can see, in his view forensic justification is not really by faith alone, but by repentance, obedience, submission, confession, and perseverance.

---

you have received a spirit of adoption as sons by which we cry out, "Abba! Father!"' Once a believer accepts what MacArthur teaches about these critical matters, he will indeed 'have received a spirit of slavery leading to fear again.' It cannot be otherwise!"

CHAPTER 20

The Way of Salvation

Introduction

Entry into a country is restricted by the laws of that country. If you lack a Passport or a Visa, you cannot simply enter any country you wish.

When the Lord Jesus returns, He will establish His own kingdom. Entrance into His kingdom will be restricted.

Jesus warned that people should enter by the narrow gate, and that few would find it (Matt 7:13-14). What did He mean? Was Jesus speaking about the way to enter *His kingdom* (cf. Matt 7:21-23)? And if so, what was He saying one must do in order to be guaranteed to spend eternity with Him in His kingdom?

Decisionism

The theme of MacArthur's introduction to this chapter is that people have a choice to make regarding their eternal destiny. A choice is a decision. MacArthur is saying that people must decide for Christ in order to be born again. Surprisingly, MacArthur is teaching *decisionism*, something which he decries as unbiblical earlier in *TGAJ*.

Until this point in *TGAJ* MacArthur has said that eternal life is *not* obtained by making a choice or by making a decision. He says that the words, "make a decision for Christ" "[are not] based on biblical terminology. They are the products of a diluted gospel. It is not the gospel according to Jesus" (p. 37).

In another chapter he says that the call to "'make a decision for Christ'...violates both the spirit and the terminology of the biblical summons to unbelievers" (p. 116). But despite these protestations, in chapter 20 he repeatedly says that regeneration is a choice or a decision:

> Each person inevitably must make *a choice*. Scripture presents *that choice* in several ways. Through Moses, God confronted the Israelites, saying, "I have set before you life and death, the blessing and the curse. So *choose life* in order that you may live" (Deut. 30:19) (p. 202, emphasis added).[1] Joshua challenged the Israelites as they entered the Promised Land, "*Choose for yourselves* today whom you will serve..." (Josh. 24:15) (p. 202, emphasis added)...[2]

> What to do with Jesus Christ is *a choice* each person must make, but it is not just a momentary *decision*. It is a once-for-all verdict with ongoing implications and eternal consequences—*the ultimate decision...a deliberate choice* of life or death, heaven or hell (p. 203, emphasis added).

Eight times in these two paragraphs MacArthur says we must choose or decide to serve Christ in order to be born again! Our eternal destiny, he says, depends on our decision.

So which is it? Do we call upon unbelievers to make a decision for Christ in order to be born again? MacArthur is being inconsistent.

The verses he cites deal with choosing *physical* life or *physical* death, not with heaven or hell. MacArthur fails to make this distinction. There are many who fail to notice that the Bible is also concerned about the things of this world, things that affect the quality of our life here and now.

---

[1] Deuteronomy 30:19 is speaking of choosing an abundant life now. But MacArthur uses it in reference to everlasting life, calling it "a deliberate choice of life or death, heaven or hell" (p. 203).

[2] While this verse in Joshua 24 refers not to choosing everlasting life, but to choosing a blessed life here and now, MacArthur cites it to support his idea that eternal salvation is "the ultimate decision," one which has "eternal consequences" (see the fourth quote given).

Does "choose life" in the pro-life movement refer to choosing everlasting life? Hardly. So too "choose life" in Deut 30:19 refers to choosing God's path which leads to fullness and length of physical life. God blesses obedience with extended and blessed life and He curses disobedience with temporal judgment and premature death (Lev 26; Deut 28-29; Eph 6:3).

The Lord Jesus never told people that believing in Him was a choice. The closest example is John 5:39-40 where He indicated that His listeners were "not willing to come to [Him] that you may have life." Coming to Jesus in John's Gospel is a synonym for believing in Him. Compare John 6:35, "He who comes to Me shall never hunger, and he who believes in Me shall never thirst." So a person's unwillingness to come to Jesus can keep them from believing in Him since they either will not listen to people share about Him, or they will not listen with an open mind. Compare also Matt 23:37 and John 7:17, both of which speak of people being willing or unwilling to believe what God says. But that is a far cry from MacArthur's decisionism.

In the first place MacArthur's decisionism is not about believing in Jesus, but about choosing to follow and serve Him (i.e., choosing to commit oneself). Thus MacArthur has works, not faith, in mind.

In the second place even the willingness to come to Jesus (John 5:39-40) is not the same as a decision to believe in Him. It is possible to choose not to go to church where the message of everlasting life is proclaimed. It is possible to decide not to listen to Christians who try to witness to you. It is possible to choose not to read the Bible. In that way belief in Christ does not occur (unless God somehow brings in the message despite the person's unwillingness). But the reason is because the person was not willing to listen, not because they heard the message and chose not to believe it. Once we hear the message we are either persuaded it is true or we are not. We can no more choose to believe in Jesus than we can choose to believe that two plus two is four or that water freezes at 32 degrees Fahrenheit.[3] The evidence either convinces us (i.e., we believe) or it does not (i.e., we do not believe).

---

[3] Pastor Paul Carpenter, who reviewed a pre-publication copy of *A Gospel of Doubt*, comments, "The bottom line regarding the place of the will with receiving eternal life is in *deciding to pursue the truth wherever it takes a person*. I think that is the point that Jesus is making in John 7:17. The classic example in the New Testament is

MacArthur says this concerning Matt 7:13-14 and the narrow way: "You will not find a plainer statement of the gospel according to Jesus anywhere in Scripture" (p. 203). But Matt 7:13-14 does not even mention believing in Jesus. How could a statement that doesn't mention faith in Jesus be the clearest statement of Jesus' gospel? Is not John 3:16 clearer? How about Eph 2:8-9? John 5:24? John 1:12-13? Acts 16:30-31? Romans 4:4-5? To say there is no clearer statement of Jesus' gospel than these verses is an incredible and unsupported claim.

MacArthur explains that "the narrow way" is the way of works: "It is a struggle, a battle, an extreme effort…entering the kingdom is like going into battle" (p. 205).[4] "Commitment is required" (p. 207). "The Lord makes the narrow path as hard as He possibly can, by demanding that those who really want to follow Him step out of the crowd and pick up a cross—an instrument of torture and death" (p. 207).

MacArthur says that the broad way is trying to enter the kingdom simply by faith, by what he calls "cheap grace or easy-believism" (p. 205). The broad way does not require commitment, obedience,

---

the case of the Bereans who 'searched the Scriptures daily *to find out* whether these things were so' (Acts 17:11). Luke then adds this telling report: 'Therefore many of them believed' (Acts 17:12). Could anything be plainer?"

[4] MacArthur points out that the word *agōnizomai* (translated as *strive*), from which we get the word *agonize*, "impl[ies] an agonizing, intense, purposeful struggle" (p. 205). He goes on to say, "It is the same word used in 1 Corinthians 9:25 of an athlete battling to win a victory" (p. 205). But the striving is *not to be born again*, as MacArthur suggests, but *to find the right gate* by which one is born again. Once a person finds the right gate, the striving is over. Of course, for some there is little if any striving needed. The Philippian jailer just had to ask, "Sirs, what must I do to be saved?" (Acts 16:30). The Apostle Paul merely had to ask, "Who are You, Lord?" (Acts 9:5). The woman at the well just had to continue talking with the Lord Jesus long enough to come to faith in Him (John 4:1-26). Of course, some had to search the Old Testament Scriptures (Acts 17:11). Since most are on the broad way of works salvation, it may take effort to find the true message of life. But the only condition of the new birth is faith in Christ. Once we come to faith, we are eternally secure and no agonizing, striving, or battling is needed to retain everlasting life. We are to fight the good fight of which MacArthur speaks, but that is for eternal rewards, not eternal destiny (1 Cor 9:24-27; 2 Tim 2:12; 4:6-8). It should also be noted that *agōnizomai* only occurs seven times in the New Testament, and it is only translated as *strive* in Luke 13:24 and Col 1:29. Translators recognize *agōnizomai* does not mean *fight* (as it does in John 18:36; 1 Tim 6:12; 2 Tim 4:7), *compete* (1 Cor 9:25), or *labor* (Col 4:12) in Luke 13:24.

and taking up the instrument of torture and death (pp. 205-207). Instead, the broad way is by grace through faith apart from works.

That's actually the opposite of what the Lord meant. We know clearly from John's Gospel, Acts, the epistles, and Revelation that the narrow way is *faith in Christ, apart from works* and the broad way is *the way of works* (e.g., John 6:28-29; Acts 15:7-11; 16:30-31; Eph 2:8-9; Titus 3:5; Rev 22:17).

The immediate context in Matthew 7 verifies that the broad way is legalism and the narrow way is faith in Jesus. At the start of the Sermon on the Mount the Lord said to enter His kingdom one must have a righteousness that exceeds that of the most religious people on earth (Matt 5:20). While He did not explain what He meant in the Sermon, the believing readers (Matthew is written for believers) know from the teachings of the Lord and His Apostles that such righteousness only comes from the imputed righteousness of Christ to the believer (John 3:16; 5:24, 39-40; 6:28-29; Rom 3:21-26; 4:3-5; 2 Cor 5:21; Phil 3:9).

And the context immediately following Matt 7:13-14 shows that the broad way is the way of legalism and works salvation. In Matt 7:15-20 the Lord shows that false prophets are identified by their false teachings, not by their works.[5] They look like sheep in terms of external behavior. But inwardly, in their beliefs and plans, they are ravenous wolves. In Matt 7:21-23 the Lord comes back to the issue of entering the kingdom which He first discussed in Matt 5:20. This time He says that those who point to their works as the reason why He should let them into the kingdom are sadly mistaken. They lack the surpassing righteousness needed which is only for believers. They are on the broad way of legalism/works salvation.

We see this repeatedly in John's Gospel too. For example, in John 6:28-29 the Lord answered a question about works and everlasting life: "What shall we do, that we may work the works of God?" Like the people in Matt 7:22, they are thinking their works should be good enough for them to get into the kingdom. Here is the Lord's answer: "This is the work of God, that you believe in Him who He

---

[5] Of course, what one says is a form of works. But in the sense of Jas 2:12, "so speak and so do," and Jas 2:14, "If someone says he has faith, but does not have works…" acts of love fall in a different category than wishing someone well ("be filled and be warmed," Jas 2:16).

sent." They asked about works (plural), the broad way. He answered about a single "work," believing in Him, the narrow way.

Over one hundred passages in the New Testament show that the narrow way is belief in Christ for everlasting life (e.g., John 1:12; 3:16; 5:24; 6:35, 37, 39, 47; 11:25-27; Acts 15:7-11; 16:30; Rom 4:4-5; Gal 2:16; 3:6-14; Eph 2:8-9; 1 Tim 1:16; 1 John 5:1, 9-13; Rev 22:17). For some sad reason, people want to earn their way into Jesus' kingdom. They must think it ridiculous that in light of the Lord Jesus dying on the cross for our sins that all we have to do to be born again is believe in Him. They even come up with derogatory names for the idea that all one must do is believe in Jesus for everlasting life. That view is pejoratively called names like *antinomianism, cheap grace,* and *easy-believism.* MacArthur uses those very names often in *TGAJ*: antinomianism (pp. 46, 197, 214, 266), cheap grace (pp. 20, 51, 68, 205, 277), and easy-believism (pp. 20, 37, 46, 52, 91, 205, 270, 276-77, 279).

Two Gates

If Matt 7:13-14 is *the plainest statement of the gospel according to Jesus,* then why does MacArthur refer to John's Gospel to explain what the narrow gate is? He cites John 10:1, 9 and 14:6 to explain that Jesus is the narrow gate. While those verses teach that Jesus (or more accurately, faith in Him) is the narrow gate, MacArthur has contradicted his statement on how plain Matt 7:13-14 is. The Lord does not indicate in Matt 7:13-14 that faith in Jesus is the narrow way. That clearly shows that Matt 7:13-14 is not the clearest statement on the gospel in Scripture.

MacArthur goes on to argue that "Entering the narrow gate is not easy...Salvation is not easy" (p. 205). Instead, "It is only for those who seek it with all their hearts" (p. 205).

These statements do not fit with MacArthur's Calvinistic ideas that faith is the gift of God and that regeneration precedes faith. If God regenerates people before they believe, and if He gives them faith, then there is no sense in which unbelievers can or do seek the narrow gate with all their hearts. Consequently, salvation would be very easy because God simply does it to us. If regeneration precedes faith, *then we have no part in that at all, not even believing, which comes later and is a gift of God.*

Yet MacArthur says that "salvation is not easy." He views salvation as difficult. He calls it "the ultimate decision" (p. 203).

Remember that MacArthur said at the start of this chapter that the decision to follow Christ "is not just a momentary decision" (p. 203). What's hard about the gospel, according to MacArthur, is that you must daily decide to follow and serve Christ until the very end of life. If you were to die during a time when you were not following Him, you'd miss the kingdom and you'd spend eternity in the lake of fire.

MacArthur says people are not born again by praying some sinner's prayer, by walking an aisle, or by raising your hand (p. 205). That is correct. Those things are man-made gimmicks. They cannot and do not save anyone. But what MacArthur calls for in their place is cut from the same cloth. He calls for an ongoing life-long decision (commitment) to follow and serve Christ. What he calls for is actually harder, for it must continue (i.e., persevere) until death. But it is the same species, decisionism and works salvation.

Two Ways

The broad way according to MacArthur has "tolerance of every conceivable sin—just as long as you say you love Jesus. Or as long as you are religious. Or whatever else you want to be" (p. 206).

He has created a straw man. While eternal life is indeed a free gift and cannot be lost, the Lord did not promote sin when He said that whoever believes in Him has everlasting life and shall never perish. There are many motivations for the eternally secure person to serve and obey God wholeheartedly (gratitude, love, desire for joy and peace and significance, desire to please God and help others, desire for eternal rewards, desire to avoid the painful and deadly consequences of a life out of fellowship with God, etc.). But fear of hell, contra MacArthur, should not be one of them. Fear of hell should be a thing of the past for the one who believes in the Lord Jesus Christ.

In MacArthur's view the narrow way, by contrast, does not tolerate anything less than wholehearted service for Christ: "Following Christ can cost your very life—it certainly costs your life in a spiritual sense. The fainthearted and compromisers need not apply" (p. 207).

The narrow way, according to MacArthur, is the way of following Christ, giving away your time, your money, and your talents. Required to make it into Jesus' kingdom is lifelong wholehearted devotion and lack of compromise. The one who hopes to get into the kingdom is one who is single-minded, hardworking, dedicated, committed, and driven.

Two Destinations

It is a misnomer to speak of heaven and hell as our two eternal destinations. The third heaven (2 Cor 12:2) is where Christians go *when they die* (2 Cor 5:8), but that is not where they will spend eternity. The eternal destiny of born-again people is *the new earth*, not heaven (Rev 21:1-27). Likewise, hell, also called Sheol or Hades, is where unbelievers go *when they die* (Rev 20:13), but that is not where they will spend eternity. The eternal destiny of unbelievers will be *the lake of fire*, not hell/Hades/Sheol (Rev 20:15).[6]

Our eternal destiny will be a physical destiny. We will not be disembodied spirits floating on clouds. We will live on the new earth with the Lord Jesus and all believers of all time.[7]

Genesis 1-3 describes God's original plan for humanity. If Adam and Eve had not sinned, mankind would have lived forever on earth. No one would ever have died. The un-cursed earth would have been mankind's home forever.

Revelation 21-22 presents God's recovery plan for humanity. Jesus' kingdom will be located not in the third heaven, but on the new earth (Rev 21:1-27). All born-again people of all time will be resurrected and will live on the new earth in glorified bodies. No one will ever die again. While believers might be able to visit the third heaven,[8] we will live on the new earth.

---

[6] For more information about the lake of fire, the place where unbelievers will spend eternity, see Robert N. Wilkin, *The Ten Most Misunderstood Words in the Bible* (Denton, TX: Grace Evangelical Society, 2012), chapter 6, "Hell," pp. 85-106.

[7] For more information about the new earth, the place where believers will spend eternity, see Wilkin, *The Ten Most Misunderstood Words in the Bible*, chapter 5, "Heaven," pp. 71-84.

[8] There are three heavens now: the air in which the birds fly (the first heaven), outer space where other galaxies are (the second heaven), and the place where God's Shekinah glory is especially present (the third heaven). In eternity the first two will still exist, though each will be new. (The "new heaven" of Rev 21:1 refers to the new outer space, that is, the new second heaven.) Possibly the third heaven will be in the

The third heaven is where regenerate people who have died reside *now*. But it is a *temporary residence* until the Rapture. After that they will live on the millennial earth and then the new earth.

Two Crowds

Like the two gates, the issue MacArthur sees in the two crowds is sin versus personal righteousness: "The broad way is the natural choice, from a human point of view. People prefer sin to righteousness" (p. 208).

MacArthur doesn't actually discuss the narrow way in this section. He mentions the narrow way, but without giving details. This final section is all about the broad way, the "easy road" (p. 209).

The idea of choice/decision, emphasized in the introduction to this chapter, is again prominent in the last section. MacArthur speaks of "the natural *choice*" and "the stark *choices*" (p. 208, emphasis added).

The message of this chapter is clear: choose today whom you will serve. Will you serve the Lord Jesus wholeheartedly, exclusively, and to the death, or will you serve Him when it is convenient, when it feels right, when you want to, when it is easy? The choice for MacArthur is clear. If you work hard for Christ your whole life, you might find out in the end that you did enough to make it into the kingdom. If you don't work hard for Christ day in and day out, then you are on the broad road that leads to the lake of fire. According to MacArthur your eternal destiny depends upon what you do, not upon faith in the Lord Jesus Christ.

Conclusion

MacArthur wants people to serve and glorify God. That is a terrific aim. But we cannot serve and glorify God by abandoning the message that Jesus preached. The Lord preached that whoever believes in Him has everlasting life. That is the narrow way. Sadly that is the way rejected by all the religions of the world. Sadder still, that is also the way rejected by many who call themselves *Christians*.

New Jerusalem. But most likely it will continue to exist as well. See *The Ten Most Misunderstood Words in the Bible*, chapter 5, "Heaven."

CHAPTER 21

The Certainty of Judgment

Introduction

MacArthur begins this chapter on "The Certainty of [Final] Judgment" not with Scripture, but by citing the Reformers' debate with the Roman Catholics. The Catholics charged the Reformers as teaching, "If the perfect righteousness of Christ is imputed to sinners solely on the basis of faith, then those who have been justified can simply live any way they please yet be guaranteed of heaven" (p. 210).[1]

The answer of the Reformers, according to MacArthur, was to introduce the need of works on the back end. That is, they went on to say that only those who persevered in faith and good works were elect and would obtain entrance into the kingdom: "The Reformers answered that charge by showing that sanctification is inevitable in the experience of every true believer" (p. 210).

In the introduction to the chapter, MacArthur quotes three passages, without explanation,[2] to support his point that holy living is

---

[1] MacArthur's acceptance of this objection is amazing. He says that righteousness is not imputed solely on the basis of faith in Christ. Ongoing good works are necessary to be "guaranteed of heaven."

[2] While he does give four sentences of discussion after he quotes Heb 12:14, it should be noted that this is his *application*, not his *explanation*. He begs the question by assuming his interpretation is correct and then applying it. He simply sees the

required for one to enter the kingdom (and to have assurance that one will enter).

MacArthur quotes Heb 12:14, which says, "Pursue peace with all people, and holiness, without which no one will see the Lord."

He also quotes Matt 7:21-23 where the Lord says,

> "Not everyone who says to Me, 'Lord, Lord,' shall enter the kingdom of heaven, but he who does the will of My Father in heaven. Many will say to Me in that day, 'Lord, Lord, have we not prophesied in Your name, cast out demons in Your name, and done many wonders in Your name?' And then I will declare to them, 'I never knew you; depart from Me, you who practice lawlessness!'"[3]

MacArthur cites Matt 5:20 as well. That is where the Lord said, "For I say to you, that unless your righteousness exceeds the righteousness of the scribes and Pharisees, you will by no means enter the kingdom of heaven."

None of those passages prove his point that a life of holiness is required to enter the kingdom. Indeed, two of the passages, Matt 5:20 and Matt 7:21-23, contradict his point. And the third passage, Heb 12:14, is not discussing this issue at all, as MacArthur himself says in his own commentary on Hebrews. There he says that the point is that "when unbelievers see a Christian's peacefulness and holiness, they are attracted to the Lord."[4] Of course, the same would be true of fellow believers in our churches. When we see believers in our churches manifesting His holiness before us, then we see the Lord in our presence.

MacArthur urges people to look to their works to see if they are truly born again so they won't be caught unawares at the final

---

word *sanctification* in the NASB (nearly every other translation has *holiness*) and then runs with that. He does not discuss the context at all.

[3] MacArthur does have three paragraphs applying Matt 7:21-23. But what he is doing is assuming his interpretation and applying it, not proving his interpretation. For example, notice that he assumes that "he who does the will of the Father" refers to the one who lives a godly life (p. 212), not to the one who believes in Jesus (cf. Matt 21:28-32; John 6:39-40). Yet he does not discuss how that fits the context (it does not). Nor does he discuss other uses of that expression in Matthew and in the other Gospels. He simply assumes his understanding.

[4] John F. MacArthur, *Hebrews*, The MacArthur New Testament Commentary (Chicago, IL: Moody Bible Institute, 1983), p. 406.

judgment. Of course, as Engelsma,[5] Zachman,[6] and many others have pointed out, if one looks to his works for assurance, he will not have assurance, but doubt. The believer is to look to Christ, not himself, for assurance of his eternal destiny.

The Final Judgment?

The title of this Chapter is "The Certainty of Judgment." Thus the theme for this chapter is judgment. By *judgment* MacArthur means "the final judgment" (p. 211) where people find out what will be "their [eternal] destiny" (p. 211).

But what about John 5:24? There the Lord promised that the one who believes in Him, the One sent by the Father, "shall not come [future tense] into judgment." That promise is surrounded by two other promises of eternal security. It is preceded by the promise that the one who believes in Jesus "has [present tense] everlasting life." It is followed by the promise that the believer "has passed [past tense] from death into life." All three promises (present, future, and past) concern the believer's security regarding everlasting life. Thus the promise that the believer "shall not come into judgment" means that no believer shall come into judgment *concerning his eternal destiny*, which is secure.

MacArthur does not mention John 5:24 in this chapter or anywhere in *TGAJ*.

Believers will be judged, but not to determine their eternal destinies. They become eternally secure the moment they believe in Jesus (John 5:24). All believers will appear at the Judgment Seat of Christ (Rom 14:10-12; 1 Cor 9:24-27; 2 Cor 5:9-10; 1 John 2:28; 4:17-19). At issue will be Christ's approval and eternal rewards, not destiny. MacArthur does not mention the Judgment Seat of Christ anywhere in this chapter or in the entire book.

---

[5] David J. Engelsma, *The Gift of Assurance* (South Holland, IL: The Evangelism Committee of the Protestant Reformed Church, 2009). For example, he says, "Puritan preaching...is forever questioning your assurance, forever challenging your right to assurance, forever sending you on a quest for assurance, and forever instilling doubt," p. 53.

[6] Randall C. Zachman, *The Assurance of Faith: Conscience in the Theology of Martin Luther and John Calvin* (Minneapolis, MN: Fortress Press), 1993. He does show, however, that Calvin and Luther opened the door for the later Puritan view of assurance (pp. 85-87, 220-23).

He also does not mention the Great White Throne Judgment or Rev 20:11-15 in this chapter or anywhere in his book.

Since he is discussing eschatological judgment in this chapter, it would seem essential that he discuss John 5:24, the Judgment Seat of Christ, and the Great White Throne Judgment. Yet he does not. Those are significant omissions.

Saying without Doing: The Sin of Empty Words

The title of this section tells the story. MacArthur believes in *salvation by doing*. For proof he turns to Matt 7:21-23, which reads:

> "Not everyone who says to Me, 'Lord, Lord,' shall enter the kingdom of heaven, but he who does the will of My Father in heaven. Many will say to Me in that day, 'Lord, Lord, have we not prophesied in Your name, cast out demons in Your name, and done many wonders in Your name?' And then I will declare to them, 'I never knew you; depart from Me, you who practice lawlessness!'"

MacArthur interprets the Lord to be saying that at the Great White Throne Judgment some will be cast into the lake of fire because they did not have a sufficient amount of good works (pp. 213-15).[7]

He does not discuss what "the will of My Father" means in this passage. He assumes that the will of the Father refers to obeying God's commandments. Thus he encourages the readers to examine their works to see if their lives reflect true holiness, that is, obedience to the commandments. MacArthur thinks the problem is these people of Matt 7:21-23 did not really serve Christ faithfully. However, his analysis is flawed. The will of the Father concerning everlasting life is not a life of obedience, but it is faith in Jesus.

The expression *the will of the Father* occurs in John 6:39-40 and means believing in Jesus: "This is the will of the Father who sent Me, that of all He has given Me I should lose nothing, but should raise it up at the last day. *And this is the will of Him who sent Me,*

---

[7] The Great White Throne Judgment passage, Rev 20:11-15, specifically says, "anyone not found in the Book of Life was cast into the lake of fire" (Rev 20:15). The basis of condemnation is not what is in the books of works (Rev 20:12). Failure to believe in Christ keeps one out of the Book of Life and hence out of the kingdom as well.

that everyone who sees the Son and believes in Him may have everlasting life; and I will raise him up at the last day" (emphasis added).

The expression *the will of the* [or his] *father* also is found in Matt 21:31a,

> "But what do you think? A man had two sons, and he came to the first and said, 'Son, go, work today in my vineyard.' He answered and said, 'I will not,' but afterward he regretted it and went. Then he came to the second and said likewise. And he answered and said, 'I go, sir,' but he did not go. Which of the two did *the will of his father*?" (Matt 21:28-31a, emphasis added).

We know that *the will of the Father* there refers to believing in Jesus because of what the Lord goes on to say in verses 31b-32,

> Jesus said to them, "Assuredly, I say to you that tax collectors and harlots enter the kingdom of God before you. For John came to you in the way of righteousness, *and you did not believe him*; but tax collectors and harlots *believed him*; and when you saw *it*, you did not afterward relent *and believe him*" (emphasis added).

John the Baptist called for his listeners to believe in Jesus (John 1:7-8; John 3:36; Acts 19:4). The Lord three times in vv 31-32 speaks of believing (or not believing) John the Baptist. The Pharisees were like the son who said he'd do the will of the father, but did not. The tax collectors and harlots are like the son who said they would not do the will of the father, but then they did. The former did not believe in Jesus. The latter did.

The will of the Father in relation to everlasting life is *that we believe in His Son.* If the will of the Father refers to obeying all His commands, then no one would ever be able to enter the kingdom because to disobey just one of God's commands shows that one is a sinner and thus unable to enter the kingdom on the basis of deeds done (i.e., behavior). James said, "For whoever shall keep the whole law, and yet stumble in one point, he is guilty of all" (Jas 2:10).

This passage actually *contradicts* Lordship Salvation. Notice that MacArthur goes on to say that we should look to our obedience to see if we are truly saved. That is what the people in Matt 7:22 did! They looked to their obedience, their works, the miracles they did in Jesus' name. And notice the Lord didn't deny that they had done works in His name. And yet, despite all the works they had done, Jesus said, "I never knew you; depart from Me, you who practice lawlessness." Comparing that statement with His statement in verse 21 about the need to do the will of the Father, it is clear that they had failed to do the will of the Father. That is, regardless of how many works they had done in Jesus' name, they had failed to believe in Jesus for everlasting life. Thus Jesus did not know them.

MacArthur thinks the fact that Jesus spoke of their "lawlessness" means they had not done enough good works. But the reason the Lord Jesus says "you who practice [or work] lawlessness" is because of the truth found in Jas 2:10. According to the world's standards, someone is good so long as his good deeds outweigh his bad deeds. Even MacArthur thinks that you can tell a true believer from a false one because their good works win out in the end.

But God has a different standard. He does not grade on the curve. The Bible says that one sin makes a person guilty of lawlessness, and no good work is ever the basis for our regeneration or our assurance. Works do not save us or assure us. While the death of Christ makes people savable, His death alone puts no one into the Book of Life. That only happens through believing in Christ. Anyone not in the Book of Life will be cast into the lake of fire (Rev 20:15) because there are only two ways, one possible and one impossible, to gain entrance into the kingdom, by faith in Christ (possible) or by sinlessness (impossible). Since no one (other than the Lord Jesus) is sinless, the only possible way to enter is by belief in Christ.

Stop and think about it. Who at the Great White Throne Judgment will point to works they have done in Jesus' name in an effort to prove they should enter into the kingdom? Would it not be those who believe in Lordship Salvation? Church Age believers will not be judged at the Great White Throne Judgment. The Lord promised that believers would not come into judgment concerning their eternal destiny (John 5:24).[8] Matthew 7:21-23 contradicts Lordship Salvation.

Many of the people who hold to Lordship Salvation formerly believed in justification by faith alone apart from works. According to his own testimony, John MacArthur himself falls in that category. Thus they remain born again and eternally secure even

---

[8] It is possible that Church Age believers *will be present* at the Great White Throne Judgment as witnesses. But we will not be judged there.

though they no longer believe the message of John 3:16. In spite of what they think, they will not be judged at the Great White Throne Judgment (John 5:24).

But sadly many people who hold to Lordship Salvation have never believed in justification by faith alone and hence have not yet been born again. Unless they believe in Christ for everlasting life before they die, they will find themselves at the Great White Throne Judgment. And when they appear before the Lord, pointing to the works they did in His name, they will be sorely disappointed.

If I cannot enter into the kingdom on the basis of faith in Christ, apart from works, then I will not enter at all. I know I'm a sinner. I fall short of God's glory every day. I don't match up to my own standards; so I know I don't match up to God's. The same is true with everyone on earth. We either will enter the kingdom by faith in Christ, apart from works, or we won't enter at all.

Periodic Doubts?

MacArthur makes a very telling statement about doubt: "Periodic doubts about one's salvation are not necessarily wrong" (p. 213). The word *periodic* means *repeated* or *happening at regular intervals*. Thus in MacArthur's view it is normal for born again people to doubt their eternal destiny over and over again until they die. But is that really normal?

Martha indicated she was sure that she had everlasting life (John 11:27). And the Lord did not rebuke her for saying she was sure.

Paul was not only sure of his own eternal destiny, he mentioned that Euodia, Syntyche, Clement, and his other coworkers were in the Book of Life (Phil 4:3). How could they have "periodic doubts about [their] salvation" if inspired Scripture says their names are in the Book of Life?

MacArthur cites 2 Cor 13:5 to try to prove that repeated doubts about one's eternal destiny are healthy and normal. Yet he fails to cite the entire context, verses 1-7.

Verse 5 starts with "Test yourselves," or the Greek order, "Yourselves test." In verses 1-4 Paul pointed out that there were some in the church of Corinth *who were testing Paul to see if he truly spoke for God*: "since you seek a proof of Christ speaking in me" (v 3). The issue was not whether they thought Paul was born again. The issue was whether they thought God was behind what he was saying.

Paul turns the tables on them and says, "Yourselves examine." Stop examining me and start examining yourselves. Are you approved by Christ? Do you speak for Him? Are you in fellowship with Him?

This is clear when we see all of 2 Cor 13:5-7 (emphasis added),

> Examine yourselves *as to* whether you are in the faith. *Test yourselves* [*dokimazete*, from *dokimazō*, related to the noun *dokimos*, approved, qualified]. Do you not know yourselves, that Jesus Christ is in you?—unless indeed you are *disqualified* [or disapproved, *adokimos*]. But I trust that you will know that we are not *disqualified* [or disapproved, *adokimos*] (emphasis added).

Repeated concepts are italicized to highlight Paul's emphasis. The issue here is not assurance of one's *eternal destiny*, but assurance of *God's approval*. Not every believer lives a life that is worthy of his Christian calling. Not every believer will be approved by Christ at His Judgment Seat. The Apostle Paul indicated that even he himself was not sure that he would be approved by Christ (1 Cor 9:27). God approves of some of his children, but not all. That depends on whether or not we use our talents well. Of course, none of this is discussed by MacArthur. He quotes verse 5, but does not explain it.

The question about whether "Jesus Christ is in you" is not one of position in this context.[9] The context concerns experience (compare 2 Cor 5:1-4; 10:7). Was Christ abiding in them? Were they in fellowship with Him? All through First and Second Corinthians Paul affirms that the readers are born again (cf. 1 Cor 1:2; 3:1; 6:19; 15:58; 2 Cor 1:1; 3:1-3; 5:1-11).

---

[9] Philip Edgcumbe Hughes argues that the issue here is position. However, he says that position is well known by Paul and the readers. He says, "If such self-examination reveals that they have experience of the grace of God, then that alone is proof irrefutable that it is none other than Christ who speaks in Paul, for it was precisely through his ministry to Corinth that they received the gospel and passed from death into life…If they know Jesus Christ to be in themselves, then they know, by simple logic, that [Paul] is the one who proclaimed Jesus Christ to them…The Corinthian Christians are veritably Paul's epistle commendatory, addressed to the world at large (3:2); they are the seal of his apostleship in the Lord (1 Cor. 9:2)" (*The Second Epistle to the Corinthians*, NICNT [Grand Rapids, MI: Eerdmans, 1962]), pp. 480-81.

The reason why *periodic doubts about salvation* are common among those whom MacArthur teaches is because he preaches that a lifetime of good works are required to be able to enter the kingdom. But how good is good enough?[10]

This is evident in a 1989 reprint of a 17th century book by Puritan Matthew Mead for which MacArthur wrote the foreword. The title is telling: *The Almost Christian Discovered.*

MacArthur writes,

> *The Almost Christian Discovered* is a rare treasure. It reveals the force and fervor of Puritan spirituality as vividly as any work I know. It delivers the kind of potent message one longs to hear—but almost never does—in this age of cheap grace and shallow conversion...
>
> His arguments are devastating, and in the end the verdict is clear. The "almost Christian" is convicted.
>
> So, by the way, are the rest of us. Everyone but the most cold-hearted reader will sense some degree of conviction.[11]

Mead's book indeed causes those who agree with his reasoning to question whether they are truly born again or not. This is precisely what Calvinist Engelsma charges that all Puritans did:

> Puritan preaching...is forever questioning your assurance, forever challenging your right to assurance, forever sending you on a quest for assurance, and forever instilling doubt. The Spirit does not work assurance by means of a gospel of doubt.[12]

In an effort to make the supposedly inevitable periodic doubts about our eternal destiny more manageable, MacArthur ends this section with a disclaimer:

> Those with true faith will fail—and in some cases, fail pathetically and frequently—but a genuine believer will, as a pattern of life, be confessing sin and coming to the Father

---

[10] *How Good Is Good Enough?* is the title of a book by Andy Stanley. His answer is that perfection is required and we only get that by Christ's imputed righteousness when we believe in Him.

[11] Matthew Mead, *The Almost Christian Discovered* (Ligonier, PA: Soli Deo Gloria Publications, 1989), pp. i, iii-iv.

[12] Engelsma, *The Gift of Assurance*, p. 53.

for forgiveness (1 John 1:9). *Perfection* is the standard; *direction* is the test. If your life does not reveal growth in grace and righteousness and holiness, you need to examine the reality of your faith—even if you believe you have done great things in the name of Christ (p. 215).

Direction is not *perfection.* If the standard is perfection, as MacArthur says, not direction, then only perfect people can enter the kingdom. Since no one is perfect in his experience, no one would enter Jesus' kingdom if what MacArthur says is correct.

But let's say that somehow God will end up imputing Christ's righteousness to us, and thus making us perfect, *if in this life we manifested a righteous "pattern of life," a godly "direction," and "growth in grace and righteousness and holiness."* Even then, there could be no assurance. As MacArthur himself says, "even if you believe you have done great things in the name of Christ" (p. 215), that is no guarantee that you are kingdom bound (see Matt 7:21-23). Besides, as many Calvinist pastors and theologians have admitted to me, they can't be sure they will persevere in faith and good works in the future. Hence they can't be sure of their own eternal destiny, let alone the destinies of the people in their churches.

The issue in assurance for Lordship Salvation is not belief, but behavior. It turns our attention away from Christ and His promise of life to our "pattern of life," our "direction," and our "righteousness and holiness." For people like MacArthur, the direction of our lives, not the declaration of the Lord of lords, determines our assurance. And the results are always the same: doubt, doubt, and more doubt.

MacArthur's gospel is what Engelsma calls, "a gospel of doubt."[13]

It is ironic that in a chapter entitled "The *Certainty* of Judgment," the author *denies the possibility that anyone can be certain of his eternal destiny.*

God doesn't want His children to live in doubt.

Are you a parent? If so, do you want your children to have periodic doubts about whether they are truly part of your family?

Do you tell your children to examine the direction of their lives so they can see if they are really your children and if they will be

---

[13] Engelsma, *The Gift of Assurance,* p. 53.

allowed to continue to live with you? Of course not. That would harm your children.

God is the ideal Father. As such He wants His children to be certain of their eternal destinies all the time. Assurance promotes gratitude, love, and an abiding desire to please God.[14] Lack of assurance is not a good thing.[15] The gospel MacArthur proclaims is not the gospel according to Jesus.

Hearing without Obeying: The Sin of Empty Hearts

The final section deals with the closing illustration from the Sermon on the Mount, the houses built on the rock and on the sand (Matt 7:24-27). MacArthur says that the illustration "contrasts those who obey and those who do not" (p. 215). "Those without genuine righteousness will not enter the kingdom of heaven" (pp. 215-16). MacArthur understands the issue here to be *personal righteousness*, not *imputed righteousness*.

The closing illustration (Matt 7:24-27) applies to both unbelievers and believers.

Unbelievers need to build their lives on the rock which is Christ by believing in Him for everlasting life.

Believers need to build their lives on Christ the rock by allowing His teachings to change their thinking and thereby transform their behavior (John 8:31; 15:7; Rom 12:2; 2 Cor 3:18).

MacArthur thinks Jesus is teaching that in order to enter the kingdom, you need "genuine righteousness." Only "those who obey" will enter. Obedience, not faith, is the issue. Of course, for MacArthur *obedience is faith*, or at least, one aspect of faith. He is convinced that faith also includes repentance, submission, commitment, and perseverance. A person who obeys Christ for a few years and then stops will not obtain entrance into the kingdom because he failed to persevere.

In addition, a person who obeyed Christ in most areas of life, but failed to repent of a major sin in another area (e.g., drunkenness),

---

[14] In contrast, MacArthur thinks that assurance of eternal security is a license to sin. His reaction is similar to the Reformers when the Catholics charged that faith alone for everlasting life would lead to loose living and sinful conduct. So-called "fire insurance" *discourages* right living in their view.

[15] Lack of assurance fosters doubt and anxiety and creates the wrong incentive for service, fear instead of love and wanting to please the Lord.

would not enter. MacArthur does not mean to imply in this section that obedience alone grants everlasting life. It is obedience combined with repentance, submission, commitment, and perseverance.

"The difference [between the saved and the unsaved] will be seen in whether obedience followed the hearing, whether *a life of righteousness* followed the profession of faith" (p. 217, emphasis added). He adds one paragraph later, "The gospel according to Jesus clearly calls for *a radical difference*—not merely a new opinion, but *a response of full commitment*" (p. 218, emphasis added).

After saying, "The crowds thought He was wonderful," MacArthur continues, "But it was not a saving response; they had already started building on the sand.[16] There was *no repentance, no expression of obedience*—only analysis" (p. 218, emphasis added).

In this closing section MacArthur mentions five of what he believes are the leading conditions of everlasting life: repentance, full commitment, profession of faith, obedience, and perseverance.

Have you responded with "full commitment"? Do you have "a life of righteousness"? Do you see "a radical difference" in your life? If so, then you *may* be on your way to the kingdom. Or not. That is the dilemma MacArthur poses. According to MacArthur your eternal destiny depends on whether your deeds are as righteous as you think they are, and whether you persevere in those things until death.

That isn't the message that the Lord Jesus preached concerning everlasting life. He said, "he who believes in Me has everlasting life" (John 6:47). He said, "whoever believes in Him should not perish but have eternal life" (John 3:16). According to the Lord Jesus, the issue in kingdom entrance is faith in Him, not our works. But according to MacArthur the issue is our commitment and a life of righteousness.

Conclusion

At the Great White Throne Judgment people from all over the world, including many from within Christendom, will hope to be eternally saved on the basis of their works. Sadly, many who loved

---

[16] The first option is a straw man. No one other than a universalist is saying that anyone who thinks Jesus is wonderful is born again. The two options are salvation by grace through faith apart from works and salvation by grace through repentance, obedience, full commitment, profession of faith, and perseverance.

MacArthur's book *The Gospel According to Jesus* will be among them. And on that day, they will hear an awful truth from the Lord, "I never knew you; depart from Me, you who practice lawlessness!"

It will come as a terrible realization that no amount of good works can earn anyone a place in eternity. Committing even one sin means we worked lawlessness. The only people who know the Lord and are known by Him are those who have done the Father's will, that is, those who have believed in the Lord Jesus Christ for everlasting life.

When thinking about "The Certainty of Judgment," we should stand upon Scripture and not tradition.

If we believe the Lord Jesus, the certainty is that we will not be judged to determine our eternal destiny (John 5:24). We know with certainty that we have everlasting life and have already passed from death into life (John 5:24). We are certain that the only "work" (i.e., action) we can do to enter the kingdom is to believe in the Son of God whom the Father sent (John 6:28-29). We are sure that all of our righteous deeds are as filthy rags before God (Isa 64:6). We know with certainly that the Lord Jesus cannot and does not lie. What He promises, He fulfills.

We are sure of our eternal destiny because we are sure that our Savior lives and our Savior keeps His promises. And that certainty produces in us a profound sense of gratitude that moves us to give our lives in service for Him. We do not serve Him so that we might get into the kingdom. We serve Him because we love Him and are certain we will spend eternity in His kingdom with Him based not on what we have done or will do, but based on what He has done for us on the cross and what He has promised us as a result.

CHAPTER 22

The Cost of Discipleship

Introduction

MacArthur says, "In previous chapters we have touched on Jesus' call to discipleship. Here we will examine it more closely" (p. 219). There is little new in this chapter, other than a more extended discussion of Matt 10:32-33 and the addition of a few new conditions of obtaining everlasting life.

Denying the Self

"Jesus' summons to deny self and follow Him," MacArthur suggests, "was an invitation to salvation" (p. 219). That may sound a bit odd to those of you who have not been paying careful attention during the first twenty-one chapters. You may still think that John 3:16 is "an invitation to salvation." Yet John 3:16 says that "whoever believes in Him...has everlasting life." It says nothing about self-denial and following Christ. If self-denial and following Christ are invitations to salvation, then John 3:16 is not, unless, of course, we understand John 3:16 to be teaching self-denial and following Christ.

MacArthur has to add things to the Biblical text or change the meaning of terms in order to support Lordship Salvation.

For instance, take belief. Normally, according to MacArthur and Lordship Salvation, the concept of believing in the Bible simply refers to believing, that is, being convinced. Believing in monotheism, believing in prophecy, believing Jesus was born in Bethlehem, believing that Jesus died on the cross for our sins, these are all propositional beliefs. You are presented with a statement, like "David was king over Israel" and you either believe that is true or you do not. MacArthur agrees with that, of course; but he thinks that *saving faith* is the lone exception.

Whenever MacArthur speaks of *saving faith* he means repentance, surrender, commitment, obedience, following Christ, self-denial, and perseverance (in discipleship). Thus Jesus' promise of everlasting life that "whoever believes in Him" in John 3:16 actually is a promise of everlasting life for "whoever *denies self, follows the Son of God, turns from his sins, commits his life to Him, surrenders to His Lordship, obeys Him, and perseveres in all these things until death* has everlasting life…"

MacArthur says,

> A Christian is not one who simply buys "fire insurance,"[1] who "accepts Christ" just to escape hell. As we have seen repeatedly, true believers' faith expresses itself in submission and obedience. Christians follow Christ. They are committed unquestionably to Christ as Lord and Savior (p. 220).

What does he mean? He means that one cannot be born again simply by believing in Jesus for the promise of everlasting life and of never perishing (John 3:16; 5:24). Instead, one must commit, submit, obey, and follow Christ.

But the Gospel of John clearly shows, as we have seen repeatedly, that the Lord Jesus taught that whoever believes in Him has everlasting life and shall never perish. He never conditioned everlasting life on commitment, submission, obedience, or following Him. The Lord Jesus fought the Pharisees and other legalists who thought they would enter the kingdom due to their commitment, submission, and obedience.

Implicit in MacArthur's comments here is the idea that if someone has assurance of eternal security simply by believing in Jesus

---

[1] Reviewer Paul Carpenter comments at this point, "What an odd thing it is that this is precisely what MacArthur's soteriology is. That is, MacArthur teaches that one buys his fire insurance through the laborious experience of persevering in the faith, which, as is turns out, is really persevering in good works.

for everlasting life, then such belief promotes an ungodly lifestyle. He seems to think that anyone who did not think that his eternal destiny depended on his own faithfulness in service would go out and live like the devil.

I actually thought that way for many years. I had been raised in an extreme Arminian group. But in spite of my reservations, I came to believe in the free gift of everlasting life by faith alone, apart from works, during the start of my senior year in college. I did not want to believe that. I was compelled to believe it. For five meetings in a row, a Campus Crusade for Christ staff member kept quoting Eph 2:8-9 over and over again: "For by grace you have been saved through faith, and that not of yourselves; it is the gift of God, not of works, lest anyone should boast."

When I believed that, I was convinced I was saved and I could never lose my salvation. Though I did not know the expressions *eternal security* or *once-saved, always-saved*, I knew I was secure no matter what I did or did not do in the future. I could see that in Eph 2:8-9. Yet I did not fall into immorality, drunkenness, drug abuse, or anything of the kind. Instead, I found that the grace of God so moved me that I changed from being pre-Med to pre-Ministry. I dedicated my life to telling others this wonderful message. That led to four years on staff with Campus Crusade for Christ, seven years at Dallas Theological Seminary (during which I served as a youth pastor, hospital chaplain, and pastor), two years teaching in Bible Colleges, and then nearly thirty years to date heading a ministry designed to promote clarity in evangelism and discipleship.

I've met untold thousands of people who are highly motivated to please the Lord even though they are certain of their eternal destiny and even though they know that nothing they do or fail to do can take away the everlasting life which is theirs.

God promises that what we sow, we will also reap (Gal 6:7). If we do not live in fellowship with Him, then we will be miserable, suffering, discontented people (Gal 5:19-21). If we live in fellowship with Him, then we will experience love, joy, peace, and so forth (Gal 5:22-23).

The sowing and reaping principle extends beyond this life as well. How we live now will determine how fully we will be able to glorify

Christ in the life to come (Luke 19:16-26).[2] Only a foolish Christian would indulge in a sinful lifestyle now, knowing that what he will reap is pain and suffering now and loss of rewards forever.

The reason that people go to twelve-step programs is because they realize that sin hurts them and their loved ones. Even atheists can see that. So can people who know themselves to be saved once and for all.

The gospel according to Jesus is not about our cross; it's about His cross. It is not about our work for Him; it's about His work for us. The gospel according to Jesus is not about what we promise to do for Him; it's about what He promises to do for us.

The issue is belief versus behavior. Is justification by faith alone, or is it by repentance, surrender, commitment, obedience, following Christ, self-denial, and perseverance in discipleship? In this chapter, as in the entire book, MacArthur argues for the latter. But the Biblical evidence does not support his view.

Confessing Christ before Others

One of my favorite passages in the Synoptic Gospels is Matt 10:32-33, where the Lord says,

> "Therefore whoever confesses Me before men, him I will also confess before My Father who is in heaven. But whoever denies Me before men, him I will also deny before My Father who is in heaven."

MacArthur asks, "Does that mean confession before others is a condition of becoming a true Christian?" He then answers, "No, but it means that a characteristic of every genuine believer is that he or she *will* profess faith in Christ unreservedly" (p. 221, emphasis his).

On the one hand MacArthur avows that confessing Christ is not a condition of everlasting life, but on the other hand, he says that if you do not confess your faith in Him, and confess Him *unreservedly*, you show you are not a "genuine believer." The inescapable conclusion is that if you do not confess Christ unreservedly, you will spend eternity in the lake of fire with all other unbelievers.

That is confusing.

---

[2] Dr. Earl Radmacher, who just went to be with the Lord, said, "I am becoming today, by what I do with what God has given me, what I will be in the life to come."

A bit later he does go on to make it clear that he believes that confessing Christ is a condition of "real discipleship," which he had earlier said (p. 219, quoted below) is itself "an invitation to salvation":

> The heart of real discipleship is a commitment to be like Jesus Christ. That means both acting as He did and being willing to accept the same treatment. It means facing a world that is hostile to Him and doing it fearlessly. *It means confessing before others that Jesus is Lord* and being confident that He will also speak on our behalf before the Father (p. 221, emphasis added).

Here is his reasoning:

Major premise:	"Jesus' call to discipleship...was an invitation to salvation" (p. 219).
Minor premise:	"The heart of real discipleship...means confessing before others Jesus is Lord" (p. 221).
Conclusion:	Confessing Christ is a key condition of discipleship and hence salvation.

As this section goes on, MacArthur attempts to soften what it means to confess Christ. A person need not confess Christ publicly *each and every time he has an opportunity*: "We have all failed to confess Christ before others more often than we would like to admit" (p. 222). If so, how do we know if we have confessed Him *enough* in order to enter the kingdom? And what happened to the need to confess Him "unreservedly" (p. 221)?

At one point MacArthur says that denying Christ means "someone whose *entire life* is a denial of Christ" (p. 222, emphasis added). He continues, "He may claim to believe, but *everything* about his way of life exudes denial (cf. Titus 1:16)" (pp. 222-23, emphasis added).

But before you feel safe, the pendulum swings back and MacArthur next says, "*Churches are filled with such people, masquerading as disciples* but denying the Lord in *some very disturbing ways*. Christ will deny them before God (Matt. 10:22)" (p. 223, emphasis added).

Which is it?

Is it *everything* about his way of life that denies Christ, or are there merely *some areas* of his life that deny Christ?

If denial is not merely a failure to confess Christ, but if it includes behavior, which actions "exude denial"?

Certainty of one's eternal destiny is impossible if what MacArthur says is true. Doubt reigns if the only people who will spend eternity with the Lord are those who unreservedly confess Him in word and deed for their entire lives.

MacArthur does not mention that Matt 10:33 is alluded to by Paul in 2 Tim 2:12. Essentially the Apostle Paul interprets Matt 10:32-33 for us. When we have an inspired interpretation of Scripture, it is wise to follow it. Here is what Paul says in 2 Tim 2:11-13,

> This is a faithful saying: For if we died with Him, we shall also live with Him. If we endure, we shall also reign with Him. *If we deny Him, He also will deny us.* If we are faithless, He remains faithful; He cannot deny Himself (emphasis added).

The portion italicized is a condensed version of Matt 10:33. The first half of verse 12 is thus an interpretation of Matt 10:32.

Paul says that "if we endure, we shall also reign with Him." That is an explanation of Jesus' words, "Therefore whoever confesses Me before men, him I will also confess before My Father who is in heaven." If we endure in our confession of Christ, then we shall reign with Him in the life to come.

If we do not endure in our confession of Christ, that is, if we deny Him, then He will deny us the privilege of ruling with Him, though of course we will enter the kingdom since all who've died with Him will live with Him (v 11) and even "if we are faithless, He remains faithful" for "He cannot deny Himself."

The issue in Matt 10:32-33 is not kingdom *entrance*, but kingdom *inheritance*, i.e., rulership and rewards in Christ's kingdom. This is a rich concept in the Old Testament. When the twelve tribes of Israel inherited the land, they *took possession of it*. Others could live there. But only the twelve tribes owned the land. It was their land. Of course, this is much discussed concerning Israel today. Whose land is it?

The one who becomes a co-heir with Christ will be a possessor of part of the kingdom in the sense that he will have a city or cities over which he will rule, and various privileges that only the heirs will enjoy (the right to the tree of life and the hidden manna, white garments, a special white stone engraved with a special name on it, etc.).

The Parable of the Minas in Luke 19:11-27 illustrates inheriting the kingdom. One of the nobleman's servants ends up ruling over ten cities (Luke 19:17); one gains rulership over five cities (Luke 19:19); and one gets into the kingdom but has no cities to rule over (Luke 19:20-26). This idea of perseverance for rulership is also found in Rev 2:26. Confession is about eternal rewards, not eternal destiny.

Getting the Priorities Straight

MacArthur moves on to Matt 10:34-37. Once again, he takes a passage on discipleship and applies it to evangelism, distorting Jesus' gospel along the way.

Jesus called for allegiance to Himself that is above that of family. If the call to discipleship is the call to everlasting life, as MacArthur says, then one condition of being born again is loving Christ more than you love your parents, spouse, or children. I wonder if that is something most would think of including in their evangelistic presentations. Probably not.

But MacArthur has now added a new condition to eternal life: loving Christ more than family. Thus the list of conditions so far includes repentance, surrender, full commitment, self-denial, following Christ, obeying Christ, unreservedly confessing Christ in word and deed as a pattern of life, loving Christ more than one's own family, and perseverance in all of the above. That is the gospel according to MacArthur, but not according to Jesus.

Taking Up the Cross

MacArthur begins this section as follows:

> Those who are not willing to lose their lives for Christ are not worthy of Him (Matt. 10:38). They cannot be His disciples (Luke 14:27). These statements cannot be made to accommodate the casual approach to conversion that is in vogue in our generation. Jesus is not asking people to add Him to the milieu of their lives. He wants disciples willing

to forsake *everything*. This calls for full-scale self-denial—even willingness to die for His sake if necessary (p. 224, emphasis his).

It sounds like MacArthur is saying that a willingness to be martyred for Christ is a requirement for salvation. But he quickly adds, "The Bible does not teach salvation by martyrdom. The Lord...was simply saying that genuine Christians do not shrink back, even in the face of death" (p. 224).

So a person does not have to *seek* martyrdom to gain everlasting life. However, when *confronted* by the choice to deny Christ or be martyred, then he must choose martyrdom to gain entrance into the kingdom. Why isn't that salvation by martyrdom—at least when you are confronted with that choice?

Of course we should take up our crosses every day and follow Christ. We should be delighted to do so. That is what pleases Him and thus that is what is best for us. Discipleship is about following Christ and pleasing Him. But the call to discipleship is not the call to everlasting life. John 3:16 does not say, "whoever denies himself, takes up his cross, and follows Him has everlasting life." The only condition of everlasting life is belief in the Lord Jesus Christ for it.

Conclusion

MacArthur puts discipleship and evangelism into a blender to come out with one unified concept, a major categorical mistake. To him discipleship and evangelism are not separate concepts. The call to discipleship is the call to salvation. The call to salvation is the call to discipleship.

While MacArthur rightly calls for people to follow Jesus, he wrongly makes following the Lord a condition for everlasting life.[3] That is not the gospel which Jesus proclaimed.

The condition for pleasing God and enjoying a healthy Christian life is following Christ. The condition for having everlasting life

---

[3] Additionally, MacArthur's explanation of how we follow Jesus is flawed. The Scriptures teach we follow Him by abiding in His Word, by having our lives transformed by the renewing of our minds (Rom 12:1-12; 2 Cor 3:18). The faith walk (2 Cor 5:7) is grounded in the certain knowledge of everlasting life by the promise alone (2 Cor 5:1-8; 1 John 2:25-26; 5:9-13). But MacArthur's idea of following Jesus relies on ongoing doubts about one's eternal destiny and on a list of things to do and another list of things to avoid. It is a sort of checklist view of following Jesus.

is believing in Jesus for that life. Blending discipleship and evangelism together is a bit like blending bleach and ammonia. While both have many excellent uses, when combined they form a toxic substance that can lead to nasty chemical burns of your eyes or lungs.

While getting burned due to the mixture of bleach and ammonia is bad, getting burned by the blending of discipleship and evangelism is much worse. No one can gain everlasting life by following Christ. Only by believing in Him can anyone have everlasting life.

A gospel centered *on us being faithful disciples of Christ* is misdirected. It is a gospel of doubt. The gospel according to Jesus is centered *on Him being faithful* to His promise of everlasting life to all who simply believe in Him.

CHAPTER 23

The Lordship of Christ

Introduction

How much do we need to know about Jesus' divinity in order to be saved? In this chapter, MacArthur goes through various aspects of Jesus' identity, such as being God, Savior, and Lord. The Lord Jesus possesses many other glorious attributes and titles besides these. The question is, how much do we need to know about the Lordship of Jesus Christ before we can be saved?

MacArthur's Thesis

The introduction is especially important in this chapter since it lays out MacArthur's thesis: "Jesus frequently made His lordship the central issue with unbelievers" (p. 227). The central issue *for what*? MacArthur continues, "Scripture reveals a number of eternal attributes encompassed in the name Lord. Salvation has no meaning or efficacy apart from them" (p. 227).

MacArthur is saying that the Lord Jesus made His Lordship the central focus with unbelievers concerning what they must do to have everlasting life. But what is his practical application in terms of evangelism? He might mean one of two things:

1. These eternal attributes are essential to who Jesus is and without them He could not give anyone everlasting life. However, understanding and believing all these attributes

is not a condition of everlasting life. It is the one doing the evangelizing who must keep these attributes in mind in order for his evangelism to be fully effective.

2. One must understand and believe all of the eternal attributes of Christ in order to be born again. It is not enough to repent, submit, fully commit, follow, obey, love Him more than your own family, and persevere in all of that. In addition, your understanding of the Lordship of Christ must not be in error on any of His essential eternal attributes.

Only at the end of the chapter do we learn which of these two options is correct. Actually we learn a third option we have not even anticipated is correct; but we will discuss that when we get there.

Jesus Is God

In these two paragraphs MacArthur is stating that Jesus is God and that He possesses all the attributes of deity.

Jesus is God. And if He were not God, then He could not have been born of a virgin, could not have lived a sinless life, could not have atoned for our sins by His death on the cross, could not be the Savior of the world, and could not give everlasting life to all who believe in Him. Being God is what made those actions effective for our salvation. And believing in His deity is a powerful reason for believing in His promise of everlasting life. But how much of His divinity do we need to know and understand in order to be saved? MacArthur doesn't say at this point.

Jesus Is Sovereign

MacArthur gives a brief presentation showing that Jesus is sovereign. His presentation is not meant to be comprehensive as whole books could be written on the subject.

Jesus is sovereign. Indeed, He holds the whole universe together (Col 1:17). He could not give anyone everlasting life if He were not sovereign. But do we need to believe He is sovereign before we can be saved? MacArthur doesn't yet say. He is building a case as to who Jesus is and later he will tell us what we need to believe about Jesus' deity and sovereignty in order to be born again.

Jesus Is Savior

In this section MacArthur touches on the cross. "The death of Christ for us…paid the penalty of our sin in full and opened the way for us to have peace with God" (p. 229). By *our*, you might be tempted to think MacArthur believes in a universal atonement, but he means Jesus' death paid the penalty for the sins *of the elect*.

In a November 7, 2004 message entitled, "The Doctrine of the Actual Atonement, Part 1," MacArthur says,

> Number one, the atonement is limited. And by "atonement" I mean the sacrifice of Christ, by which He paid the penalty for sin. The atonement is limited.[1]

Sixty-two times in that message he used the word *limited* to describe the atonement. Thirteen times he specifically said, "the atonement is limited." Six other times he simply said, "it is limited."

His discussion in *TGAJ* of the cross and what it accomplishes is brief. The cross of Christ must not have fully removed sin as a barrier (contra John 1:29; 1 John 2:2), since MacArthur believes that one must turn from his sins to be born again.

MacArthur says that we are to "invite people to receive Christ as Savior…" (p. 229). Receiving Christ as Savior is a vague expression that seems at odds with all of the rest of the conditions for everlasting life which MacArthur has explained in *TGAJ*.

We cannot receive Him as Savior. He *is* the Savior whether we believe in Him or not. If we believe in Him, what we receive is everlasting life. So we don't receive a Savior; we receive everlasting life because He is the Savior who gives everlasting life to all who believe in Him.

Jesus Is Lord

No one calling himself a Christian disputes the fact that Jesus is Lord. However, MacArthur's emphasis in this section is not on Jesus' Lordship, but on *the response* that people should have to His Lordship: "The signature of saving faith is surrender to the lordship of Jesus Christ" (p. 231). He continues, "The definitive test of

---

[1] The transcript of the sermon is posted on his *Grace to You* website: http://www.gty.org/resources/sermons/90-277/the-doctrine-of-actual-atonement-part-1?Term=Nov%207%202004. Accessed January 15, 2015.

whether a person belongs to Christ is a willingness to bow to His divine authority" (p. 231).

What is "a willingness to bow to His divine authority"? It is more than simply saying, "Jesus is Lord." MacArthur explains that bowing to His divine authority "includes acknowledging Him as Lord by obeying Him, by surrendering one's will to His lordship, [and] by affirming Him with one's deeds as well as one's words..." (p. 232).

So the issue is neither of the two points we mentioned at the start of this chapter:

1. These eternal attributes are essential to who Jesus is and without them He could not give anyone everlasting life. However, understanding and believing all these attributes is not a condition of everlasting life.

2. One must understand and believe all of the eternal attributes of Christ in order to be born again. It is not enough to repent, submit, fully commit, follow, obey, and persevere if your understanding of the Lordship of Christ is defective on any of His essential eternal attributes.

The issue is a third point:

3. One must *live in a manner consistent* with the eternal attributes of Christ in order gain entrance into Jesus' kingdom. The issue is not that one must believe some or all of His eternal attributes (option 2). *The issue is that one must live out His eternal attributes.* We must be good, faithful, true, just, loving, and so forth in order to escape eternal condemnation.

MacArthur moved from the fact that Jesus is Lord and the second member of the Trinity to the supposed idea that saving faith is "obeying Him, surrendering one's will to His lordship, [and] affirming Him with one's deeds as well as one's words" (p. 232). Obedience and deeds are works. Saving faith according to MacArthur is works.

Conclusion

The Pharisees were constantly opposing the Lord Jesus. The free gift of everlasting life to whoever believes in Jesus didn't sit well with them because it did not require works, but faith in Jesus (John 5:39-40; 6:28-29). Like the Pharisees, MacArthur argues that our deeds (turning from our sins and then persevering until death in a life characterized by obedience) are the issue in evangelism. The issue is not really the Person or work of the Lord Jesus Christ, except in the sense that His holiness shows us our sinfulness and points us to the way we must live in order to gain kingdom entrance.

The example view of the atonement says that by His sacrificial death on the cross the Lord Jesus showed us how to live so that we might gain everlasting life. While MacArthur says he believes in substitutionary atonement, his words argue otherwise.

Who can be sure his actions accurately reflect Jesus' divine attributes? Only those who are convinced that they are good, holy, loving, kind, just, and so forth could be sure of his eternal destiny if what MacArthur says is this chapter is true. But no one can be sure of that. Doubt, doubt, and more doubt. That is the legacy of MacArthur's gospel.

CHAPTER 24

Tetelestai!: The Triumph Is Complete

Introduction

MacArthur's final chapter has almost nothing to do with Lordship Salvation. But it does contain a final, glaring contradiction.

A Show of Strength in Dying

MacArthur tells us that Jesus willingly went to the cross and gladly laid down His life for us as our substitute. All true. His death was "a show of strength" (p. 237).

At this point MacArthur does not explain how Jesus' death is linked with us being born again. He is simply establishing that Jesus willingly went to the cross because this was "the Father's will" and was "the divine plan" (p. 238).[1]

It Is Finished!

Only in the last paragraph in this section do we find any hint of Lordship Salvation, and what we find is a last ditch attempt to convince the reader that everlasting life is not for those who believe

---

[1] Jesus' death on the cross makes everyone savable (John 1:29; Titus 2:11; 1 John 2:2). In addition, His death and resurrection are the ultimate proofs that He indeed gives everlasting life to all who simply believe in Him (John 2:18-22; 3:14-16).

in Jesus, but is instead for those "who will surrender to Him in humble, repentant faith" (p. 241).

As MacArthur says, Jesus's final words were, "It is finished!" But what did the Lord mean? Did the Lord Jesus Christ indeed pay the full price? Did He finish the work the Father sent Him to do? MacArthur says here that He did. He rightly says that "no works of human righteousness can expand on what Jesus accomplished for us" (p. 240). But with those words MacArthur contradicts himself, for in the final paragraph of this chapter and throughout his book MacArthur says something completely different.

MacArthur repeatedly says that we must buy everlasting life for ourselves. He says that we must pay the price and must persevere in obedience in order to be saved. He even says that we must take up our crosses, or we cannot be saved. At every opportunity, MacArthur has denied that Jesus' work is complete apart from any works we do. In every chapter of *TGAJ* he has argued that we must work wholeheartedly for Christ until death in order to be saved.

In Jesus' death on the cross and His cry, "It is finished!" we learn that He is the one who bought our salvation by laying down His life for all of mankind. There is nothing left for us to pay. No works are required of anyone to be born again. All one needs to do is believe in Him who died in his place.

Let's be clear. The issue in the gospel, according to MacArthur, is not faith in the Lord Jesus. The issue is submission, repentance, confession, works, obedience, and perseverance. According to MacArthur, *we must finish the work* that the Father has for us in order to enter into Jesus' kingdom. Jesus' finished work is a vital truth in MacArthur's understanding of the gospel. But his understanding treats Jesus' work as incomplete in itself. Jesus' finished work needs to be supplemented by our own works as MacArthur says repeatedly in *TGAJ*.

MacArthur's emphasis from beginning to end in his book has been on what we must do, what we must suffer, what we must buy, and what we must finish. MacArthur's gospel is primarily about us being able to say at the end of our lives, "It is finished!"

Remember the game young girls would play, plucking the petals off a daisy? "He loves me," one said, plucking one petal. "He loves me not," plucking another. This went on until she got to the last petal. She hoped she ended with "He loves me."

That is MacArthur's hope. He might be a Calvinist (TULIP)[2], but what he actually promotes is what Engelsma calls, "a gospel of doubt," the Daisy Theology of Puritanism. MacArthur hopes that when he dies he can shout, "It is finished!" and that the Lord will indeed accept him.

In *TGAJ* MacArthur teaches his readers to embrace doubt. He calls them to strive to fight the good fight and finish the race so that they might obtain entrance to Jesus' kingdom.[3] He teaches the readers to examine their own lives and behavior to see if they love God and if they will be permitted to spend eternity with God.

Conclusion

MacArthur is zealous for good works. He loves God and is concerned about people. His ability to move people with his preaching and with his writing is extraordinary. He is obviously extremely gifted and extremely influential.

But if he is getting the message of life wrong, and he is, then he is misleading multitudes. I do not say that with any animosity for MacArthur. I have prayed for him that God would bring him back to the truth he once championed. It would be fantastic if he renounced Lordship Salvation and proclaimed the free gift of

---

[2] The letters in TULIP stand for Total depravity, Unconditional Election, Limited Atonement, Irresistible grace, and the Preservation and Perseverance of the Saints. Total depravity is understood to mean that unbelievers are like rocks and can only respond to God if He regenerates them first. In this view the new birth precedes faith. Unconditional election is the idea that God chose a small percentage of humanity to be born again. The rest He passed over. Limited atonement means that Christ did not die for everyone. He only died for the elect. All others cannot be saved because Christ did not die for their sins. Irresistible grace means that anyone God draws comes to faith. Calvinists reject the idea that God is drawing all. Preservation of the saints is once saved, always saved. Perseverance of the saints is the teaching that all who are elect will persevere until death in faith and good works. Hence, according to Calvinists, if a believer falls away (without turning back to the Lord), then he proves he is not one for whom Christ died and he will end up in the lake of fire.

[3] While we are to fight the good fight and finish the race set before us as Paul says in 1 Cor 9:24-27 and 2 Tim 4:6-8, the reason is not so that we can gain entrance into Jesus' kingdom. That is guaranteed for all who simply believe in the Lord Jesus Christ (John 3:16; 5:24; 1 Thess 5:10). The reason we are to fight the good fight and finish the race is in order to please the Lord, gain His approval, and gain the eternal rewards which will be given to overcoming believers, especially ruling with Christ forever in His kingdom. While all believers will be in the kingdom, only believers who endure will reign with Him (2 Tim 2:12).

everlasting life to all who simply believe in the Lord Jesus Christ. What a great proponent he would be of the grace of God.

"He loves me." Pluck.

"He loves me." Pluck.

"He loves me." Pluck.

The real gospel according to Jesus says that the moment anyone simply believes in the Lord Jesus, he has everlasting life and is forever secure in His love. That is good news. The amazing promise of John 3:16—not any works we do—is the basis for assurance. That assurance is the foundation of holiness. That assurance is the inspiration for good works. That promise and the assurance which arises from believing it is the *real* gospel according to Jesus.

The Gospel According to the Apostles

Introduction

Most of what MacArthur says in the introduction to this appendix is correct. The message of everlasting life starts with the teaching of the Lord Jesus. There is indeed no contradiction between the message of life which the Lord Jesus preached and the message which His Apostles preached as well—as long as we interpret each correctly.

That is the problem. MacArthur does not interpret the Lord or the Apostles correctly.

MacArthur wrongly thinks that the Lord's evangelistic messages are found in the discipleship teaching found in Matthew, Mark, and Luke (which are the books MacArthur primarily considers in *TGAJ*). The Lord's evangelistic ministry is recorded in John's Gospel (see John 20:30-31). John's Gospel is evangelistic in purpose. The Synoptic Gospels are written to believers about discipleship.

MacArthur is incorrect when he says that the call to discipleship is the call to everlasting life. MacArthur is able to come up with Lordship Salvation in the teachings of Jesus because he merges justification and sanctification.

He also misinterprets what the Apostles have to say about justification and regeneration. When MacArthur considers the writings of Paul, Peter, James, John, and the author of Hebrews, he turns to discipleship and sanctification teachings in their epistles, rather than to texts in which they deal with justification or the promise of everlasting life.

Paul

MacArthur's first sentence concerning the Apostle Paul is great except that he leaves out one word: "The apostle Paul was a champion of the great doctrine of justification by faith" (p. 246). It is noticeable that he does not say "the great doctrine of justification by faith *alone*." The Reformation cry of *sola fide*, justification *by faith alone*, that is, justification by faith apart from works, is reduced to *fide* (by faith) by MacArthur, justification by faith.

Yet for a passage that clearly teaches justification by faith MacArthur does not go to Gal 3:6-14 or Rom 3:21-31 or Rom 4:1-5. Instead, he starts with Rom 10:9-10 which doesn't even mention justification directly (though it does say that righteousness is by faith).

The second verse he cites is Eph 2:10; he does not cite Eph 2:8-9 to show that salvation/regeneration/justification is not of works. Instead he points to Eph 2:10 to show "the place of works in a believer's life" (p. 246), evidently implying that good works are necessary for a person to have what some theologians call *final justification*.[1]

The third verse MacArthur cites is Rom 3:28, "Therefore we conclude that a man is justified by faith apart from the deeds of the law." But in the very same sentence, after a semicolon, he adds, "while James wrote, 'You see that a man is justified by works, and not by faith alone' (James 2:24)." What does he mean? It sounds like he thinks that Paul and James contradict each other.

MacArthur explains this seeming contradiction by saying, "Paul was saying that human works cannot earn favor with God, and James was saying that true faith must always result in good works" (p. 246).

Yet that is not what James says. James plainly says, "Was not Abraham our father justified by works when he offered up Isaac his son on the altar?" (Jas 2:21). Paul said the same thing in Rom 4:2, "If Abraham was justified by works, he has something to boast about,

---

[1] Justification, like salvation, is final and secure the very moment anyone believes in Jesus. There is no time of probation.

but not before God." Both Paul and James teach that Abraham was justified, or vindicated, *before men*, when he offered up Isaac. Both men quote Gen 15:6 to say that Abraham was justified *before God* when he believed.

James 2:24, cited by MacArthur, actually should be translated, "You see then that a man is justified by works, and not only by faith." James is saying that there are two justifications, one before men by works and one before God by faith alone. Paul, of course, speaks of those same two different justifications in Rom 4:1-5.

MacArthur went on from here to produce more verses which speak about works in order to try to prove that Paul taught justification by faith that works.

MacArthur does not believe in justification by faith *alone*.[2] He believes that works must be joined to faith in order for justification to occur.

Unfortunately, this sort of theological doublespeak is quite common today. Many pastors and theologians argue as MacArthur does.

Dear reader, examine carefully what MacArthur says and what he doesn't say about justification and compare it with what Paul says in Rom 3:21-31; 4:1-5; Gal 2:17.

Peter

There are a number of places in Acts and in Peter's two epistles where the Apostle Peter speaks of justification or salvation by faith alone, apart from works. But MacArthur cites none of those.

He could have cited Peter's famous words from the Jerusalem Council in Acts 15: 7-11:

> "Men and brethren, you know that a good while ago God chose among us, that by my mouth the Gentiles should hear the word of the gospel and believe. So God, who knows the

---

[2] A search of the entire book in Google Books shows that he mentioned justification by faith *alone* only once, and then not when stating his own view, but when indicating that he was not "repudiating the great Reformation emphasis on justification by faith alone" (p. 14). That paragraph began with the words, "The original edition (of *TGAJ*) had no treatment of the doctrine of justification by faith" (p. 13). By contrast, he speaks of "justification by faith" a total of eight times (pp. 13, 176 [favorable citation of Ironside], 195, 210, 211 [favorable citing of Lloyd-Jones], 247, 255, 258).

heart, acknowledged them by giving them the Holy Spirit, just as *He did* to us, and made no distinction between us and them, purifying their hearts by faith. Now therefore, why do you test God by putting a yoke on the neck of the disciples which neither our fathers nor we were able to bear? But we believe that through the grace of the Lord Jesus Christ we shall be saved in the same manner as they."

Most likely the reason MacArthur fails to mention this passage is because it speaks of salvation by faith alone, apart from works, which contradicts his Lordship Salvation view of justification as being by faith joined with works.

MacArthur instead cites places in which Peter called his listeners/readers to repent and to live holy lives. Holy living is the condition of eternal life for MacArthur, not faith in Christ.

James

Next up is James and salvation by faith plus works. According to MacArthur, James taught that faith without works will not save anyone from eternal condemnation. Why is this not works salvation? The answer is evidently because "all this is a work of God" (p. 250).[3]

James uses the word *save* five times (1:21; 2:14; 4:12; 5:15, 20). All five refer to salvation *from physical death and from temporal judgment*. That MacArthur sees all of them except Jas 5:15 as dealing with how one escapes eternal condemnation contradicts the contexts. However, it does make it possible for him to find Lordship Salvation in James.

John

John, who in his Gospel made it clear that regeneration is by faith alone, supposedly in his first epistle reversed course and taught that assurance of everlasting life was found not simply in what we believe (what MacArthur calls "the doctrinal test"), but also and especially in our obedience ("the moral test"). MacArthur insists,

---

[3] This is the same argument that even Roman Catholics make today. See Michael P. Barber, "A Catholic Perspective: Our Works Are Meritorious at the Final Judgment Because of Our Union with Christ by Grace," in *Four Views on the Role of Works at the Final Judgment* (Grand Rapids, MI: Zondervan, 2013), pp. 161-84.

"For John, a true believer could never ultimately fail to overcome" (p. 251).

What about 1 John 5:9-13, where John says that we know we have everlasting life because we believe God's testimony concerning His Son? Those verses are not mentioned, possibly because they do not fit MacArthur's faith-plus-works paradigm.

The Writer of Hebrews

MacArthur believes that progressive sanctification and personal holiness are necessary in order to enter Christ's kingdom (pp. 251-52).

Is it any wonder that Mormons, Romans Catholics, Eastern Orthodox, Churches of Christ, and all who believe in works salvation love *The Gospel According to Jesus*? In this first appendix, as in the entire book, MacArthur plainly argues that in order to enter the kingdom and escape eternal condemnation one must have personal holiness, personal righteousness, and sufficient works to justify his spending eternity with the Lord.

Sadly the first appendix underscores his view that certainty of one's eternal destiny is impossible prior to death. MacArthur's gospel of doubt is quite evident in this appendix.

The Gospel According to Historic Christianity

D oes the history of the Church support Lordship Salvation? If so, is that a good thing or a bad thing?

MacArthur starts his second appendix with these words:

> Those who want to eliminate Jesus' lordship from the gospel message often insinuate that it is heresy equal to Galatian legalism to demand that sinners *forsake their sins, commit themselves to Christ, obey His commands,* and *surrender to him* [sic] (p. 253, emphasis added).

MacArthur says those who disagree with Lordship Salvation "want to eliminate Jesus' lordship from the gospel message" (see above). That claim is quite offensive; and it is quite wrong.

The reason why John 3:16 is true is because Jesus is Lord. If He were not Lord, then He could not die on the cross *for our sins* and He could not give everlasting life to those who believe in Him. But it is one thing to say that the Lord Jesus gives everlasting life to those who believe in Him (Acts 16:31). It is something else entirely to proclaim that the Lord Jesus gives everlasting life to those who forsake their sins, commit themselves to Him, obey His commands, and surrender to Him.

Notice that faith is not even mentioned by MacArthur when he speaks of the four things one must do ("forsake their sins, commit themselves to Christ, obey His commands, and surrender to him [sic]"). Instead the issues are repentance, commitment, obedience, and surrender. What happened to the "five essentials of genuine conversion" which MacArthur spoke of in Chapter 10 (p. 118)? There he said the five essentials were humility, revelation, repentance, faith, and submission. Now in this appendix there are four essentials, leaving out not only faith, but also leaving out humility and revelation.

If those things are *essentials*, then what MacArthur claims are the essentials in this chapter is inaccurate.

The gospel according to MacArthur is indeed one of works, like the Judaizers who attacked the churches of Galatia (Gal 1:6-9; 5:4). Like them, MacArthur teaches justification by works.

MacArthur wrongly summarizes a quotation from Hodges as supposedly suggesting that "the concept that faith necessarily produces obedience is a new invention…" (p. 253). Yet that is not what Hodges wrote or believed. He did not give any discussion of the history of this controversy. MacArthur merely quotes Hodges as speaking about "modern assaults on the integrity of the gospel" (p. 253).[1] Hodges did not attempt to discuss whether these assaults occurred in times past.

Thomas F. Torrance discussed the issue of soteriology in the early church in his book *The Doctrine of Grace in the Apostolic Fathers*. The Apostolic Fathers were the writers who followed the Apostles and wrote in the late first century and in the second century. They included Clement of Rome, Ignatius of Antioch, Polycarp of Smyrna, the Didache, and the Shepherd of Hermas.

Torrance shows that to a man the Apostolic Fathers departed from the concept of grace. They all taught works salvation.

That MacArthur wishes to align his theology with the Didache, Ignatius, and Clement—MacArthur quotes all three as agreeing with him—is quite revealing. None of those writers believed in justification by faith alone. None of them believed that everlasting life is by grace through faith apart from works.

After citing the Apostolic Fathers, MacArthur cites Augustine, fifth century, and then he jumps to Luther in 1517. The very fact that he leaves out 1,000 years of church history shows that he considers his view different than that held by the Eastern (Orthodox) or Western (Roman Catholic) churches from 500 till 1500. If that

---

[1] The original source is Zane C. Hodges, *The Gospel Under Siege* (Dallas, TX: Redención Viva, 1981), p. 4.

is so, then does he not concede that his view is not the view of "historic Christianity"?

Or, might it be fair to say that his view is essentially that of Roman Catholicism and Eastern Orthodoxy, but he simply does not want to admit that?

He can't have it both ways. MacArthur's position is either inconsistent with Catholicism and Orthodoxy, and hence his position is not the view of historic Christianity, or else his position is consistent with Rome and Constantinople and hence his position is that of historic Christianity.

It is apparent that MacArthur's position is the one taught by the Apostolic Fathers, Roman Catholicism, Eastern Orthodoxy, the Reformers (at times), the Puritans, and most Evangelicals in the twentieth and twenty-first centuries.

The reason MacArthur wishes to claim his view is that of historic Christianity is because he assumes that historic Christianity is correct. But if historic Christianity has been wrong, then MacArthur is hereby admitting he is wrong.

MacArthur rightly says, "Lordship salvation is…the heart of historic Christian soteriology" (p. 271). And he is right when he says, "To teach anything else is to withdraw from the mainstream of church teaching through the ages" (p. 271).

The Bible declares that justification is by faith alone, apart from works. That is what the Reformers initially taught. It is unfortunate that once the Apostles died, this truth has never been the majority position in the church. Yet there are many individuals and movements that have agreed with the grace message, like the Marrow Controversy, John Glas, Andrew Croswell (*What Is Christ to Me, If He Is Not Mine?*), John Nelson Darby, C. H. MacIntosh, Robert Sandeman, Dispensationalism, Doc Latham, AWANA Youth Ministries, New Tribes Missions, Lewis Sperry Chafer, Charles Ryrie, Earl Radmacher, J. Irwin Oberholtzer (Child Evangelism Fellowship), Zane Hodges, R. B. Thieme, Jr. and Doctrinal Churches, Florida Bible College, Greater Grace Churches, and so on. But the number of people who have agreed with the grace view over the years is far less than those who agree with MacArthur and Lordship Salvation.[2]

---

[2] It should be noted that the winners write the history. Hence it should not be surprising that there are no surviving works that promote justification by faith

That MacArthur wishes to find cover under the mistaken notion that the majority is right and most in historic Christianity have been on the narrow path that leads to everlasting life is surprising given his view that the way is narrow that leads to life *and few find it* (Matt 7:13-14, emphasis added).[3]

If you wish to be in the mainstream, become a Roman Catholic. If you wish to please God, become a Berean (Acts 17:11). Search the Scriptures for yourself to see what is true. Do not take the words of the Apostolic Fathers or anyone else for that matter. Take God's Word on the issue and His Word alone.

If you follow the crowd, you will not be sure of your eternal destiny. You will be another victim of the gospel of doubt. But if you believe God's Word, you will be sure you have everlasting life simply because you believe in the Lord Jesus Christ for it.

---

alone (with the possible exception of Augustine, but he was far from consistent on this issue) before the sixteenth century. Surely many people held that view in every generation. But the first surviving writings of that type we have are from Luther and Calvin.

[3] The Bible teaches that the majority is rarely correct. The ten spies were wrong. Joshua and Caleb were right. Nearly the entire nation agreed with the ten spies. Only Moses, Aaron, and Miriam sided with Joshua and Caleb.

Answers to Common Questions

There was no third appendix in the first edition of *TGAJ*. MacArthur answers seventeen questions that he received after he wrote the first edition, but before he published the second edition. No new questions were added after the second edition.

These are excellent questions.

1. Immediate assurance?

A reader asks,

> If your view of salvation is correct, how can we lead people to Christ and offer them immediate assurance? You seem to be saying people need to seek assurance in their works (p. 272).

MacArthur follows the approach of the Westminster Confession that the foundation of assurance is both objective (the promises of God's Word to the believer) and subjective (the works of the Spirit in our lives and the inner witness of the Holy Spirit). In his view the basis of assurance is not simply believing the promises in the Bible.

According to MacArthur (and the signers of the Westminster Confession) certainty of one's eternal destiny is impossible prior to death. While the promises are indeed objective, MacArthur offers two reasons why the promises by themselves cannot grant anyone assurance.

In the first place, faith according to MacArthur is not objective. One can know if he believes in the deity of Christ or in Jesus' death on the cross in our place, but one cannot know if he believes in Jesus for everlasting life since saving faith is not faith, but is defined by MacArthur to be repentance, commitment, submission, obedience, and perseverance. Thus while the promise may be objective for "the believer," there is no objective way to know if you are a believer.

In the second place, according to MacArthur the way one gains "a measure of assurance" (p. 272)—a very revealing expression, is by looking for evidences of faith, that is, looking for subjective evidences of repentance, commitment, submission, obedience, and perseverance. The more sensitive a person is, the less likely he will have "a measure of assurance" based on his works.

Assurance is part of "the lifelong growth process of the Christian life" (p. 273).

MacArthur points the reader to his book *Saved without a Doubt*, *(SWD)*. In that book he discusses "how you can tell whether you are truly a Christian" in Chapter 5 (pp. 67-91). His answer is that there are eleven tests that the Apostle John gives and if you pass all eleven tests, then you can tell you are a true Christian. Here are the eleven tests:

- "Have you enjoyed fellowship with Christ and with the Father?" (*SWD*, pp. 69-70).

- "Are you sensitive to sin?" (*SWD*, pp. 70-72).

- "Do you obey God's Word?" (*SWD*, pp. 72-73).

- "Do you reject this evil world?" (*SWD*, pp. 73-75).

- "Do you eagerly await Christ's return?" (*SWD*, pp. 75-76).

- "Do you see a decreasing pattern of sin in your life?" (*SWD*, pp. 76-79).

- "Do you love other Christians?" (*SWD*, pp. 79-83).

- "Do you experience answered prayer?" (*SWD*, pp. 83-84).

- "Do you experience the ministry of the Holy Spirit?" (*SWD*, pp. 85-86).

- "Can you discern between spiritual truth and error?" (*SWD*, pp. 86-89).

- "Have you suffered rejection because of your faith?" (*SWD*, pp. 89-91).

There is not a person on earth who can pass all those tests all the time. For example, no one "obeys God's Word" perfectly (1 John 1:8, 10). None one loves other Christians all the time. No one receives yes answers to all his prayers.

No matter how much you think you've enjoyed fellowship with the Lord, you know that what you think is fellowship with Him may not be. I remember Dr. Norm Geisler railing against a line in the famous hymn "He Lives." It is the last line in the chorus: "You ask me how I know He lives: He lives within my heart."

Dr. Geisler says that we don't know that Jesus lives by some feeling we have. We know that He lives because the Bible tells us so. He makes a good point.

In the same way, no matter how sensitive you are to sin, you cannot be sure that your sensitivity is enough or too much or is truly from God. Aren't some unregenerate people very sensitive to sin too?

You may think you obey God's Word, but you know you sin and fall short of God's glory (Rom 3:23; 1 John 1:8, 10). You'd be a liar if you claimed you obeyed God's Word perfectly. But if you don't obey His Word perfectly, then you don't obey it (Jas 2:10).

Every one of these eleven tests is subjective and cannot provide assurance. To modify what Dr. Geisler said a bit, "You ask me how I know I'm His: the Bible tells me so." The Bible tells me that whoever believes in the Lord Jesus has everlasting life. I believe in the Lord Jesus. Therefore, the Bible tells me I have everlasting life. There are no additional tests to determine whether we are born again. The only test is whether you believe the testimony concerning the Lord Jesus (1 John 5:9-13).

2. Proofs that one is unsaved?

The second question also concerns assurance:

> You acknowledge that believers can and do sin for extended
> periods of time. How can such people know whether their
> sin is a temporary failure or proof that they are unsaved?
> (p. 273).

MacArthur admits, "even in Scripture we see that believers sometimes sinned grievously and over long periods of time" (p. 273).

According to MacArthur, sinning for extended periods of time
does not prove one is unregenerate. But it clearly does not prove one
is born again either. If assurance is not found in God's Word, then
our sinful works can't provide assurance. That is what MacArthur
goes on to say: "No one who persists in willful, deliberate sin and
rebellion against the Lord should be encouraged with any promise of assurance...Such a person may be clinging to a false hope"
(p. 274).

Lordship Salvation, a gospel of doubt, provides ways in which a
person can be fairly confident that he is *not* born again, but no way
in which a person can be sure that he is actually born again.

3. Should I doubt my salvation?

Assurance continues to be the concern of the third question:

> I love Christ, but struggle constantly with sin in my life.
> Should I doubt my salvation? (p. 274).

A theme is beginning to emerge in the questions. Lordship
Salvation is a gospel of doubt. It makes such assurance impossible
for those who accept its teachings.

MacArthur says that a person should not doubt his salvation
simply because he constantly struggles with sin in his life: "It is
those who *do not* struggle—those who deliberately and eagerly
revel in their sin—who need to have their false sense of security
shaken" (p. 274, emphasis his).

This contradicts what MacArthur said in answer to the first two
questions above and what he writes in an earlier book, *Saved without a Doubt.* Assurance is found in one's works. Perhaps he means
that the mere fact that one struggles with sin does not prove he is

not born again. But it certainly does not prove that he is, either. The questioner is still left to wonder if he is really born again.

4. Romans 12:1-2?

This question is interesting in discussing Lordship Salvation:

> If all Christians have already yielded to Christ's lordship, why did Paul write Romans 12:1-2, commanding believers to make a once-for-all surrender? (p. 274).

MacArthur's answer about Rom 12:1-2 is fine *in part*. There is nothing in Rom 12:1-2 that requires this to be "a once-for-all surrender."

However, MacArthur is wrong to suggest that people are transformed at the new birth. Second Corinthians 5:17 does not say that.[1]

Romans 12:1-2 and 2 Cor 3:18 both say that transformation of one's life comes by the renewal of a believer's mind via the teaching of God's Word (primarily in the local church).

In addition, MacArthur is wrong to suggest that yielding to Christ's Lordship is a condition of everlasting life. The sole condition of everlasting life is believing in Jesus (Rom 4:4-5; Gal 2:16; Eph 2:8-9).

5. Turning people away from Christ?

The fifth question is about perception:

> Why do you use language like "forsake everything," "death to self," and "unconditional surrender"? The absoluteness of those demands is intimidating. Aren't you afraid you'll turn people away from Christ? (p. 275).

MacArthur is not concerned that he is turning people away from Christ by saying that one must forsake everything, die to self, and unconditionally surrender. He should be concerned about that, however. James 3:1 tells us that teaching God's Word is a very serious matter since teachers will have a stricter judgment at the Judgment Seat of Christ.

---

[1] See p. ??? above for my discussion of 2 Cor 5:17. SHAWN, PUT THE PAGE NUMBER HERE.

MacArthur confuses Jesus' teaching on discipleship with His teaching on evangelism. Thus Christian living truth becomes new birth truth.

6. Imperfect obedience?

Here we are back to another question that impinges on assurance:

> You acknowledge that no one can obey perfectly. Doesn't that dampen the force of the demand for absolute surrender? (p. 275).

If absolute surrender is required to be born again and my obedience is imperfect, then how can I have assurance?

MacArthur's answer is that it is humanly impossible to be born again, but it is possible with God. But now we are back to wondering if we believe or not, since for MacArthur belief is not belief but is absolute surrender, repentance, lifelong obedience, etc.

There is, of course, no once-for-all absolute surrender (as MacArthur himself says in his answer to question 4 above) because no one can obey perfectly. The questioner has pointed out a major flaw in Lordship Salvation.

7. Room for failure?

This is yet another question about assurance:

> Where in the Bible is it taught that all believers will be spiritually fruitful? Does this mean there is no room for failure in the Christian life? (p. 276).

If all believers are spiritually fruitful, then it would seem there is no room for failure in the Christian life. But as the questioner implies, all Christians fail at times.

MacArthur gives another subjective answer: "We all experience *some degree of failure*" (p. 276, emphasis added). On question 1 he spoke of "a measure of assurance." Now he finds "some degree of failure" is possible. How much? He does not say. But "*ultimate* failure—returning permanently to unbelief and wanton sin—is not possible for true Christians" (p. 276, emphasis his).

Since no one, MacArthur and I included, can be sure he will continue in belief or will avoid "returning permanently to unbelief and wanton sin," assurance is impossible prior to death under MacArthur's view of salvation.

8. Abandoning Dispensationalism?

This reader asks:

> You seem to blame dispensationalism for the deficiencies of modern evangelicalism. Are you abandoning dispensationalism? (p. 277).

MacArthur attempts to show that Dispensationalism is not linked to justification by faith alone, which he calls *easy-believism* and *cheap grace* in his answer to this question. His brief discussion is unconvincing. The men he mentions as in favor of his view, Ironside, Barnhouse, and Feinberg, did not believe in or teach Lordship Salvation as MacArthur suggests. They all taught essentially the same message proclaimed by Lewis Sperry Chafer and Charles Ryrie, men whom MacArthur indicates did not teach Lordship Salvation.[2]

9. Lordship Salvation for children?

This too is another assurance-related question:

> How can I explain the gospel to my children without toning down the hard demands of Christ? Must a child understand Jesus' lordship to be saved? (p. 278).

MacArthur says that a child must do exactly what an adult must do to be born again. That is correct. However, the Bible says that a person simply needs to believe in Jesus in order to be born again.

Contrary to Scripture MacArthur says, "trusting Jesus means obeying Him" (p. 279). So if by "trusting Jesus" MacArthur means believing in Jesus, which he surely does, then he is saying that adults and children must obey Jesus in order to be born again.

So we are back to regeneration by works, both for children and adults. Since no one's obedience is perfect, no one can have certainty of everlasting life according to MacArthur. Doubt of one's eternal destiny is the fruit of Lordship Salvation and *TGAJ*.

---

[2] See *TGAJ*, pp. 19 n. 1, 39-40, 46, 47 n. 29, 104, 253 n. 1.

10. Carnal Christians?

This question is a good one:

> How can you deny the existence of carnal Christians when
> Paul himself uses that expression in 1 Corinthians 3 (KJV)?
> (p. 279).

MacArthur's answer is quite brief and unsatisfying.

If "Christians can be carnal" (p. 279), then it follows that while they are carnal they are carnal Christians. Is that not what the expression "carnal Christians" means?

MacArthur says believers cannot remain in a state of carnality. Yet 1 Cor 3:3 says that they can. So does Heb 5:12-14.

It is true that "Christians...are never carnal by nature" (p. 279). But nature and behavior are two different things.

This too is related to assurance. If a person finds himself thinking and acting like unbelievers think and act (1 Cor 3:3), then he should wonder if he is born again according to MacArthur's teaching. He might be able to take a small measure of comfort ("a measure of assurance," question 1) in the supposed fact that a born again person can be carnal *for a time*. But if he remains that way for very long (and no one knows how long is too long), then he proves he is probably not born again. Once again, MacArthur's view of those who are born again is a matter of behavior, not belief.

11. Are easy-believism people saved?

What a fantastic question this is:

> What about those who come to Christ after hearing a mes-
> sage of easy-believism? Do you regard their salvation as
> questionable? (p. 279).

Again, assurance is in view. Unfortunately, MacArthur beats around the bush instead of answering it directly.

MacArthur is saying this: God's elect will be born again no matter what. But the message of "easy-believism" allows people who are not elect to think that they are, giving them false assurance.

Actually the question was about everlasting life, not election. Since MacArthur is a Puritan, he brings such discussions back to election.

So what if an elect person hears and believes the message MacArthur calls *easy-believism*? Is the person born again now, or must his regeneration wait until he hears the message of Lordship Salvation? Though MacArthur does not say directly, he seems to hold the view that there is no salvation apart from Lordship Salvation. Hence in his view elect people can be delayed, from a human standpoint, in being born again, by believing in *easy-believism*. But in his view they will eventually believe in salvation by repentance, submission, confession, obedience, and perseverance.

The odd thing is that according to justification by faith alone (i.e., what MacArthur calls *easy-believism*), a person who ever believed that message, as MacArthur once did, is still born again even though he no longer believes it. But according to Lordship Salvation, a person who once believed Lordship Salvation but departed into "easy-believism" proves that he was never really born again in the first place.

12. Implicitly counting the cost to be saved?

This is another excellent question in light of MacArthur's teaching on the need to count the cost of following Christ in order to be born again:

> Can a person be saved who does not *consciously* count the cost of following Christ at the time of conversion? (p. 279).

MacArthur's answer to this question must be bothersome for many who hold to Lordship Salvation. If one must count the cost to be born again as MacArthur argues throughout *TGAJ* (see, for example, pp. 25-36, 37-48, 219-25), then how can he now say, "A person might be truly born again without explicitly considering the cost of following Christ" (p. 279)? He then continues, "but no one can be saved who counts the cost and is unwilling to pay it" (p. 279).

This is confusing. Must someone count the cost of following Christ or not?

If *explicit counting of the cost is not required*, does that mean that *implicit cost counting* is required? If so, what is *implicit cost counting*?

And what does this say about evangelism? Should the evangelist tell people to whom he witnesses that they need to count the cost of discipleship in order to be born again?

If one need not count the cost unless a person tells him that he must do so, then wouldn't it be best for evangelists to avoid telling people they need to count the cost? By telling them that they need to count the cost you make them culpable. But if they don't know, then they can be born again without explicitly counting the cost.

Of course, as we've seen many times, in *TGAJ* MacArthur says that one must count the cost to be born again. Thus in his own evangelism MacArthur does tell people they need to count the cost. Every reader of *TGAJ* is now responsible to count the cost of discipleship as one step in the path that might lead to being born again.

In the last sentence of his answer, MacArthur comes back to another vague comment about degree: "But the work of the Holy Spirit in the heart of a true believer prompts *some degree of surrender to Christ's authority even at the inception of the new birth*" (p. 280, emphasis added). What is "some degree of surrender to Christ's authority?" How much surrender is enough? 50%? 75%? 90%?

This question also concerns assurance. Over and over again people attracted to MacArthur's teaching doubt whether they are really born again. That is what his teaching does.[3] That is why his teaching is rightly called *a gospel of doubt*.

13. Backsliding?

Here's another question about how we can identify *a true Christian*:

Can a true Christian "backslide"? (p. 280).

As with question 10 on carnality, MacArthur says that "true Christians can 'backslide,'" but that "true Christians [cannot] abandon the faith completely" (p. 280). So backsliding *for a time* is deplorable but somewhat normal, but backsliding that continues until death proves you were never born again in the first place.

This too is an assurance question. So far most of the questions concern assurance.

Once again, if what MacArthur says here is true, then certainty of one's eternal destiny is impossible prior to death. Someone who

---

[3] Pastor Paul Carpenter comments, "And don't forget, this doubt is on purpose. To MacArthur the greatest threat to Christian living is the certain knowledge of everlasting life."

shares MacArthur's views, R. C. Sproul, once famously wrote, "being uncomfortable with Jesus was better than any other option."[4]

14. First Corinthians 3:11-15?

Another reader wonders about works and assurance:

> Does 1 Corinthians 3:11-15 prove that a true Christian might live a wholly fruitless life? (p. 280)

MacArthur may be correct[5] when he says that "Those verses in no way imply that a Christian can be devoid of fruit or works" (p. 280).[6] But he goes too far when he says,

> In fact, they teach the opposite—that every Christian will have works of some sort (ministry, service, evangelism, etc.) but that the works may vary as to their quality. Some people's good works are cluttered with wrong motives or unbiblical methods, so our rewards will differ (pp. 280-81).

The issue in 1 Cor 3:11-15 is not that some works were done "with wrong motives" or with "unbiblical methods." Remember that Paul in 1 Cor 3:5-15 is using himself and Apollos (see 3:5-6) as examples of *wise master builders* (1 Cor 3:10). Paul is not discussing Christians in general. He is discussing highly effective Christians in particular. His point that whatever even he, Apollos, and wise master builders like them do that lacks eternal value will be burned

---

[4] *Tabletalk Magazine*, November 6, 1989, p. 20.

[5] Many people think that the word *saved* in 1 Cor 3:15 refers to salvation from eternal condemnation and the reference to *work* refers to all the person did in his life as a believer. I don't agree on either point. See the next two footnotes.

[6] The Parable of the Four Soils suggests that all believers who live even a day or two after the new birth will have some good works. (Certainly there must have been at least a few people in Church History who died at the very moment of faith. If so, there would a small number of Christians with no good works at all. But that is not what MacArthur is discussing in his answer to this question.) Remember that the sprout came out of the ground. While other humans might not be able to recognize the good works as something which is a product of the new birth, God can. But that is far different from MacArthur's contention that all Christians *will persevere* in a life *characterized by* good works. Indeed, the second soil in the Parable of the Four Soils shows that is not true. And the third soil shows that there are believers who are half-hearted in the works that they do, resulting in immature fruit.

up at the Judgment Seat of Christ and there will be no reward for those works which are burned up.[7]

The issue here is works with enduring quality, works that remain after a fiery examination (gold, silver, precious stone) versus works that lack enduring quality, works that are burned up in the fire of judgment (wood, hay, straw). Only works with eternal value will be rewarded.

Amazingly, MacArthur in his answer contradicts what he said earlier in *TGAJ*. Notice that in the quote cited above he says, "Our rewards will differ" (p. 281). Yet in Chapter 14, "The First and Last," he said, "Everyone crosses the finish line in a dead heat" (p. 152), "A dying convert inherits the same glories of eternal existence as an apostle" (p. 154), "The issue here is equality of eternal life" (p. 155), and "in the end all enjoy the fullness of eternal life to the maximum" (p. 157). It is disturbing that MacArthur makes dogmatic statements in one place in *TGAJ* only to reverse himself elsewhere and say the opposite things just as forcefully.

MacArthur's answer engenders doubt about one's eternal destiny because he argues that every Christian will have effective ministries, but that there may be some level of wrong motives or methods. How much ministry is needed to show I am born again? That is not stated. If I find wrong motives or wrong methods, then clearly that is not good. But since *some* wrong motives and *some* wrong methods are possible even for born-again folks according to MacArthur, one is back to examining his works and his motives to see if there is enough evidence to lead to the conclusion that he is probably or at least possibly born again.

15. Judging the salvation of others without being judgmental?

TGAJ produced another assurance question, this time concerning others:

> How should we act toward those who profess to be Christians but seem indifferent to spiritual things? (p. 281).

---

[7] The word *saved* in 1 Cor 3:15 probably means *spiritually healthy* (compare 1 Cor 5:5). Eternal salvation from hell is *a present possession* as Paul makes clear in Eph 2:8-9 ("you have been saved," a past action with an abiding result). The "salvation" Paul speaks of in 3:15 is clearly future and will be meted out at the Judgment Seat of Christ (the Bema). The wise master builder will be *approved by Christ* at the Bema (cf. 1 Cor 9:27), though some of his works will end up not being found worthy of reward.

Twelve of the first fifteen questions deal with assurance. Lordship Salvation undercuts assurance of everlasting life. It produces doubt.

This question applies not only to judging the salvation of others at our churches, but to our own children, brothers and sisters, parents, aunts and uncles, cousins, co-workers, friends at school, etc.

MacArthur says we should avoid two extremes when "assessing the spiritual state of others": 1) "we must realize that we are not ultimately the judge of anyone's salvation" and 2) "we must hold firmly to the truth of God's Word concerning salvation and not offer false assurance to people who may not truly be saved" (p. 281).

Yet he goes on to say that if you have doubts about the salvation of a friend or family member you are morally bound to "speak frankly to that person about your concerns" (p. 281).

Let's imagine the conversation:

> "Son, you know that God will judge us all. I will not judge you or anyone else. However, I love you and I've got some concerns about whether you are really born again or not?"
>
> "But Dad, you know I believe in Jesus and you know that I came to faith in Him when I was ten."
>
> "I know you *profess to believe* now and that you first *professed faith* when you were ten. But now you are twenty-one and I have doubts because frankly you do not seem to be fully submitted to Christ."
>
> "What are you saying, Dad?"
>
> "Well, I notice that you seem jealous of some of the other guys on the baseball team. I've observed outbursts of anger from time to time. Sometimes you seem to look a little too long at pretty girls. Your heart does not seem to be in worship. You go to church, but you don't seem all there. You don't spend much time in the Word or in prayer or in witnessing as far as I can tell."
>
> "But Dad, the Lord Jesus said that whoever believes in Him has everlasting life. The issue is belief, not behavior. Right?"
>
> "Son, have you come to believe in easy-believism?"
>
> "Well, Dad, I got involved with Navigators and now I do base my assurance on my faith in Christ, not on my works. But I don't call that *easy-believism*. In any case, I am following Christ and I don't understand your concerns."

"Son, I will pray for you. If you continue in this easy-believism, you will prove you were never born again in the first place. Only those who count the cost and submit everything to Christ will make it into the kingdom. Please repent and submit and obey before it is too late."

Some people after hearing such concerns will lose their assurance and will be moved to spend more time in church, more time in Bible study, and more time reading Lordship Salvation books.

Others will lose their assurance and will spend less time in church, less time in Bible study, and less time reading Christian books of any kind. The pain of loss of assurance drives some people to legalism and others to despair.

Some will stand firm in their assurance and might pray for their parents or whoever is questioning their salvation. They might view that conversation as suffering for Jesus.

Are such conversations a good idea? It is hard to see how even for those who believe in Lordship Salvation this sort of interaction is helpful.

Is it really helpful for you to question the eternal destiny of your own child (or sibling or parent or friend) based on your conclusions about his commitment, his zeal, and his works? Might not such a conversation drive a wedge between you? Might not the conversation actually hurt his walk with the Lord (if he is born again)? And if he is an unbeliever, might not your words lead him to believe that what he needs is a lifetime of good works, not faith in Christ, in order to spend eternity with the Lord?

Even if someone believes what MacArthur believes, he should not be comfortable questioning the eternal destiny of those he loves based on his perception of their commitment and works.[8]

---

[8] I went to MacArthur's Shepherd's Conference in 2002. There I heard two Pastors from MacArthur's Grace Community Church speak about doubts they had about whether some of their own teenage children were born again. I found the discussion uncomfortable. Why should a youth Pastor be telling strangers that he has doubts about the salvation of some of his own children because of their works? I had a similar sort of experience in 1985 when I spoke at a Bible Church in Paris, TX. Between the morning and evening services I spent time with a family of four. The two boys were around 12 to 14. The parents told me, with their sons listening, that they did not have enough evidence to know if their boys were born again. They said until they went off on their own and were not under parental control would they get enough evidence to decide if they were probably elect or not. I felt very uncomfortable for the boys that day. I doubt that is a good memory for them.

16. Why did MacArthur change his view?

A reader asks this perceptive question:

> What caused you to change your views on the gospel? Your book seems like a total departure of what I thought you believed (p. 281).

MacArthur denies changing his view.[9] This is untenable based on statements he has made on the radio. Prior to 1980 he had no category for people whom he led to faith in Christ and discipled one on one and who later fell away from the faith. But after 1980 he had a category.[10] He changed his view and came to believe that such a fall proved they were false professors.[11]

In 1989 I spoke with a group of people who had been in his church for over 20 years at that time. They all told me that he changed his understanding of the condition of everlasting life in 1980.

It really is of no consequence to this issue whether he changed or not. However, it is odd that he so adamantly says he did not change.

17. Since Lordship Salvation is divisive, shouldn't you just avoid teaching it and instead promote harmony?

This an interesting question on which to end:

> Don't you believe it is better to ignore divisive issues like the lordship controversy and keep harmony in the body of Christ? (p. 282).

MacArthur is correct that the issue is not whether Lordship Salvation is divisive. The issue is whether it is what the Bible teaches. If it is, then MacArthur and all of us should teach it boldly and

---

[9] However, see the Preface to the Anniversary Edition where he indicates that when he preached through Matthew (1978 to circa 1983) "those years in Matthew brought my doctrinal convictions into sharp focus and amplified several truths in my heart and mind…starting with the gospel message itself" (p. 9). While he tries to present it as a mere sharpening and amplification of his theology and his gospel message, his views changed radically.

[10] I heard him say this on his *Grace to You* radio program circa 1989. However, I cannot find it via a search of the *Grace to You* archives as they only go back to 2005.

[11] The Wikipedia article on John F. MacArthur says, "In December of 1989 the Bible Broadcasting Network terminated MacArthur's "Grace to You" [radio] program…[because of] a drift by Dr. MacArthur." The article points out that the drift, or change, was to Lordship Salvation/Hyper-Calvinism.

accept any persecution that comes. If not, then none of us should teach it.

Doctrine divides. The only way to have harmony among people who have major doctrinal differences is to overlook our differences. As MacArthur says, that is acceptable for things like mode of baptism, church government,[12] whether women need to wear head coverings in church, which version of the Bible we use, etc. In nonessentials there should be liberty and differences of opinion in such areas should not hinder our unity. However, on essential truths, like what we must do to have everlasting life, there must be unity. If people disagree with us on what one must do to be born again, then we should be in different churches.

If the Bible teaches that we are to look to our works over the course of our lifetimes to see if we are born again, as MacArthur says, then we should live each day with doubts about our eternal destiny. So be it. If that is what God wants, then that is what is good for us. If the gospel according to Jesus is a gospel of doubt, then we should believe and proclaim a gospel of doubt.

However, if the Bible teaches that we are not to look to our works for assurance, but only look to the promises in God's Word to the believer, then we can and should live each day with the joyful certainty that we are eternally secure. As long as we keep our eyes on the Lord's promise and His faithfulness, we will remain sure and that certainly can and should produce a lifelong profound sense of gratitude that will drive us to long to hear Him say, "Well done, good servant" (Luke 19:17).

MacArthur's *TGAJ* promotes doubt because Lordship Salvation is a gospel of doubt. My prayer for everyone who holds to Lordship Salvation, including John MacArthur, is that they will discover (or re-discover) certainty of everlasting life in the simple promise of John 3:16 and that as a result they would glorify Christ in what they say and do and thus that one day soon they would hear those blessed words, "Well done, good servant."

---

[12] Though I do not consider mode of baptism and type of church government as the most important fundamental issues, I would not use these as examples of non-essentials either. These are important issues. I would be reluctant to be a part of a church that did not practice elder rule and believer's baptism by immersion. However, I agree that these issues are not *as essential* as issues like the deity of Christ, substitutionary atonement, justification by faith alone, the soon return of Christ, and inerrancy.

Subject Index

Scripture Index

Made in the USA
San Bernardino, CA
16 April 2016